Bauwelt Fundamente 156

Series editors:
Elisabeth Blum
Jesko Fezer
Günther Fischer
Angelika Schnell

Neil Brenner

Critique of Urbanization:
Selected Essays

Bauverlag
Gütersloh · Berlin

Birkhäuser
Basel

The Bauwelt Fundamente series was founded in 1963 by Ulrich Conrads; it was edited from the early 1980s to 2015 jointly with Peter Neitzke. Editorial supervision of this volume: Elisabeth Blum.

Image credit for front and back cover: David Maisel, *Oblivion, 8N/9N,* 2004. http://davidmaisel.com/. Reproduced with the generous permission of the artist and Yancey Richardson Gallery, New York City; Haines Gallery, San Francisco; Mark Moore Gallery, Los Angeles.

Image credits for section divider pages (pages 14-5, 40-1, 184-5): David Maisel, *Oblivion 5N, 14N, 15N,* 2004. http://davidmaisel.com/. Reproduced with the generous permission of the artist and Yancey Richardson Gallery, New York City; Haines Gallery, San Francisco; Mark Moore Gallery, Los Angeles.

Library of Congress Cataloging-in-Publication data
A CIP catalog record for this book has been applied for at the Library of Congress.

Bibliographic information published by the German National Library
The German National Library lists this publication in the Deutsche Nationalbibliografie; detailed bibliographic data are available on the Internet at http://dnb.dnb.de.

This publication is also available as an e-book (ISBN PDF 978-3-0356-0795-6).

© 2017 Birkhäuser Verlag GmbH, Basel
P.O. Box 44, 4009 Basel, Switzerland
Part of Walter de Gruyter GmbH, Berlin/Boston
and Bauverlag BV GmbH, Gütersloh, Berlin

bau| | |**verlag**

Printed on acid-free paper produced from chlorine-free pulp. TCF ∞
Printed in Germany

ISBN 978-3-0356-1011-6
9 8 7 6 5 4 3 2 1

www.birkhauser.com

Contents

For Ignacia

Preface

Martín Arboleda

The Pacific Trash Vortex is a gyre of garbage located in the central North Pacific Ocean whose size, according to conservative estimates, is around 700,000 square kilometers (roughly equivalent to the state of Texas). A "spectacle of disintegration," as McKenzie Wark refers to it, this infamous continent of plastic is composed of miniscule fragments of furniture, refrigerators, water bottles, television sets, and cigarette lighters, among many other objects that populate the everyday fabric of contemporary urban life.[1] Such circling constellations of flotsam puncturing the water's surface, reshaping the biochemical composition of the ocean and the maritime food chain as they refuse to biodegrade, are woven together by the increasingly complex, mind-boggling process of urban metabolic transformation that defines our current epoch. Far from episodic, the fragmentation of the gyre is then both metaphor and mirror reflection of the sheer plunder, unevenness and disintegration that also abounds in densely populated areas of the world. The same forces that project millions of tons of solid waste into the ocean each year also produce marginality and social disintegration in densely populated agglomerations. The very economic processes that fill the cityscapes of the world with luxurious gated communities also generate job insecurity, gentrification and the unrelenting growth of slums on the outskirts of megacities. The same financial mechanisms that circulate billions of dollars in asset-backed securities have often induced catastrophic busts which inflict mass foreclosures, increased insecurity and public health crises in working-class neighborhoods and suburbs.

In the face of this sublimely complex, deeply interconnected social reality, how should we approach the study of urban processes and transformations, as well as the suppressed possibilities for social emancipation that are contained with the landscapes of urban life? How should we even begin to grasp a phenomenon that seems to elude us as it transgresses all imaginable boundaries? In addition to its sheer breadth and geographical extent, the contradictory inner rhythms and discontinuous dynamics of the global urban system make this an extremely difficult object of theoretical inquiry. The urban *problematique* has been gaining increasing relevance in recent years, especially after two United Nations (UN) agencies declared in 2007 that half the world's population was living in cities. Mainstream urban epistemologies, however, advance positivistic methods which construe the urban as a statistical artifact that can be delineated, measured and socially engineered by a supposedly external, value-free observer. Such epistemologies tend to underpin technoscientific and corporate-developmentalist policy approaches that are ill-equipped to grasp, let alone to reshape, the broader political-economic processes that actually produce urban inequalities, governance failures, legitimation crises and socioecological disasters. A genuinely transformative urban epistemology needs to overcome such narrowly technoscientific or profit-driven orientations, and to elaborate forms of knowledge and practice that directly address the inherently politicized, socially antagonistic, crisis-riven and ecologically disruptive dynamics that shape and reshape urban geographies at multiple spatial scales.

The overarching motivation that drives and weaves together the carefully selected, timely collection of essays presented in this book is the need to overcome the fragmentation that abounds in positivistic, empiricist and city-centric epistemologies of the urban and thus to grasp the multiple determinations that produce historically and geographically specific formations of the urban environment. As Marshall Berman once argued, the vividness, resonance and depth of the modern city is sometimes lost among a cacophony of voices speaking incommensurably private languages; consequently, we attain only a partial understanding of what living in a modern urban world really means.[2] Throughout the following pages, the reader will find an invitation to supersede the immediacy of such experiences, and to explore the perspectives opened up by critical urban theory to decipher the manifold layers of political struggle, ideological projection, regulatory contestation, and sociopolitical antagonism that define the places we inhabit in our everyday lives.

The process of urbanization, however, needs to be understood as much more than a mere shorthand for the built environment of capital and its associated forms of uneven geographical development. This is because, in creating pathways and opportunities for encounter and assembly, urbanization also enables the possibility for a politics of space; it reasserts the creative capacities of life and in so doing, engenders myriad possibilities for coming together and appropriating the world in order to transform it. For this reason, the chapters contained in this volume steer away from unilinear, mechanistic readings of urban transformation and reaffirm Henri Lefebvre's profoundly hopeful reading of the urban as a vast whirlpool in which exclusion and marginalization coexist with playfulness, strategic opportunity, and liberating potential.[3] As many of the chapters included in this book suggest, even in the midst of the enclosures, market fundamentalisms and privatizations associated with recent rounds of neoliberalization, the urban can still reassert itself as a space of social experimentation in which new ways of sharing resources and developing the commons are invented.

For example, the recent financial crisis of 2010 in Spain, which sent shockwaves across the European Union and beyond, and left behind hundreds of thousands of evictions and foreclosures, also engendered the conditions for an emancipatory politics and for alternative, collectivist forms of producing, experiencing, and inhabiting urban space. Neighbors, workers, pensioners and migrants joined in association to conceive new forms of political organization that facilitated the blocking of evictions, the occupation of empty, bank-owned property and the provision of aid to evicted families. In precisely this sense, critical theory is more than an antagonistic orientation towards the existing state of things. As several chapters contained in this volume demonstrate, critique demands a relentless excavation of the radical, alternative sociospatial imaginations that are embedded within, but often suppressed by, current sociospatial and institutional arrangements. The immanent critique of urban configurations inherited from the past can thus contribute powerfully to enhancing the emancipatory content and potential of emergent forms of urban thought and action.

One of the most analytically crucial and politically urgent challenges for contemporary urban interventions is to expand their field of vision beyond inherited, naturalized jurisdictional and sociological visions of the city to address newly emergent geographies of urbanization that are unevenly traversing erstwhile hinterlands, rural zones, and even wilderness areas. To this end, several chapters of this book build upon the metaphor of implosion/explosion to describe the contradictory dialectic between concentrated and extended urbanization under capitalism: urbanization entails not only the growth of large population centers and metropolitan agglomerations, but the construction and continual creative destruction of operational landscapes (industrialized hinterlands) to support their core metabolic operations.[4] The constellations of plastic waste circling around the Pacific Vortex are therefore not the ontological "other" of the urban, but are instead among its constitutive, "internal" elements. Revealing the hidden socionatural relations that underlie the ebb and flow of modern urban life, especially if they are beyond the purview of predominant urban epistemologies, is perhaps one of the most politically pressing intellectual agendas that this book pushes forward. A simple focus on cities obfuscates the broader processes of infrastructural and socioecological transformation that urbanization exerts upon the entire planetary landscape.

The explosion of the city, in all its material and aesthetic exuberance, thus needs to be understood foremost as a question of sociospatial differentiation, at all imaginable scales, from the molecular to the planetary. When mediated by capitalist social relations, urbanization becomes a pulsing, powerful engine for the production of sheer geographical unevenness that ricochets destructively across places, territories and scales to create new forms of socioecological suffering, but also new opportunities for the collective appropriation of the urban potentials it unleashes. Politicizing and making visible such uneven geographies, and their suppressed emancipatory potentials, should therefore be at the forefront of any critical-theoretical project, urban or otherwise. Every building, every infrastructure and every regulatory framework is traversed by power relations, ideological visions and institutionalized exclusions that benefit some populations at the expense of others. The tendency of the urban, at least in its modern, capitalist expression, to universalize itself is but the material basis for the expansion of capitalist social relations on a world scale. The critique of this twofold movement, Neil Brenner reminds us in this selection of his works, must assert itself as the horizon that drives thought and action in an increasingly urbanized planet.

Notes

1   Mc Kenzie Wark, *The Spectacle of Disintegration: Situationist Passages out of the Twentieth Century* (London: Verso, 2013).

2   Marshall Berman, *All That Is Solid Melts into Air: The Experience of Modernity* (New York: Verso, 1982).

3   Henri Lefebvre, *The Urban Revolution*, trans. Robert Bononno (Minneapolis: University of Minnesota Press, 2003).

4   The notion of implosion/explosion is derived from the work of Henri Lefebvre, as discussed in Chapter 12 in the present volume. See also Neil Brenner, ed., *Implosions/Explosions: Towards a Study of Planetary Urbanization* (Berlin: Jovis, 2014); Neil Brenner and Christian Schmid, "Towards a New Epistemology of the Urban," *CITY* 19, no. 2–3 (2015): 151–82; and Neil Brenner, "Theses on Urbanization," *Public Culture* 25, no. 1 (2013): 86–114.

Framings

1 The *Problematique* of Critique

This book assembles a series of texts devoted to the critique of urbanization. Most of the articles, essays, interventions, manifestos and dialogues contained herein were produced since 2009; two chapters stem from the early 2000s; about half were coauthored with other critical urban researchers, who have generously permitted their inclusion here. All reflect a concerted, collaborative and still ongoing effort to develop a critical approach to understanding emergent forms of urban transformation. Just as crucially, the analyses gathered in this book grapple with the changing conditions of possibility for the very critique of urbanization they advance. In this sense, this book is not only an attempt to develop critical perspectives on specific patterns and pathways of urban restructuring, but a series of sustained reflections on how, why and in what forms such a critique might be articulated, even as the geographies of urbanization are continuously transformed before our eyes, at every imaginable spatial scale.

The chapters that follow are grounded upon a specific, if evolving, normative-political orientation – the goal of facilitating the collective imagination and radically democratic appropriation of the "right to the city," or what I term *alter-urbanizations,* by the inhabitants of our rapidly urbanizing planet. Crucially, however, the critique of urbanization proclaimed in this book's title is not intended merely to signal a specific criticism of emergent urban formations – for instance, due to their manifestly unjust, exclusionary, undemocratic, militarized, fragmented or environmentally destructive character. Nor, for that matter, do I propose here a specific alternative framework for reorganizing the life of cities, regions and territories – for instance, based upon more substantive forms of redistribution, inclusion, participation, security, solidarity or sustainability. While such agendas are, obviously, absolutely essential to the work of critical urban theory and research, including to the texts presented here, this book explores a still more wide-ranging *problematique*: the multifaceted critique of urbanization that, under modern capitalist conditions, persistently animates everyday life, counterpublics, insurgent social movements, counter-hegemonic political strategies, radical planning and design interventions, and the writings of critical urban scholars, generating new, if always ideologically contested, horizons for interpreting, representing, imagining, shaping, regulating, governing and appropriating the variegated, urbanizing landscapes of our planet.

As conceived here, then, the critique of urbanization is a *problematique* that emerges from within, and conflictually co-evolves with, the very urban transformations towards which its subversive energies, dissident analyses and counter-hegemonic visions are directed. This book is focused upon that *problematique* itself. Its goal is not only to develop critical perspectives on the neoliberalizing, increasingly planetary forms of market-disciplinary urban transformation that have been unfolding since the 1980s, but to track the vicissitudes of critique that have been provoked by, and that have actively shaped, those transformations.

In the expanded sense proposed here, the critique of urbanization is necessarily multidimensional, at once in spatial, institutional and political terms. It includes everyday forms of experimentation, resistance, rebellion and insurgency, as well as organized political strategies, reflexive design projects, and small- and large-scale planning interventions that, in some way, call into question the necessity, rationality or legitimacy of hegemonic spatial arrangements. Such critiques may be directed, for instance, at the commodification of housing; the class-based and racial polarization of social space; the enclosure and privatization of public space; speculation-driven approaches to property development; the lack of public investment in key infrastructures for social reproduction (including housing, transportation, education, health care and other public goods); the insulation of key planning and design decisions from relays of democratic control and accountability; the legal institutionalization or cultural normalization of spatial exclusions based on class, race, gender or sexuality; the dispossession of local inhabitants from common, community-based resources; the concentration of environmental risk, public health hazards and social vulnerability among low-income, minority or historically oppressed communities; or the intensifying degradation of our planetary environmental commons in pursuit of endless capital accumulation. Across diverse arenas, territories and scales of politico-ideological contestation, however, what such critiques share is the relentless insistence that "things could be otherwise" – or, as I argue in several chapters below, the notion that *another urbanization is possible*.

This proposition lies at the heart of the idea of alter-urbanization, the goal of which is not only to pursue alternative models of spatial organization, whether within streetscapes, neighborhoods, cities, regions or territories, but to envision alternative *processes* for the common appropriation and transformation of the shared, intensely interconnected urban world we all now inhabit. This emphasis on processes rather than spatial forms or territorial units necessarily requires a sustained critical interrogation of the political institutions, regulatory frameworks and legal rule-regimes that govern the production of spatial configurations and modes of interspatial connection under modern capitalism. In the absence of new institutional spaces – or, more precisely, new institutional *processes* – alter-urbanizations are impossible to imagine, much less to pursue. This politico-epistemological orientation lies at the heart of the dialectical approach to radical sociospatial transformation famously encapsulated in Henri Lefebvre's concept of the production of space, and more recently elaborated by David Harvey.[1] Its implications are explored in several chapters of this book which critically evaluate the prospects for more socially just, radically democratic, territorially balanced and ecologically viable interventions into emergent patterns and pathways of urban restructuring.

The pursuit of alter-urbanizations is grounded, above all, in everyday life, social mobilization and political struggle, but it is necessarily mediated through and animated by questions of ideology – in Stuart Hall's terms, "the languages, the concepts, categories, imagery of thought and the systems of representation" through which "different classes and social groups [...] make sense of, define, figure out and render intelligible the way society works."[2] Such frameworks of interpretation saturate everyday life and spatial practices with meaning while also, as Hall emphasizes, serving as a "material force" insofar as they may "stabilize a particular form of power and domination" or, by contrast, "move the masses of the people into historical action against the prevailing system."[3]

It is for this reason, I believe, that the work of critical urban theory is essential to the project of pursuing alter-urbanizations, since its proper task is precisely to investigate the historically contingent social and institutional sources of human suffering – "social suffering," in Pierre Bourdieu's memorable phrase – underlying spatial arrangements that, in mainstream political discourse, are represented as natural, necessary or optimal.[4] While the historical, institutional and ideological mechanisms of this generalized projection of "false necessity" are a matter of considerable controversy,[5] its deconstruction, both in theory and in practice, is surely a shared goal among all critical urban researchers, whether of a neo-Marxian, post-Marxist, anti-racist, feminist, poststructuralist, postcolonial, queer-theoretical, ecosocialist or anarchist orientation. Indeed, in contrast to mainstream or "traditional" forms of urban research, which produce knowledge in the service of dominant political-economic institutions oriented towards profit-maximization, labor discipline, social control, political tranquilization, militarization, cultural normalization, consumerism and/or ecological self-obliteration, each of these broadly allied streams of critical urban studies aims explicitly to destabilize the hegemonic urban institutions, practices and ideologies that sanctify, naturalize or legitimate extant sociospatial arrangements and the manifold injustices, dispossessions, dislocations, degradations and irrationalities upon which they are grounded.[6]

Against the background of this broader agenda, the chapters assembled in this book aim, in particular, to illuminate the spatial operations of power and ideology that underpin the capitalist form of urbanization, especially in the wake of the successive waves of crisis-induced and crisis-inducing neoliberalization that have radically, if unevenly, reterritorialized and rescaled the urban landscapes of the world since the 1980s, generally with socially and ecologically disastrous consequences.[7] The opening and closing chapters of the section on *Urban Strategies, Urban Ideologies* (Chapters 3 and 10) result from my long-term collaboration with Nik Theodore and Jamie Peck. Positioned as theoretical bookends for this section of the book, these essays propose a framework through which to decipher the variegated spatial, politico-regulatory and discursive dynamics of neoliberalization processes, across regions, territories, scales and contexts. This framework strongly informs the other contributions to that section of the book, which include coauthored essays with Roger Keil (Chapter 4), David Wachsmuth (Chapter 5) and Peter Marcuse and Margit Mayer (Chapter 9). Here, with my colleagues, I mobilize the tools of critical urban theory to contextualize, assess and deconstruct some of the hegemonic urban keywords of our time – including "global cities," "territorial competitiveness," "good governance," "open city," "tactical urbanism" and "post-neoliberalism," among several others. Such ideological discourses naturalize, and thus depoliticize, the spatial (il)logics and enclosures of neoliberal urbanism.[8]

Precisely because, as Stuart Hall notes, ideology serves as a "material force" which can "reconcile or accommodate the mass of the people to their subordinate place in the social formation," its sustained critique, including through the rigorous, often abstract, work of critical theory, can also help transform the "terrain of ideological struggle," facilitating the production of "new forms of consciousness [and] new conceptions of the world" that may, in turn, animate new forms of social experimentation, alternative spatial practices and oppositional political mobilization.[9] For this reason, these chapters are intended not only to serve deconstructive purposes; they are presented in the hope of offering some measure of intellectual, normative and political orientation to those social forces and political alliances struggling to envision and to realize some of the "possible urban worlds" which such hegemonic, depoliticizing and normalizing spatial ideologies systematically hide, devalorize, stigmatize, repress or criminalize.[10] Such dialectical, always shifting connections between theory and practice (and, inversely: from practice back to theory) are of particularly central concern in Chapters 9 and 10, where my coauthors and I reflect on the prospects for alternative pathways of urbanization and regulation following the global financial crises of the post-2008 period.

Here arises a further, equally essential contrast between traditional or mainstream approaches to urban knowledge and the form of critical urban theory espoused in this book. Mainstream approaches to the urban question tend to presuppose what Andrew Sayer has termed an epistemology of "naïve objectivism," in which the city and the urban are conceived as self-evident empirical entities that can be transparently understood and instrumentally manipulated by a neutral observer occupying a vantage point external to the sites and processes being investigated.[11] In contrast, as I elaborate in Chapter 2, one of the hallmarks of any form of critical social theory, including critical urban theory, is its emphasis on the practical situatedness of all forms of knowledge and on a rigorous epistemological reflexivity regarding the changing contexts, conditions and mediations of that situatedness in relation to ongoing processes of historical-geographical restructuring. Accordingly, building upon the epistemological foundations developed by Frankfurt School social theorists, I argue that the work of reflexive critique requires a continual interrogation of the changing historical conditions of possibility for such an orientation. Rather than presupposing a rigid separation between subject (knower) and object (the site or context under investigation), reflexive approaches emphasize their mutual constitution, practical interdependence and ongoing transformation through social relations, including in the contested realm of interpretation and ideology. In Margaret Archer's more general formulation, a reflexive approach to social theory involves "a subject considering an object in relation to itself, bending that object back upon itself in a process which includes the self being able to consider itself as its own object."[12]

In the context of critical urban studies, this philosophical requirement involves not only the constant interrogation of changing urban conditions, but the equally vigilant analysis and revision of the very conceptual frameworks being used to investigate the urban process itself. For any reflexive approach to urban theory, therefore, the categories, methods and cartographies of urban analysis are themselves important focal points of inquiry: understanding their conditions of emergence and intelligibility, as well as the possibility of their destabilization or obsolescence, represent essential, ongoing, and potentially transformative research priorities. Simply put, reflexive approaches to urban theory must constantly subject their own epistemic assumptions and categories of analysis to critical interrogation, even as the latter are being mobilized in ongoing research endeavors.

The texts assembled in the final section of the book, *New Urban Geographies,* put this epistemological imperative into action in order to explore the possibility that some of the most entrenched categories, cartographies and methods within the field of urban theory – in particular, those associated with inherited notions of the city, the urban/rural divide and the hinterland – today require systematic reinvention under rapidly mutating planetary conditions. This analysis builds upon my ongoing collaborative work with Christian Schmid on the *problematique* of "planetary urbanization." In our writings thus far, we have mobilized this concept to critically interrogate the inherited metageographical assumptions of twentieth-century urban theory, and on this basis, to demarcate the limitations and blind spots of contemporary triumphalist ideologies of city-centric capitalism and the "urban age." Just as importantly, our theorization of planetary urbanization is intended to help illuminate the variegated, profoundly uneven geographies of urban restructuring around the world, at once within expanding megacities and large-scale metropolitan regions, as well as across the landscapes of erstwhile rural zones, inherited hinterlands and even wilderness areas that are now increasingly being integrated within, and operationalized by, planetary-scale urban-industrial strategies, mega-infrastructural configurations and intercontinental logistics corridors.[13]

Following a programmatic overview of this wide-ranging agenda in a short text written with Christian Schmid (Chapter 11), subsequent chapters explore some of its contours through engagements with several key terrains of analysis in contemporary urban studies – including debates on the notion of an urban revolution (Chapter 12), the transformation of inherited hinterlands into operational landscapes (Chapter 13), the agency of design under conditions of neoliberalized, planetary urbanization (Chapter 14), and the uses and potential hazards of actor-network theory in critical urban studies (Chapter 15; coauthored with David J. Madden and

David Wachsmuth). In a brief manifesto produced to orient work in the Urban Theory Lab, a research platform I established at the Harvard GSD, I reflect upon the challenges of pursuing theoretically speculative, postdisciplinary, cartographically experimental and unapologetically critical approaches to urbanism in a global academic and political climate that systematically prioritizes the modalities of application-oriented, policy-driven research (Chapter 16). This section contains two "dialogues" with my colleagues, Daniel Ibañez and Martín Arboleda, which further elaborate some of the book's core arguments in relation to contemporary urban discourse and research practice in the social sciences, urban planning and the design disciplines (Chapters 14 and 17).

Taken together, then, the contributions to this book advocate a constant reinvention of the framing categories, methods and assumptions of critical urban theory in relation to the rapidly, unevenly mutating geographies of capitalist urbanization, especially in the contemporary era of hyperfinancialized, planetary-scale spatial, institutional and ecological transformation. If urbanization is, at core, a process of producing and transforming space, then the moment of critique is, in practice, already contained within it, while also itself being recurrently, relentlessly transformed through the cascading dynamics of creative destruction that underpin and articulate this process. As understood here, therefore, critique is not simply an oppositional orientation towards extant spaces, institutions and ideologies; it is a pulse of subversion *and* transcendence that is embedded within, yet suppressed by, the apparent facticity of the present. In this sense, the moment of critique is not produced from a standpoint external to the process of urbanization; it is immanently contained within the latter, as an animating force that at once internalizes the enclosures, dispossessions, crisis tendencies and contradictions of the current urban configuration, while also pointing beyond them, towards alternative possible futures. In precisely this sense, I believe, critique is a mode of counter-interpretation that – to return once again to Stuart Hall's phrase – can operate as a "material force" shaping and continuously reshaping the process of urbanization itself.[14]

Through its irreducible abstraction, then, critique is an essential moment within the ongoing struggle to imagine and to pursue alter-urbanizations – alternative pathways for the collective production and appropriation of space. As the process of capitalist urbanization continues its relentless, if systemically uneven, forward movement of creative destruction across places, territories and scales, the meanings and modalities of critique must be continually reinvented, and so too must the parameters for imagining, mapping and pursuing alter-urbanizations. This is, from my point of view, one of the major intellectual and political challenges confronting critical urban theorists today, and it is accordingly a central concern animating the texts assembled in this book. Only a theory that is dynamic – which is constantly, reflexively being transformed in relation to the restlessly, unevenly evolving social worlds and territorial landscapes it aspires to grasp – can be a genuinely *critical* theory.

Notes

1 Henri Lefebvre, *The Production of Space*, trans. Donald Nicholson-Smith (Oxford: Blackwell, 1991); David Harvey, *Spaces of Hope* (Berkeley: University of California Press, 2000).
2 Stuart Hall, "The Problem of Ideology: Marxism without Guarantees," *Journal of Communication Inquiry* 10, no. 2 (1986): 29.
3 Ibid., 30.
4 Pierre Bourdieu, *The Weight of the World: Social Suffering in Contemporary Society,* trans. Priscilla Parkhurst Ferguson (Stanford, Ca: Stanford University Press, 2000).
5 Roberto Mangabeira Unger, *False Necessity: Anti-Necessitarian Social Theory in the Service of Radical Democracy* (London: Verso, 2004).
6 On the distinction between traditional and critical theory, see Max Horkheimer, "Traditional and Critical Theory," in *Critical Theory: Selected Essays,* trans. Matthew O'Connell (New York: Continuum, 1982), 188–243.
7 David Harvey, *A Brief History of Neoliberalism* (New York: Oxford, 2010).
8 Other urban-ideological keywords could be added to this list – including, in more recent years, "creative cities," "smart cities," "sustainable cities" and "resilient cities." For powerful critical contextualizations and deconstructions of such terms, see Jamie Peck, "Struggling with the Creative Class," *International Journal of Urban and Regional Research* 29, no. 4 (2005): 740–70; Adam Greenfield, *Against the Smart City* (New York: Do projects, 2013); Timothy Luke, "Neither Sustainable nor Development: Reconsidering Sustainability in Development," *Sustainable Development* 13 (2005): 228–38; and Susan Fainstein, "Resilience and Justice," *International Journal of Urban and Regional Research* 39, no. 1 (2015): 157–67.
9 Hall, "The Problem of Ideology," 30–31.
10 The concept of "possible urban worlds" is developed in David Harvey, *Justice, Nature and the Geographies of Difference* (Oxford: Blackwell, 1995).
11 Andrew Sayer, *Method in Social Science: A Realist Approach*, 2nd ed. (London: Routledge, 1992).
12 Margaret Archer, *Making Our Way Through the World: Human Reflexivity and Social Mobility* (Cambridge: Cambridge University Press, 2007), 72.
13 These arguments are developed at length in several coauthored texts that are not included in this volume, as well as in several other collaborative writing projects. See, in particular, Neil Brenner and Christian Schmid, "The 'Urban Age' in question," *International Journal of Urban and Regional Research* 38,

no. 3 (2014): 731–55; and Neil Brenner and Christian Schmid, "Towards a New Epistemology of the Urban," *CITY* 19, no. 2–3 (2015): 151–82. See also Neil Brenner, ed., *Implosions/Explosions: Towards a Study of Planetary Urbanization* (Berlin: Jovis, 2014).

14   Hall, "The Problem of Ideology," 30.

2 What Is Critical Urban Theory?

What is *critical* urban theory? This phrase is generally used as a shorthand reference to the writings of leftist or radical urban scholars during the post-1968 period – for instance, those of Henri Lefebvre, David Harvey, Manuel Castells, Peter Marcuse and a legion of others who have been inspired or influenced by them.[1] Critical urban theory rejects inherited disciplinary divisions of labor and statist, technocratic, market-driven and market-oriented forms of urban knowledge. In this sense, critical theory differs fundamentally from what might be termed "mainstream" urban theory – for example, the approaches inherited from the Chicago School of urban sociology, or those deployed within technocratic or neoliberal forms of policy science. Rather than affirming the current condition of cities as the expression of transhistorical laws of social organization, bureaucratic rationality or economic efficiency, critical urban theory emphasizes the politically and ideologically mediated, socially contested and therefore malleable character of urban space – that is, its continual (re)construction as a site, medium and outcome of historically specific relations of social power. Critical urban theory is thus grounded on an antagonistic relationship not only to inherited urban knowledges, but more generally, to existing urban formations. It insists that other, more democratic, socially just and sustainable forms of urbanization are possible, even if such possibilities are currently being suppressed through dominant institutional arrangements, practices and ideologies. In short, critical urban theory involves the critique of ideology (including social-scientific ideologies) *and* the critique of power, inequality, injustice and exploitation, at once within and among cities.

However, the notions of critique, and more specifically of critical theory, are not merely descriptive terms. They have determinate social-theoretical content that is derived from various strands of Enlightenment and post-Enlightenment social philosophy, especially within the work of Hegel, Marx and the Western Marxian tradition.[2] Moreover, the focus of critique in critical social theory has evolved significantly during the course of the last two centuries of capitalist development.[3] Therefore, it is worth revisiting some of the key arguments developed within the aforementioned traditions, particularly that of the Frankfurt School, which arguably provide a crucial, if often largely implicit, reference point for the contemporary work of critical urbanists.

One of the main points to be emphasized in this chapter is the historical specificity of any approach to critical social theory, urban or otherwise. The work of Marx and the Frankfurt School emerged during previous phases of capitalism – liberal-competitive and Fordist-Keynesian, respectively – that have now been superseded through the restless, creatively destructive forward motion of global capitalist development.[4] A key contemporary question, therefore, is how the conditions of possibility for critical theory have changed today, in the early twenty-first century, in the context of an increasingly neoliberalized, financialized formation of capitalism.[5]

Such considerations also lead directly into the thorny problem of how to position urban questions within the broader project of critical social theory. With the significant exception of Walter Benjamin's *Passagen-Werk* (*Arcades Project*), none of the main figures associated with the Frankfurt School devoted much attention to urban questions. For them, critical theory involved the critique of commodification, the state and the law, including their mediations, for instance, through family structures, cultural forms and social-psychological dynamics.[6] This orientation was typical for many Euro-American social theorists working during the competitive and Fordist-Keynesian phases of capitalist development, in which urbanization was widely viewed as a straightforward spatial expression of other, purportedly more fundamental social forces, such as industrialization, class struggle and state regulation. I argue, however, that such an orientation is untenable in the early twenty-first century, as we witness nothing less than an urbanization of the world – the planetary "urban revolution" anticipated in the 1970s by Henri Lefebvre.[7] Under conditions of increasingly generalized, worldwide urbanization, the project of critical social theory and that of critical urban theory have been mutually intertwined as never before.

Critique and critical social theory

The modern idea of critique is derived from the Enlightenment and was developed most systematically in the work of Kant, Hegel and the Left Hegelians.[8] But it assumed a new significance in Marx's work, with the development of the notion of a critique of political economy.[9] For Marx, the critique of political economy entailed, on the one hand, a form of *Ideologiekritik* (critique of ideology), an unmasking of the historically specific myths, reifications and antinomies that pervade bourgeois forms of knowledge. Just as importantly, Marx understood the critique of political economy not only as a critique of ideas and discourses about capitalism, but as a critique of capitalism itself, and as a contribution to the collective effort to transcend it. In this dialectical conception, a key task of critique is to reveal the contradictions within the historically specific social totality formed by capitalism.

This approach to critique is seen to have several important functions. First, it exposes the forms of power, exclusion, injustice and inequality that underpin capitalist social formations. Second, for Marx, the critique of political economy is intended to illuminate the landscape of ongoing and emergent sociopolitical struggles: it connects the ideological discourses of the political sphere to the underlying (class) antagonisms and social forces within bourgeois society. Perhaps most crucially, Marx understood critique as a means to explore, both in theory and in practice, the possibility of forging alternatives to capitalism. A critique of political economy thus served to show how capitalism's contradictions simultaneously undermine the system, and point beyond it, towards other ways of organizing societal capacities and society/nature relations.

During the course of the twentieth century, Marx's critique of political economy has been appropriated within diverse traditions of critical social analysis, including the traditional Marxism of the Second International and the alternative strands of radical thought associated with Western Marxism.[10] It was arguably within the Frankfurt School of critical social theory, however, that the concept of critique was explored most systematically as a methodological, theoretical and political problem. In confronting this issue, the major figures within the Frankfurt School also developed an innovative, intellectually and politically subversive research program on the political economy, social-psychological dynamics, evolutionary trends and inner contradictions of modern capitalism.[11]

It was Max Horkheimer who, writing from exile in New York City in 1937, introduced the terminology of "critical theory."[12] The concept was subsequently developed and extended by his associates Theodor Adorno and Herbert Marcuse, and later, in different directions, by Jürgen Habermas, up through the 1980s. In the Frankfurt School conception, critical theory represented a decisive break from the orthodox forms of Marxism that prevailed under the Second International, with its transhistorical ontology of labor and its invocation of proletarian class struggle as the privileged basis for social transformation under capitalism. Additionally, during the course of the mid-twentieth century, the Frankfurt School of critical theory was animated by several other contextually specific concerns and preoccupations – including the critique of fascism in Germany and elsewhere; the critique of technology, mass consumerism and the culture industry under postwar capitalism in Europe and the USA; and, particularly in the later work of Herbert Marcuse, the critique of suppressed possibilities for human emancipation latent with present institutional arrangements.

The Frankfurt School notion of critical theory was initially elaborated as an epistemological concept. In Horkheimer's classic 1937 essay "Traditional and Critical Theory," it served to demarcate an alternative to positivistic and technocratic approaches to social science and bourgeois philosophy.[13] This line of analysis was famously continued by Adorno in the 1960s, in the *Positivismusstreit* (positivism dispute) with Karl Popper, and again in a different form in his philosophical writings on dialectics and aesthetic theory.[14] The notion of critical theory was developed in yet another new direction by Habermas in his debate on technocracy with Niklas Luhmann in the early 1970s, and in a still more elaborate, mature form in his magnum opus, *The Theory of Communicative Action*, in the mid-1980s.[15]

The most politically charged vision of critical theory was arguably presented by Herbert Marcuse in the mid-1960s, above all in his 1964 classic, *One-Dimensional Man*. For Marcuse, critical theory entailed an immanent critique of capitalist society in its current form: it is concerned, he insisted, with "the *historical alternatives* which haunt the established society as subversive tendencies and forces [italics added]."[16] There is thus a direct link between Marcuse's project and a central aspect of Marx's original critique of political economy – the search for emancipatory alternatives latent within the present, due to the contradictions of existing social relations.[17]

Key elements of critical theory: four propositions

There are, of course, profound epistemological, methodological, political and substantive differences among writers such as Horkheimer, Adorno, Marcuse and Habermas. Nonetheless, it can be argued that their writings collectively elaborate a core, underlying conception of critical theory.[18] This conception can be summarized

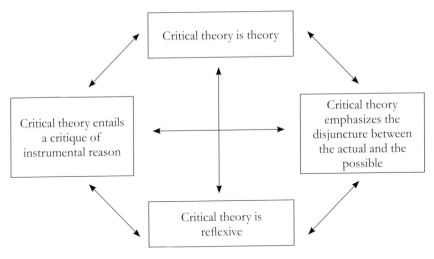

Figure 2.1: Four mutually constitutive propositions on critical theory

with reference to four key propositions: critical theory is theory; it is reflexive; it involves a critique of instrumental reason; and it is focused on the disjuncture between the actual and the possible. These propositions should be understood as being inextricably intertwined and mutually constitutive; the full meaning of each can only be grasped in relation to the others (Figure 2.1).

Critical theory is theory

In the Frankfurt School, critical theory is unapologetically abstract. It is characterized by epistemological and philosophical reflections; the development of formal concepts, generalizations about historical trends; deductive and inductive modes of argumentation; and diverse forms of historical analysis. It may also build upon concrete research, that is, upon an evidentiary basis, whether organized through traditional or critical methods. As Marcuse writes, "In order to identify and define the possibilities for an optimal development, the critical theory must abstract from the actual organization and utilization of society's resources, and from the results of this organization and utilization."[19] It is, in this sense, a *theory*.

Critical theory is thus not intended to serve as a formula for any particular course of social change; it is not a strategic map for social change; and it is not a practical manual for social movements. It may – indeed, it *should* – have mediations to the realm of practice, and it is explicitly intended to inform the strategic perspective of progressive, radical or revolutionary social and political actors. But, at the same time, crucially, the Frankfurt School conception of critical theory is focused on a moment of abstraction that is analytically prior to the famous Leninist question of "What is to be done?"

Critical theory is reflexive

In the Frankfurt School tradition, theory is understood to be at once enabled by, and oriented towards, specific historical conditions and contexts. This conceptualization has at least two key implications. First, critical theory entails a total rejection of any standpoint – positivistic, transcendental, metaphysical or otherwise – that claims to be able to stand "outside" of the contextually specific time/space of history. All social knowledge, including critical theory, is embedded within the dialectics of social and historical change; it is thus intrinsically contextual. Second, Frankfurt School critical theory transcends a generalized hermeneutic concern with the situatedness of all knowledge. It is focused, more specifically, on the question of how oppositional, antagonistic forms of knowledge, subjectivity and consciousness may emerge within an historical social formation.

Critical theorists confront this issue by emphasizing the fractured, broken or contradictory character of capitalism as a social totality. If the totality were closed, noncontradictory or complete, there could be no critical consciousness of it; there would be no need for critique; and indeed, critique would be structurally impossible. Critique emerges precisely insofar as society is in conflict with itself, that is, because its mode of development is self-contradictory. In this sense, critical theorists are concerned not only to situate themselves and their research agendas within the historical evolution of modern capitalism. Just as crucially, they want to understand what it is about modern capitalism that enables their own and others' forms of critical consciousness.

Critical theory entails a critique of instrumental reason

As is well known, the Frankfurt School critical theorists developed a critique of instrumental reason.[20] Building on Max Weber's writings, they argued against the societal generalization of a technical rationality oriented towards the purposive-rational (*Zweckrationale*), an efficient linking of means to ends, without interrogation of the ends themselves. This critique had implications for various realms of industrial organization, technology and administration, but most crucially here, Frankfurt School theorists also applied it to the realm of social science. In this sense, critical theory entails a forceful rejection of instrumental modes of social scientific knowledge – that is, those designed to render existing institutional arrangements more efficient and effective, to manipulate and dominate the social and physical world, and thus to bolster current forms of power. Instead, critical theorists demanded an interrogation of the ends of knowledge, and thus, an explicit engagement with normative-political questions.

Consistent with their historically reflexive approach to social science, Frankfurt School scholars argued that a critical theory must make explicit its practical-political and normative orientations, rather than embracing a narrow or technocratic vision. Instrumentalist modes of knowledge necessarily presuppose their own separation from their object of investigation. However, once that separation is rejected, and the knower is understood to be embedded within the same practical social context that is being investigated, normative questions are unavoidable. The proposition of reflexivity and the critique of instrumental reason are thus directly interconnected.

Consequently, when critical theorists discuss the so-called theory/practice problem, they are *not* referring to the question of how to "apply" theory to practice. Rather, they are thinking this dialectical relationship in exactly the opposite direction – namely, how the realm of practice (and thus, normative-political considerations) always already inform the work of theorists, even when the latter remains on an abstract level. As Habermas wrote in 1971, "The dialectical interpretation [associated with critical theory] comprehends the knowing subject in terms of the relations of social praxis, in terms of its position, both within the process of social labor and the process of enlightening the political forces about their goals."[21]

Critical theory emphasizes the disjuncture between the actual and the possible

As Therborn argues, the Frankfurt School embraces a dialectical critique of capitalist modernity – that is, one that affirms the possibilities for human liberation that are opened up by this social formation while also criticizing its systemic exclusions, oppressions, injustices and irrationalities.[22] The task of critical theory is therefore not only to investigate the forms of domination, scarcity and waste associated with modern capitalism, but equally, to excavate the emancipatory possibilities that are embedded within, yet simultaneously suppressed by, this very system.

In much Frankfurt School writing, this orientation involves a "search for a revolutionary subject," that is, the concern to find an agent of radical social change that could realize the possibilities unleashed yet suppressed by capitalism. However, given the Frankfurt School's abandonment of any hope for a proletarian-style revolution, their search for a revolutionary subject during the postwar period generated a rather gloomy pessimism regarding the possibility for social transformation and, especially in the work of Adorno and Horkheimer, a retreat into relatively abstract philosophical and aesthetic concerns.[23]

Marcuse, by contrast, presents a very different position on this issue in the opening chapter of *One-Dimensional Man*. Here, he agrees with his Frankfurt School colleagues that, in contrast to the formative period of capitalist industrialization, late twentieth-century capitalism lacks any clear "agents or agencies of social change"; in other words, the proletariat was no longer operating as a class "for itself." Nonetheless, Marcuse insists forcefully that "the need for qualitative change is as pressing as ever before [...] by society as a whole, for every one of its members."[24] Against this background, Marcuse proposes that the rather abstract quality of critical theory, during the time in which he was writing, was organically linked to the absence of an obvious agent of radical, emancipatory social change. He argues, moreover, that the abstractions associated with critical theory could only be blunted or dissolved through concrete-historical struggles: "The theoretical concepts," Marcuse suggests, "terminate with social change."[25] This powerful proposition thus returns us to the idea of critical theory as theory. Just as the *critical* thrust of critical theory is historically conditioned and historically oriented, so too is its *theoretical* orientation continuously shaped and reshaped through ongoing social and political transformations.

Marcuse's position is reminiscent of Marx's famous claim that all science would be superfluous if there were no distinction between reality and appearance.[26] Similarly, Marcuse suggests, in a world in which radical or revolutionary social change were occurring, critical theory would be effectively marginalized or even dissolved – not in its critical orientation, but as *theory:* it would become concrete practice. Or, to state this point differently, it is precisely because revolutionary, transformative, emancipatory social practice remains so tightly circumscribed and constrained under contemporary capitalism that critical theory remains critical *theory* – and not simply everyday social practice. From this point of view, the so-called theory/practice divide is an artifact not of theoretical confusion, epistemological inadequacies or a penchant for abstraction, but of the alienated, contradictory social formation in which critical theory is embedded. There is no theory that can overcome this divide, because, by definition, it cannot be overcome theoretically; it can only be overcome in practice.

Critical theory and the urbanization question

While Marx's work has exercised a massive influence on the post-1968 field of critical urban studies, few, if any, contributors to this field have engaged directly with the writings of the Frankfurt School. Nonetheless, I believe that most authors who position themselves within the intellectual universe of critical urban studies would endorse, at least in general terms, the conception of critical theory that is articulated through the four propositions summarized above:

- they insist on the need for abstract, theoretical arguments regarding the nature of urban processes under capitalism, while rejecting the conception of theory as being subservient to immediate, practical or instrumental concerns;
- they view knowledge of urban questions, including critical perspectives on the latter, as being historically specific and mediated through power relations;
- they reject instrumentalist, technocratic and market-driven forms of urban analysis that promote the maintenance and reproduction of extant urban formations; and
- they are concerned to excavate possibilities for alternative, radical and emancipatory forms of urbanism that are latent, yet suppressed, within contemporary cities.

Of course, any given contribution to critical urban theory may be more attuned to some of these propositions than to others, but they appear, cumulatively, to constitute an important epistemological foundation for the field as a whole. In this sense, critical urban theory has developed on an intellectual and political terrain that had already been tilled extensively not only by Marx, but also by the various theoreticians of the Frankfurt School. Given the rather pronounced, even divisive character of methodological, epistemological and substantive debates among critical urbanists since the consolidation of this field in the early 1970s, it is essential not to lose sight of these broad areas of foundational agreement.[27]

However, as the field of critical urban studies continues to evolve and diversify in the early twenty-first century, its character as a putatively "critical" theory deserves to be subjected to careful scrutiny and systematic debate. In an incisive feminist critique of Habermas, Nancy Fraser famously asked, "What's critical about critical theory?"[28] Fraser's question can also be posed of the field of study under discussion here: what's critical about critical *urban* theory? Precisely because the process of capitalist urbanization continues its forward movement of creative destruction and socioterritorial transformation on a world scale, the meanings and modalities of critique can never be held constant; they must be continually reinvented in relation to the unevenly evolving political-economic geographies of this process and the diverse conflicts it engenders. This is one of the major intellectual and political challenges confronting critical urban theorists today.

As indicated above, the concept of critique developed by Marx and the vision of critical theory elaborated by the Frankfurt School were embedded within, and conditioned by, historically specific formations of capitalism. Consistent with their requirement for reflexivity, each of these approaches explicitly understood itself to be contextually embedded, and was oriented self-consciously towards subjecting its own historical context to critique. This requirement for reflexivity must also figure centrally in any attempt to appropriate or reinvent critical theory, urban or otherwise, in the early twenty-first century.

However, as Moishe Postone has forcefully argued, the conditions of possibility for critical theory have been thoroughly reconstituted under post-Fordist, post-Keynesian, post-developmentalist capitalism.[29] The nature of the structural constraints on potentially emancipatory forms of social change, and the associated imagination of alternatives to capitalism, have been qualitatively transformed through the acceleration of geoeconomic integration, the intensified financialization of capital, the crisis of the Keynesian-developmentalist model of state power, the still ongoing neoliberalization of state forms, the deepening of planetary ecological crises and a host of parallel geopolitical, technological and geocultural shifts.[30] The most recent global financial crisis – the latest expression of a roller-coaster of catastrophic regional crashes that have been rippling across the world economy for several decades – has generated a new round of worldwide, crisis-induced restructuring that has still further rearticulated the epistemological, political and institutional conditions of possibility for any critical social theory.[31] While the four aforementioned elements of critical theory surely remain urgently relevant in the early twenty-first century, their specific meanings and modalities need to be carefully reconceptualized. The challenge for those committed to the project of critical theory is to do so in a manner that is adequate to the continued forward motion of capital, its associated crisis tendencies and contradictions, and the struggles and oppositional impulses it is generating across the variegated landscapes of the world economy.

Confronting this task hinges, I submit, on a much more systematic integration of urban questions into the analytical framework of critical social theory as a whole. As mentioned previously, the problematic of urbanization received relatively scant attention within classical Frankfurt School analyses; and it is only relatively recently that Walter Benjamin's wide-ranging sketches on the capitalist transformation of nineteenth-century Paris have engendered significant scholarly interest.[32] Clearly, even during the liberal-competitive and Fordist-Keynesian phases of capitalist development, urbanization processes – manifested above all in the consolidation and territorial expansion of large-scale urban regions – figured crucially in the dynamics of capital accumulation and in the organization of everyday social relations and political struggles. Under present geohistorical conditions, however, the process of urbanization has become increasingly generalized on a world scale. Urbanization no longer refers simply to the expansion of the "great towns" (Friedrich Engels) of industrial capitalism, to the sprawling metropolitan production centers, suburban settlement grids and regional infrastructure configurations of Fordist-Keynesian capitalism, or to the linear expansion of city-based human populations and informal settlements in the world's megacities to create a "planet of slums" (Mike Davis).[33] Instead, as Lefebvre presciently anticipated, the capitalist form of urbanization now increasingly unfolds through the uneven stretching of an urban fabric across the entire planet: it is composed not only of large, dense agglomerations and their immediate hinterlands, but of variegated configurations of industrial land use, infrastructural investment, logistical connectivity and socio-environmental transformation extended throughout the world economy, including within relatively "remote," low-population and/or low-density landscapes.[34] Urbanization is, to be sure, still manifested in the continued, massive expansion of cities, city-regions and megacity regions, but it now equally entails the intensification of land use, and associated large-scale infrastructure investments, to metabolize the accelerating industrialization of capital through extraction, cultivation, logistics and environmental management across diverse places, territories and landscapes. We are witnessing, in short, nothing less than the intensification and extension of capitalist urbanization at all spatial scales, across planetary space as a whole, including not only the earth's terrestrial surfaces, but the underground, the oceans and even the atmosphere itself.[35]

As during previous phases of global capitalist development, the geographies of urbanization are profoundly uneven, but their parameters are no longer confined to any single type of settlement space, whether defined as a city, a city-region, a metropolitan region or even a megacity-region. Consequently, under contemporary circumstances, the urban can no longer be viewed as a distinct, relatively bounded site; it has instead become a generalized, planetary condition in and through which the accumulation of capital, the extension of industrial infrastructure, the regulation of political-economic life, the reproduction of everyday social relations, the production of socionatures and the contestation of humanity's possible futures are simultaneously organized and fought out. In light of this, it is increasingly untenable to view urban questions as merely one among many specialized subtopics to which a critical theoretical approach may be applied – alongside, for instance, the family, social psychology, education, culture industries and the like. Instead, each of the key methodological and political orientations associated with critical theory, as discussed above, today requires sustained engagement with contemporary world-wide patterns of capitalist urbanization and their far-reaching consequences for social, political-economic and socioenvironmental relations.

This is an intentionally provocative assertion, and this chapter has offered no more than a modest attempt to demarcate the need for such an engagement, and some of the broad intellectual parameters within which it might occur. Clearly, the effective elaboration of this *urbanization*-theoretical reorientation of critical theory will require further theoretical reflection, extensive concrete and comparative research, as well as creative, collaborative strategizing to nourish the politico-institutional conditions required for an effervescence of critical knowledges about historical and contemporary urbanization. I argued above that critical urbanists must work to clarify and continually redefine the "critical" character of their theoretical engagements, orientations and commitments in light of early twenty-first century processes of urban restructuring. Given the far-reaching transformations associated with such processes, the time seems equally ripe to integrate the problematic of urbanization more systematically and comprehensively into the intellectual architecture of critical theory as a whole.

It is to these tasks that the various studies and explorations presented in this book are devoted. They aspire to mobilize the tools of critical urban theory to decipher some of the dynamics of urban transformation and contestation – infrastructural, regulatory and ideological – since the global economic crises of the 1970s. Just as importantly, these investigations are animated by a persistent concern to update, and even to reinvent, the categories, methods and framing assumptions of critical urban theory in relation to the volatile, conflictual, rapidly mutating worlds of capitalist urbanization.

Notes

1   Ira Katznelson, *Marxism and the City* (New York: Oxford University Press, 1993); Andy Merrifield, *Metromarxism* (New York: Routledge, 2002).

2   Reinhart Koselleck, *Critique and Crisis: Enlightenment and the Pathogenesis of Modern Society* (Cambridge, MA: MIT Press, 1988); Moishe Postone, *Time, Labor and Social Domination: A Reinterpretation of Karl Marx's Critical Social Theory* (New York: Cambridge University Press, 1993); Craig Calhoun, "Rethinking Critical Theory," in *Critical Social Theory: Culture, History, and the Challenge of Difference* (Cambridge, MA: Blackwell, 1995).

3   Göran Therborn, "Dialectics of Modernity: On Critical Theory and the Legacy of Twentieth-Century Marxism," *New Left Review* 215 (January/February 1996): 59–81.

4   Postone, *Time, Labor and Social Domination*. See also Moishe Postone, "Contemporary Historical Transformations: Beyond Postindustrial Theory and Neo-Marxism," *Current Perspectives in Social Theory* 19 (1999): 3–53; and Moishe Postone, "Political Theory and Historical Analysis," in *Habermas and the Public Sphere,* ed. Craig Calhoun (Cambridge, MA: MIT Press, 1992), 164–80.

5   Göran Therborn, *From Marxism to Post-Marxism?* (London: Verso, 2008).

6   Douglas Kellner, *Critical Theory, Marxism and Modernity* (Baltimore: Johns Hopkins University Press, 1989); Martin Jay, *The Dialectical Imagination* (Boston: Little, Brown & Co, 1973); Rolf Wiggershaus, *The Frankfurt School,* trans. Michael Robertson (Cambridge, MA: MIT Press, 1995).

7   Henri Lefebvre, *The Urban Revolution,* trans. Robert Bononno (Minneapolis: University of Minnesota Press, 2003 [1970]). See also Edward Soja and Juan Miguel Kanai, "The Urbanization of the World," in *The Endless City,* ed. Ricky Burdett and Deyan Sudjic (London: Phaidon Press, 2007), 54–69; and Neil Brenner, ed., *Implosions/Explosions: Towards a Study of Planetary Urbanization* (Berlin: Jovis, 2014).

8   Jürgen Habermas, *Theory and Practice,* trans. John Viertel (Boston: Beacon Press, 1973); Herbert Marcuse, *Reason and Revolution: Hegel and the Rise of Social Theory* (London: Humanities Press, 1954); Jay, *The Dialectical Imagination;* Calhoun, "Rethinking Critical Theory"; and Therborn, "Dialectics of Modernity."

9   Postone, *Time, Labor and Social Domination.*

10   Leszek Kolakowski, *Main Currents of Marxism: The Golden Age,* vol. 2 (Oxford: Oxford University Press, 1981); Martin Jay, *Marxism and Totality* (Berkeley: University of California Press, 1986).

11   Andrew Arato and Eike Gebhardt, eds., *The Essential Frankfurt School Reader* (New York: Continuum, 1990); Stephen Bronner and Douglas Kellner, eds., *Critical Theory and Society: A Reader* (New York: Routledge, 1989); and Wiggershaus, *The Frankfurt School.*

12   Max Horkheimer, "Traditional and Critical Theory," in *Critical Theory: Selected Essays,* trans. Matthew O'Connell (New York: Continuum, 1982), 188–243.

13   Ibid.

14   Theodor Adorno et al., *The Positivist Dispute in German Sociology,* trans. Glyn Adey and David Frisby (London: Heinemann, 1976). See also Brian O'Connor, ed., *The Adorno Reader* (Oxford: Wiley-Blackwell, 2000).

15   Jürgen Habermas and Niklas Luhmann, *Theorie der Gesellschaft oder Sozialtechnologie – was leistet Systemforschung?* (Frankfurt: Suhrkamp Verlag, 1971); Jürgen Habermas, *The Theory of Communicative Action,* vol. 1, trans. Thomas McCarthy (Boston: Beacon Press, 1985); Jürgen Habermas, *The Theory of Communicative Action,* vol. 2, trans. Thomas McCarthy (Boston: Beacon Press, 1987).

16   Herbert Marcuse, *One-Dimensional Man* (Boston: Beacon Press, 1964), xi–xii.

17   As emphasized systematically by Postone, *Time, Labor and Social Domination.*

18   For an alternative but compatible reading, see Calhoun, "Rethinking Critical Theory."

19   Marcuse, *One-Dimensional Man,* xi.

20   See Habermas, *Theory of Communicative Action.*

21   Habermas, *Theory and Practice,* 210–11.

22   Therborn, *From Marxism to Post-Marxism.*

23   Postone, *Time, Labor and Social Domination.*

24   Marcuse, *One-Dimensional Man,* xii.

25   Ibid.

26   "But all science would be superfluous if the outward appearance and the essence of things directly coincided." See Karl Marx, *Capital,* vol. 3, chapter 48, "The Trinity Formula," accessible at: https://www.marxists.org/archive/marx/works/1894-c3/ch48.htm.

27   See, for instance, Peter Saunders, *Social Theory and the Urban Question,* 2nd ed. (New York: Routledge, 1986); Mark Gottdiener, *The Social Production of Urban Space,* 2nd ed. (Austin: University of Texas Press, 1985); Jennifer Robinson, *Ordinary Cities* (London: Routledge, 2006); Neil Brenner and Roger Keil, eds., *The Global Cities Reader* (New York: Routledge, 2006); and Edward Soja, *Postmetropolis* (Cambridge, MA: Wiley-Blackwell, 2000).

28   Nancy Fraser, *Unruly Practices* (Minneapolis: University of Minneapolis Press, 1989).

29   Postone, "Contemporary Historical Transformations"; Postone, *Time, Labor and Social Domination.*

30   David Harvey, *The New Imperialism* (New York: Oxford University Press, 2005); Robert Albritton, ed., *Phases of Capitalist Development* (New York: Palgrave, 2001).

31   Neil Brenner, Jamie Peck and Nik Theodore, *The Afterlives of Neoliberalism.* Civic City Cahiers (CCC) (London: Bedford Press/Architectural Association, 2012).

32   Walter Benjamin, *The Arcades Project,* ed. Rolf Tiedemann, trans. Howard Eiland and Kevin McLaughlin (Cambridge, MA: Harvard University Press, 2002). See also Susan Buck-Morss, *The Dialectics of Seeing* (Cambridge, MA: MIT Press, 1991).

33   See Friedrich Engels, *The Condition of the Working Class in England* (London: Penguin Classics, 2009 [1845]); and Mike Davis, *Planet of Slums* (London: Verso, 2006).

34   Lefebvre, *The Urban Revolution.*

35   This argument is elaborated further in the final section of this book, *New Urban Geographies.* See also Brenner, *Implosions/Explosions.*

Urban Strategies, Urban Ideologies

3 Cities and the Geographies of Actually Existing Neoliberalism

with Nik Theodore

The lynchpin of neoliberal ideology is the belief that open, competitive and unregulated markets, liberated from all forms of state interference, represent the optimal mechanism for economic development. Although the intellectual roots of this "utopia of unlimited exploitation" can be traced to the postwar writings of Friedrich Hayek and Milton Friedman, neoliberalism first gained widespread prominence during the late 1970s and early 1980s as a strategic political response to the sustained global recession of the preceding decade.[1] Faced with the declining profitability of traditional mass production industries and the crisis of Keynesian welfare policies, national and local states throughout the older industrialized world began, if hesitantly at first, to dismantle the basic institutional components of the postwar settlement and to mobilize a range of policies intended to extend market discipline, competition and commodification throughout all sectors of society. In this context, neoliberal doctrines were deployed to justify, among other projects, the deregulation of state control over major industries, assaults on organized labor, the reduction of corporate taxes, the privatization of public services, the shrinking or dismantling of welfare programs, the enhancement of international capital mobility, the intensification of interlocality competition and the criminalization of the urban poor.

If Thatcherism and Reaganism represented particularly aggressive programs of neoliberal restructuring during the 1980s, more moderate forms of a neoliberal politics were also mobilized during this same period in traditionally social democratic or social-christian democratic states such as Canada, New Zealand, Germany, the Netherlands, France, Italy and Sweden. Following the debt crisis of the early 1980s, neoliberal programs of restructuring were extended globally through the efforts of the USA and other Group of Seven (G7) states to subject peripheral and semi-peripheral states to the discipline of capital markets. Bretton Woods institutions such as the General Agreement on Tariffs and Trade (GATT), the International Monetary Fund (IMF) and the World Bank were subsequently transformed into the agents of a transnational neoliberalism and were mobilized to institutionalize this extension of market forces and commodification in the Third World through various structural adjustment and fiscal austerity programs. By the mid-1980s, in the wake of this dramatic U-turn of policy agendas throughout the world, neoliberalism had become the dominant political and ideological form of capitalist globalization.

The global imposition of neoliberalism has, of course, been highly uneven, both socially and geographically, and its institutional forms and sociopolitical consequences have varied significantly across spatial scales and among each of the major zones of the world economy. While recognizing the polycentric, multiscalar character of neoliberalism as a geopolitical and geoeconomic project, this chapter explores the role of neoliberalism in ongoing processes of *urban* restructuring. The supranational and national parameters of neoliberalism have been widely recognized in the literatures on geopolitical economy. However, the contention that neoliberalism has also generated powerful impacts at subnational scales, within cities and city-regions, deserves to be elaborated more systematically.

This chapter provides a first cut towards theorizing the variegated institutional, geographical and social interfaces between neoliberalism and urban restructuring. We begin by presenting the conceptual and methodological foundations for an approach to the geographies of what we term "actually existing neoliberalism." In contrast to neoliberal ideology, in which market forces are assumed to operate according to immutable laws no matter where they are unleashed, we emphasize the contextual embeddedness of neoliberal restructuring projects, insofar as they have been produced within national, regional and local contexts defined by the legacies of inherited institutional frameworks, policy regimes, regulatory practices and political struggles. An understanding of actually existing neoliberalism must therefore explore the path-dependent, contextually specific interactions between inherited regulatory landscapes and emergent neoliberal, market-oriented restructuring projects at a range of geographical scales.

These considerations lead to a conceptualization of contemporary neoliberalization processes as catalysts and expressions of an ongoing creative destruction of political-economic space at multiple geographical scales. While the neoliberal restructuring projects of the 1980s and 1990s failed to establish a coherent basis for sustainable capitalist growth, they nonetheless profoundly reworked the institutional infrastructures upon which the postwar configuration of Fordist-Keynesian-developmentalist capitalism had been grounded. The concept of creative destruction is presented to describe the geographically uneven, socially regressive and politically volatile trajectories of institutional-spatial change that have crystallized under these conditions. We conclude by discussing the role of urban spaces within the contradictory and chronically unstable geographies of actually existing neoliberalism. Throughout the world, we suggest, cities have become strategically crucial geographical arenas in which a variety of neoliberal initiatives, along with closely intertwined strategies of crisis displacement and crisis management, have been articulated.

Towards a political economy of "actually existing neoliberalism"

The 1990s was a decade in which the term "neoliberalism" became a major rallying point for a broad range of anti-capitalist popular struggles, from the Zapatista rebellion in Chiapas, the subsequent series of Gatherings for Humanity and Against Neoliberalism and the December 1995 mass strikes in France, to the mass protests against the IMF, the World Bank, the World Trade Organization (WTO) and the World Economic Forum (WEF) in Davos, Genoa, London, Melbourne, Mumbai, Nice, Prague, Seattle, Sydney, Washington, DC, and Zurich, among many other locations. As such struggles continue to proliferate in the new millennium, anti-capitalist forces throughout the world have come to identify neoliberalism as a major target for oppositional mobilization.

Among activists and radical academics alike, there is considerable agreement regarding the basic elements of neoliberalism as an ideological project. For instance, Kim Moody has described neoliberalism concisely as "a mixture of neoclassical economic fundamentalism, market regulation in place of state guidance, economic redistribution in favor of capital (known as supply-side economics), moral authoritarianism with an idealized family at its center, international free trade principles (sometimes inconsistently applied), and a thorough intolerance of trade unionism."[2] However, as Moody and others have emphasized, there is also a rather blatant disjuncture between the ideology of neoliberalism and its everyday political operations and societal effects. On the one hand, while neoliberalism aspires to create a "utopia" of free markets liberated from all forms of state interference, it has in practice entailed an intensification of coercive, disciplinary forms of state intervention in order to impose market rule upon all aspects of social life. On the other hand, whereas neoliberal ideology implies that self-regulating markets will generate an optimal allocation of investments and resources, neoliberal political practice has generated pervasive market failures, new forms of social polarization and a dramatic intensification of uneven spatial development at all spatial scales. In short, as Stephen Gill explains, "the neoliberal shift in government policies has tended to subject the majority of the population to the power of market forces whilst preserving social protection for the strong."[3]

During the last two decades, the dysfunctional effects of neoliberal approaches to capitalist restructuring have been manifested in diverse socioinstitutional arenas and at a range of spatial scales.[4] Indeed, as many studies have demonstrated, the disjuncture between the ideology of self-regulating markets and the everyday reality of persistent economic stagnation, intensifying inequality, destructive interplace competition, generalized social insecurity and deepening environmental crisis has been particularly blatant in precisely those political-economic contexts in which neoliberal doctrines have been imposed most extensively.[5]

Crucially, the manifold disjunctures that have accompanied the worldwide imposition of neoliberalism – between ideology and practice; doctrine and reality; vision and consequence – are not merely accidental side-effects of this disciplinary project of imposing a new market civilization; they are among its essential features. For this reason, a purely definitional approach to the political economy of neoliberal restructuring contains significant analytical limitations: we are dealing here less with a coherently bounded "ism" or end-state, than with a process of *neoliberalization*.[6] Hence, in the present context, the somewhat elusive phenomenon that needs "definition" must be construed as an historically specific, still ongoing and internally contradictory process of market-driven sociospatial and institutional transformation, rather than as a fully actualized policy regime, ideological form or regulatory framework. From this perspective, an adequate understanding of contemporary neoliberalization processes requires not only a grasp of their politico-ideological foundations, but just as importantly, a systematic inquiry into their multifarious institutional forms, their hybrid political valences, their developmental tendencies, their diverse sociopolitical effects and their multiple contradictions.

For purposes of this chapter, we describe these ongoing neoliberalization processes through the concept of *actually existing neoliberalism*. This concept is intended not only to underscore the contradictory, destructive character of neoliberal policies, but to highlight the ways in which neoliberal ideology systematically misrepresents the wide-ranging effects of such policies on the macroinstitutional structures and evolutionary trajectories of capitalism. In this context, two issues deserve particular attention. First, rather than recognizing the politically con-structed character of all "economic" relations, neoliberal doctrine represents states and markets as if they were based upon diametrically opposed ontologies of social organization. Second, rather than recognizing the extraordinary variegations that arise as neoliberal policies are mobilized within contextually specific institutional landscapes, neoliberal doctrine is premised upon a "one-size-fits-all" model which assumes that basically identical results will (eventually) follow the implementation of market-oriented reforms.[7]

Our approach to the political economy of actually existing neoliberalism is grounded upon five core premises which, taken together, provide a methodological basis on which to circumvent these ideological pitfalls.

1. *The problem of capitalist regulation.* The social relations of capitalism are permeated by tensions, antagonisms and conflicts that continually destabilize the accumula-tion process. Capitalist regulation occurs as systems of rules, habits, norms and compromises are established within particular institutions, thereby embedding these conflictual social relations within relatively stabilized, routinized and sustain-able spatiotemporal frameworks.[8] The latter in turn endow the capitalist system with a marked, if constantly evolving, institutional coherence. Since the industria-lization and urbanization of capital on a large scale during the course of the nine-teenth century, the survival of capitalism within each national territory has been secured through the production of historically specific institutional landscapes composed of at least five basic dimensions: (i) *the wage relation* – the structure of capital/labor relations in the spheres of production and reproduction; (ii) *the form of intercapitalist competition* – the framework within which capitalists jostle for mar-ket share and technological advantages; (iii) forms of monetary and financial regulation – the organizational structure of capital circulation; (iv) the state and other forms of governance – the ensemble of institutionalized political compro-mises through which the basic contradictions of capitalist society are negotiated; and (v) the international configuration – the mechanisms through which national and subnational economic relations are articulated with worldwide processes of capital accumulation.[9]

2. *The unstable historical geographies of capitalism.* The process of capital accumulation and its associated regulatory problems are always articulated in territory-, place-

and scale-specific forms.[10] Capitalist development therefore necessarily unfolds through the production of historically specific patterns of sociospatial organization in which particular territories, regions, places and scales are mobilized as productive forces – whether in the form of agglomeration economies, regional production systems, infrastructural configurations, transportation and communications networks, or spatial divisions of labor.[11] It is in this sense that the long-term survival of capitalism is premised upon the "production of space."[12] Yet, due to its inherent dynamism, capital continually renders obsolete the very geographical landscapes it creates, and upon which its own reproduction and expansion hinges. Particularly during periods of systemic crisis, inherited frameworks of capitalist territorial organization may be destabilized as capital seeks to transcend sociospatial infrastructures and systems of social relations that no longer provide a secure basis for sustained accumulation. As the effects of devaluation ripple through the space-economy, processes of *creative destruction* ensue in which the capitalist geographical landscape is thoroughly transformed: the configurations of territorial organization that underpinned the previous round of capitalist expansion are junked and reworked in order to establish a new locational grid for the accumulation process. It should be noted, however, that the creative destruction of capitalist territorial organization is unpredictable and deeply contested. Even within industrial landscapes that have been systematically devalued by capital, social attachments to place persist as populations struggle to defend the everyday practices and institutional compromises from which capital has sought to extricate itself.[13] At the same time, capital's relentless quest to open up fresh spaces for accumulation is inherently speculative insofar as the establishment of a new spatial fix is never guaranteed; it can occur only through "chance discoveries" and provisional compromises in the wake of intense sociopolitical struggles.[14]

3. *Uneven geographical development.* Each round of capitalist development is associated with a distinctive, historically specific geographical landscape in which some places, territories and scales are systematically privileged over and against others as sites for capital accumulation. The resultant patterns of core-periphery polarization and territorial inequality exist at all spatial scales; their contours are never inscribed permanently upon the geographical landscape, but are continually reworked through capital's dynamic of uneven spatial development.[15] Uneven

development is endemic to capitalism as an historical-geographical system: it is a key expression of capital's relentless drive to mobilize particular territories and places as forces of production; it is a basic geographical medium through which intercapitalist competition and class struggle are fought out; and it is an evolving spatial-institutional scaffolding within which processes of devalorization and revalorization unfold.[16]

4. *The regulation of uneven geographical development.* Each historical pattern of uneven development is in turn associated with a series of basic regulatory dilemmas: for the uneven development of capital serves not only as a basis for the accumulation process but may also, under certain circumstances, operate as a *barrier* to the latter. For this reason, uneven development is associated not only with new opportunities for capital but also with any number of potentially destabilizing effects that may undermine the structured coherence upon which sustainable capital accumulation depends. In response to these persistent dilemmas, capitalist states have mobilized a variety of spatial policies intended to regulate the uneven development of capital. Strategies of territorial development and place promotion may be introduced in order to channel economic capacities into particular locations and scales. Alternatively, strategies of territorial redistribution and other compensatory regional policies may be introduced in order to equalize the distribution of industry and population across a particular territory, and thus to alleviate the more pernicious, polarizing effects of uneven spatial development.

5. *The evolving geographies of state regulation.* State strategies to regulate uneven development evolve continually in conjunction with contextually specific political-economic circumstances and sociopolitical struggles.[17] Nonetheless, during successive phases of capitalist development, specific forms of state spatial policy have been institutionalized, albeit in divergent (national) forms, and have come to provide a key regulatory infrastructure for industrial development. In this sense, the geographies of state institutions and policies are closely intertwined with evolving processes of uneven capitalist development: states provide a relatively stable regulatory landscape within which capital's locational dynamics are articulated; at the same time, states provide a key institutional arena in and through which new approaches to the regulation of uneven spatial development may be introduced. Particularly during periods of systemic capitalist crisis, when uneven development

threatens to undermine normalized patterns of accumulation and social reproduction, pressures to junk and rework extant institutional frameworks and regulatory strategies become particularly intense. Under these circumstances, a period of institutional searching and regulatory experimentation ensues in which diverse actors, organizations and alliances promote competing hegemonic visions, restructuring strategies and developmental models. The resultant "search for a new institutional fix" generally entails the partial dismantling or reworking of inherited institutional landscapes in order to "open up a space" for the deployment and institutionalization of new regulatory strategies.[18] Regulatory landscapes are continually made and remade through this intensive, politically contested interaction between inherited institutional forms and policy frameworks, and emergent strategies of state spatial regulation.[19]

These methodological premises provide a useful starting point from which to analyze the turbulent geographies of actually existing neoliberalism during the post-1970s period. The preceding considerations suggest that an analysis of actually existing neoliberalism must begin by exploring the entrenched landscapes of capitalist regulation, derived from the Fordist-Keynesian-developmentalist period of capitalist expansion, within which neoliberal programs were first mobilized following the geoeconomic crises of the early 1970s. From this perspective, the impacts of neoliberal restructuring strategies cannot be understood adequately through abstract, decontextualized debates regarding the relative merits of market-based reform initiatives or the purported limits of particular forms of state policy. Instead, an understanding of actually existing neoliberalism requires an exploration of: (a) the historically specific regulatory landscapes and political settlements that prevailed within particular (national) territories during the Fordist-Keynesian-developmentalist period of capitalist development; (b) the historically specific patterns of crisis formation, uneven development and sociopolitical contestation that emerged within those territories following the systemic crisis of the Fordist-Keynesian developmental model in the early 1970s; (c) the subsequent interaction of market-oriented, neoliberal initiatives with inherited regulatory frameworks, patterns of territorial development and sociopolitical alliances; and (d) the concomitant evolution of neoliberal policy agendas and restructuring strategies through their conflictual interaction with contextually specific political-economic conditions, regulatory arrangements and power-geometries.

In the remainder of this chapter, we analyze the spatiotemporalities of contemporary neoliberalization processes in three closely related steps – first, by emphasizing the path-dependent character of neoliberal reform initiatives; second, by examining the destructive and creative "moments" of neoliberal policies and institutional changes; and third, by considering the ways in which cities have become strategically crucial arenas for neoliberal forms of policy experimentation and institutional restructuring. The goal of this endeavor is to offer a conceptual and methodological framework through which contextually specific patterns and pathways of neoliberalization, along with the contradictions and contestations they unleash, might be investigated through more concrete forms of research.

Spaces of neoliberalization (1): Path-dependency

As scholars in the French regulationist tradition have indicated, the Fordist-Keynesian configuration of capitalist development was grounded upon an historically specific set of regulatory arrangements and political compromises that provisionally stabilized the conflicts and contradictions that are endemic to capitalism.[20] Although the sources of this unprecedented "golden age" of capitalist expansion remain a matter of considerable academic dispute, numerous scholars have emphasized the key role of the *national* scale as the preeminent geographical basis for capital accumulation and for the regulation of political-economic life during this period.[21] Of course, the exact configuration of regulatory arrangements and political compromises varied considerably according to the specific model of capitalism that was adopted in each national context. Nonetheless, a number of broad generalizations can be articulated regarding the basic regulatory-institutional architecture that underpinned Fordist-Keynesian capitalism across the older industrialized world.[22]

– *Wage relation.* Collective bargaining occurred at the national scale, often through corporatist accommodations between capital, labor and the state; wage labor was extended and standardized with the spread of mass production systems throughout national social formations; and wages were tied to productivity growth and tendentially increased in order to underwrite mass consumption.
– *Form of intercapitalist competition.* Monopolistic forms of regulation enabled corporate concentration and centralization within major national industrial sectors;

competition between large firms was mediated through strategies to rationalize mass production technologies; and national states mobilized various forms of industrial policy in order to bolster the world-market positions of their largest firms as "national champions."

- *Monetary and financial regulation.* The money supply was regulated at a national scale through the US-dominated Bretton Woods system of fixed exchange rates; national central banks oversaw the distribution of credit to corporations and consumers; and long-term investment decisions by capital were enabled by a stabilized pattern of macroeconomic growth.

- *The state and other forms of governance.* National states became extensively engaged in managing aggregate demand, containing swings in the business cycle, generalizing mass consumption, redistributing the social product through welfare programs and mediating social unrest.

- *International configuration.* The world economy was parcelized among relatively autocentric national economies and policed by the US global hegemon; meanwhile, as the Fordist accumulation regime matured, global interdependencies among national economic spaces intensified due to enhanced competition among transnational corporations, the expansion of trade relations and the ascendancy of the US dollar as world currency.

- *The regulation of uneven spatial development.* National states introduced a range of compensatory regional policies and spatial planning initiatives intended to alleviate intranational sociospatial polarization by spreading industry and population across the surface of the national territory; entrenched world-scale patterns of uneven development were nonetheless maintained under the rubric of US global hegemony and Cold War geopolitics.

During the early 1970s, however, the key link between (national) mass production and (national) mass consumption was shattered due to a range of interconnected trends and developments, including: the declining profitability of Fordist manufacturing sectors; the intensification of international competition; the spread of deindustrialization and mass unemployment; and the abandonment of the Bretton Woods system of national currencies. Subsequently, the Fordist-Keynesian system was subjected to a variety of pressures and crisis tendencies, leading to a profound shaking up and reworking of the forms of territorial organization that had underpinned the long wave of postwar economic prosperity and national developmentalism. The global political-economic transformations of the post-1970s period radically destabilized the Fordist accumulation regime, decentered the entrenched role of the national scale as the predominant locus for state regulation, and undermined the coherence of the national economy as a real and imagined target of state policies. This "reshuffling of the hierarchy of spaces" has arguably been the most far-reaching geographical consequence of the crisis of North Atlantic Fordism in the early 1970s.[23]

In a seminal discussion that spatializes some of Antonio Gramsci's key concepts, Alain Lipietz has underscored the ways in which processes of capitalist restructuring are articulated in the form of struggles between "defenders of the old space" (to which he refers as the "conservative bloc") and proponents of a "new space" or a "new model of development" (to which he refers as "the modernist bloc").[24] For Lipietz, the production of new spaces occurs through the conflictual interaction of conservative/preservationist and modernizing or restructuring-oriented political forces at various scales, generally leading to a new territorial formation that eclectically combines elements of the old geographical order with aspects of the "projected spaces" sought by the advocates of (neoliberal or progressive) modernization.

This conceptualization provides a useful basis for examining the political, institutional and geographical transformations that unfolded following the crisis of Fordist-Keynesian capitalism in the 1970s. Throughout the subsequent decade, intense conflicts between preservationist and restructuring-oriented political blocs proliferated at a range of spatial scales, with highly uneven impacts upon the nationalized frameworks for accumulation and regulation that had been consolidated during the postwar period.[25] On the one hand, at the national scale, conservative/preservationist blocs initially mobilized diverse strategies of crisis management in order to defend the institutional infrastructures of the Fordist-Keynesian order. From the first oil shock of 1973 until around 1979, traditional recipes of national demand management prevailed throughout the OECD zone as central governments desperately tried to recreate the conditions for a Fordist virtuous circle of growth. However, as Bob Jessop remarks of the British case, such countercyclical tactics ultimately amounted to no more than an "eleventh hour, state-sponsored Fordist modernization," for they were incapable of solving, simultaneously, the dual problems of escalating inflation and mass unemployment.[26]

On the other hand, particularly following the "monetarist shock" of the early 1980s, a variety of modernizing, restructuring-oriented political alliances emerged within advanced capitalist countries that sought at once to dismantle existing regulatory frameworks and to establish a new institutional infrastructure for economic rejuvenation.[27] Since this period, such modernizing blocs have promoted a variety of regulatory experiments in their ongoing search for a new institutional fix; however, their strategies to revamp the regulatory infrastructures of capitalism should be understood as an open-ended, trial-and-error process of institutional searching rather than as the basis for a stabilized "post-Fordist" mode of social regulation.[28] These aspirationally modernizing projects have been associated with a variety of political ideologies and restructuring strategies, including: (a) neocorporatist programs that attempt to modernize industry while renegotiating social compromises; (b) neostatist programs that attempt to revitalize the economy through *dirigiste,* state-led projects to guide industrial transformation; and (c) neoliberal programs that attempt to impose new forms of market discipline upon all aspects of social, political and economic life.[29] In practice, however, these strategies have rarely appeared in such "pure" forms. Instead, real-world projects of regulatory restructuring are generally articulated as complex politico-ideological hybrids derived from contextually specific adaptations, negotiations, struggles and unintended consequences within particular political-economic conjunctures.

Even though only a relatively small number of ruling political alliances explicitly adopted an orthodox neoliberal ideology during the post-1980s period, projects of neoliberalization have, in practice, exercised tremendous influence upon the trajectories of regulatory restructuring in a broad range of supranational, national and subnational institutional arenas. This influence can be attributed, on the one hand, to the dominant role of supranational institutions such as the IMF, the World Bank and the European Commission, which are aggressively oriented towards neoliberal goals such as deregulation, enhanced capital mobility, trade liberalization and expanded commodification. On the other hand, core neoliberal priorities such as "lean" bureaucracy, fiscal retrenchment, enhanced labor market flexibility, territorial competitiveness and the free flow of capital have been extensively integrated into mainstream political programs, often through references to supposedly ineluctable trends such as "globalization," or through purportedly apolitical reform initiatives such as the New Public Management, "good governance" or, in more recent years, "smart cities." For this reason, neoliberalism cannot be understood merely as one among many possible "varieties" of state/economy relations that national governments may opt to promote within their territories. While it would be problematic to subsume neocorporatist and neostatist approaches to regulatory restructuring under an encompassing neoliberal rubric, it would be equally misleading to treat those strategies as being formally analogous to neoliberalism in terms of their political influence, ideological reach or institutional shape. At the present time, neoliberalism represents an actually existing, constantly mutating framework of disciplinary political authority that is enforcing market rule over an ever wider range of institutional arenas throughout the world economy. As such, it imposes determinate, if evolving, discursive, ideological and institutional-legal parameters around other "varieties" of regulatory reform, including those that may appear distinct from, or even opposed to, the market-fundamentalist precepts of neoliberalism.[30] Accordingly, the notion of actually existing neoliberalism is intended to encompass not only the immediate impact of neoliberal political programs upon specific regulatory environments, but also to characterize their more "subversive" role in transforming the geopolitical fields and geo-ideological frames within which struggles over the future shape of capitalist political economies are being fought out at a range of spatial scales.[31]

Most crucially here, the notion of actually existing neoliberalism is intended to illuminate the variegated, contested ways in which neoliberal restructuring strategies *interact* with preexisting uses of space, institutional configurations, regulatory arrangements and constellations of sociopolitical power. Neoliberal programs of regulatory restructuring are rarely, if ever, imposed in a pure form, for they are always introduced within politico-institutional contexts that have been molded significantly by earlier regulatory arrangements, institutionalized practices, social struggles and political compromises. In this sense, the evolution of any politico-institutional configuration following the imposition of neoliberal policy reforms is likely to demonstrate strong properties of path-dependency in which established institutional arrangements canalize the scope and trajectory of reform.

It is worth emphasizing, finally, that neoliberal policy agendas have themselves been transformed through their conflictual interaction with inherited institutional landscapes and power configurations. As Jamie Peck and Adam Tickell indicate, neoliberalism has evolved considerably during the last four decades, from a relatively abstract economic doctrine (1970s) and a means of dismantling or "rolling back" established Keynesian welfarist arrangements (1980s), into a reconstituted form of market-guided regulation intended not only to release "bursts" of economic growth, but to manage the sociopolitical and environmental contradictions induced through earlier waves of neoliberal policy intervention (1990s).[32] In the present context, the key point is that these politico-ideological shifts have crystallized along a strongly path-dependent evolutionary trajectory. While first deployed as a strategic response to the crisis tendencies of an earlier political-economic framework (Fordist-Keynesian-developmentalist capitalism), neoliberal policies were subsequently modified and extended to confront some of the governance failures, crisis tendencies and contradictions that were unleashed through earlier rounds of neoliberalization. The transition from the orthodox, radically anti-statist neoliberalisms of Reagan and Thatcher in the 1980s to the more socially moderate neoliberalisms of Blair, Clinton and Schröder during the 1990s may therefore be understood as a path-dependent reconstitution of neoliberal strategies in response to their own endemic regulatory failures and disruptive sociopolitical effects.

Spaces of neoliberalization (2): Creative destruction

In order to decipher the path-dependent interactions between existing institutional forms and emergent neoliberal projects, we interpret the spatiotemporalities of actually existing neoliberalism with reference to two dialectically intertwined but analytically distinct "moments" – first, the (partial) *destruction* of extant institutional arrangements and political compromises through market-oriented reform initiatives; and second, the (tendential) creation of new politico-institutional infrastructures for market-oriented economic growth, commodification and the rule of capital. Two important caveats must be immediately added to clarify this conceptualization of actually existing neoliberalism as a process of institutional creative destruction.

First, while our emphasis on the tendentially creative capacities of neoliberalism is at odds with earlier studies that underscored its overridingly destructive character, we suggest that this double-pronged, dialectical conceptualization can productively illuminate the complex, often highly contradictory trajectories of institutional change that have been generated through neoliberalization processes. The point of this emphasis, however, is not to suggest that neoliberalism could somehow provide a basis for stabilized, reproducible capitalist growth, but to offer a basis for exploring its wide-ranging, transformative impacts upon inherited politico-institutional configurations and geographical infrastructures. This issue, we argue, must be explored independently of the classic French-regulationist question of whether or not a given institutional form promotes or undermines sustainable capitalist growth. Even when neoliberal policy reforms fail to generate short- or medium-term bursts of capitalist expansion, they may nonetheless impose more lasting evolutionary ruptures within the institutional frameworks, policy environments and geographies of capitalist regulation.

Second, the destructive and creative moments of institutional change within actually existing neoliberalism are inextricably interconnected in practice. Our use of the term "moments" to describe these interconnections is intended in the Hegelian-Marxian sense of conflictual yet mutually related elements within a dynamic, dialectical process, rather than as a description of distinct temporal units within a linear transition.

Building upon the conceptualization of capitalist regulation developed above, Figure 3.1 summarizes the core elements within these intertwined moments of neoliberalization. As the figure illustrates, a sustained critique of the institutional forms, regulatory arrangements and political compromises associated with the Fordist-Keynesian order, and a concerted program to dismantle the latter, lie at the heart of neoliberalism as a multiscalar project of politico-institutional transformation. At the same time, in practice, actually existing neoliberalism has been premised upon the mobilization of a wide range of institutional reforms for promoting the unfettered rule of capital and a utopian vision of "market society." Most crucially, both the destructive and the creative moments of actually existing neoliberalism have been mobilized through distinctively *geographical* strategies within each of the major institutional arenas in which capitalist regulation occurs. In the most general sense, therefore, Figure 3.1 is intended to illuminate the ways in which, across diverse institutional arenas, the geographies of actually existing neoliberalism have involved a dynamic transformation of regulatory space from the nationally configured frameworks that prevailed during the Fordist-Keynesian-developmentalist period to a rescaled configuration of global-national-regional-local interaction in which no single scale serves as the primary pivot for accumulation, regulation or sociopolitical struggle.

Figure 3.1: Destructive and creative moments of actually existing neoliberalism

Site of regulation	Moment of destruction	Moment of creation
Wage relation	– Assaults on organized labor and national collective bargaining agreements – Dismantling of the family wage and the spread of generalized economic insecurity – Downgrading of national regulations ensuring equal employment opportunity, occupational safety and workers' rights	– Competitive deregulation: atomized renegotiation of wage levels and working conditions combined with expanded managerial discretion – New forms of the social wage and new gender divisions of labor – Promotion of new forms of labor "flexibility"
Form of intercapitalist competition	– Selective withdrawal of state support for leading national industries – Dismantling of national protectionist policies – Dismantling of national barriers to foreign direct investment	– New forms of state support for "sunrise" industries – Extension of global commodities markets through trade liberalization policies codified in the WTO, IMF, EU, NAFTA and other supranational bodies – Establishment of global capital markets through GATT negotiations
Form of financial and monetary regulation	– Dismantling of Bretton Woods global monetary system and deregulation of money markets – Erosion of national states' capacity to control exchange rates – Dismantling of the regulatory constraints impeding monetary and financial speculation in global markets – Separation of financial and credit flows from productive sources of investment	– Creation of speculation-driven currency markets and "stateless monies" outside national regulatory control – Expanded role of global regulatory bodies (such as the Bank for International Settlements) in the monitoring of global financial transactions – Creation of offshore financial centers, international banking facilities and tax havens
The state and other forms of governance	– Abandonment of Keynesian forms of demand management – Dismantling of traditional national relays of welfare service provision – "Hollowing out" of national state capacities to regulate money, trade and investment flows – Decentering of traditional hierarchical-bureaucratic forms of governmental control – Dismantling of traditional relays of democratic control at national and subnational levels	– "Rolling forward" of supply-side and monetarist programs of state intervention – Devolution of social welfare functions to lower levels of government, the social economy and households – Mobilization of strategies to promote territorial competitiveness, technological innovation and internationalization – Establishment of public-private partnerships and "networked" forms of governance – Creation of "new authoritarian" state apparatuses and "quangos" that are insulated from public accountability and popular-democratic control

	- Strategies to "hollow out" the autocentric national economy as a target of state intervention - Erosion of traditional managerial-redistributive functions of national and subnational administrative agencies - Imposition of fiscal austerity measures aimed at reducing public expenditures - Shrinking of public sector employment	- Rescaling of state economic intervention to privilege strategic supranational and subnational spaces of accumulation - Underwriting the costs of private investment through state subsidies - Transfer of erstwhile forms of public employment to the private sector through privatization
International configuration	- Decentering of the national scale of accumulation, regulation and sociopolitical struggle - Undercutting of regulatory standards across localities, regions, national states and supranational economic zones	- "Relativization of scales" as relations among subnational, national and supranational institutional forms are systematically rearranged - Introduction of policies to promote market-mediated, competitive relations among subnational (regional and local) levels of state power
Uneven spatial development	- Selective withdrawal of state support for declining regions and cities - Destruction of traditional relays of compensatory, redistributive regional policy ("spatial Keynesianism")	- Mobilization of new forms of state policy to promote capital mobility within supranational trade blocs and to encourage capital (re)investment within strategic city-regions and industrial districts - Establishment of new forms of sociospatial inequality, polarization and territorial competition at global, national and subnational scales

This framework provides a schematic starting point for deciphering the dynamics of politico-institutional creative destruction associated with neoliberalization processes. For purposes of simplification, the destructive tendencies sketched in the figure refer to those vestiges of the Fordist-Keynesian settlement that have been most directly threatened or undermined through the neoliberal offensive. Concomitantly, the creative tendencies depicted in the figure refer to various institutional realignments and political adjustments that have imposed new forms of market discipline upon global, national and local social relations. As indicated, however, we conceive this dynamic of creative destruction not as a unilinear transition from one complete, coherently bounded regulatory system to another, but as an uneven, multiscalar, multidirectional, contested and open-ended restructuring process that generates pervasive governance failures, crisis tendencies and contradictions of its own. As Lipietz likewise emphasizes, the dynamic of regulatory creative destruction never occurs on a blank slate in which the "old order" is abruptly obliterated and the "new order" is unfurled as a fully formed totality.[33] It occurs, rather, on an aggressively contested, unevenly organized institutional landscape in which newly emergent, projected spaces interact with inherited regulatory arrangements, leading in turn to new, unforeseen and often unstable relayerings of political-economic space.[34] These newly combined amalgamations of inherited and emergent institutional arrangements may then provide political arenas in and through which subsequent struggles over the regulation of accumulation, and its associated contradictions, can be articulated and fought out.

Spaces of neoliberalization (3): Cities

The preceding discussion has underscored the ways in which the worldwide ascendancy of neoliberalism since the early 1980s has been intertwined with a pervasive rescaling of capital-labor relations, intercapitalist competition, financial and monetary regulation, state power, the international configuration and uneven development. As the taken-for-granted primacy of the national scale was undermined in each of these arenas, inherited formations of urban governance were likewise systematically reconfigured. While the processes of institutional creative destruction associated with actually existing neoliberalism have clearly been transpiring at all spatial scales, they have been occurring with strategic intensity at the urban scale, and especially within major cities and city-regions.

On the one hand, cities are today embedded within an uncertain geoeconomic environment characterized by monetary chaos, speculative movements of financial capital, global corporate location strategies and intensifying interlocality competition.[35] Under these conditions, most local governments have been constrained, independently of their political orientation and national context, to adjust to heightened levels of economic uncertainty by engaging in short-termist forms of regulatory undercutting and aggressive place-marketing in order to attract investments and jobs.[36] Meanwhile, the retrenchment of national welfare regimes and intergovernmental systems has imposed new fiscal constraints upon municipal governments, leading to significant budgetary cuts during a period in which local regulatory challenges and problems of social reproduction have dramatically intensified.

On the other hand, in many cases, neoliberal programs have been directly interiorized into urban policy regimes as newly formed territorial alliances attempt to rejuvenate local economies through a "shock therapy" of deregulation, privatization, liberalization and enhanced fiscal austerity. In this context, major urban regions have become increasingly important geographical targets and institutional laboratories for a variety of neoliberal policy experiments, from place-marketing, enterprise and empowerment zones, local tax abatements, urban development corporations, public-private partnerships and new forms of local boosterism to workfare policies, property redevelopment schemes, business incubator projects, new strategies of social control, policing and surveillance, and a host of other institutional modifications within local and regional state apparatuses. The overarching goal of such neoliberal urban policy experiments has been to mobilize city space as an arena both for market-oriented economic growth and for elite consumption practices, while transferring the social and financial burdens of economic restructuring more directly onto marginalized, vulnerable population segments – especially the poor, communities of color and immigrants. Figure 3.2 illustrates some of the major politico-institutional mechanisms through which neoliberal projects have been localized within North American and Western European urban regions during the post-1980s period, distinguishing their constituent (partially) destructive and (tendentially) creative moments.

Figure 3.2: Destructive and creative moments of neoliberal localization

Mechanisms of neoliberal localization	Moment of destruction	Moment of creation
Recalibration of intergovernmental relations	– Dismantling of earlier systems of central government support for municipal activities	– Devolution of new tasks, burdens and responsibilities to municipalities; creation of new incentive structures to reward local entrepreneurialism and to catalyze 'endogenous growth'
Retrenchment of public finance	– Imposition of fiscal austerity measures upon municipal governments	– Creation of new revenue collection districts and increased reliance of municipalities upon local sources of revenue, user fees, and other instruments of private finance
Restructuring the welfare state	– Local relays of national welfare service provision are retrenched; assault on managerial-welfarist local state apparatuses	– Expansion of community-based sectors and private approaches to social service provision – Imposition of mandatory work requirements on urban welfare recipients; new (local) forms of workfare experimentation

Reconfiguring the institutional infrastructure of the local state	− Dismantling of bureaucratized, hierarchical forms of local public administration − Devolution of erstwhile state tasks to voluntary community networks − Assault on traditional relays of local democratic accountability	− "Rolling forward" of new networked forms of local governance based upon public-private partnerships, "quangos" and the "new public management" − Establishment of new institutional relays through which elite business interests can directly influence major local development decisions
Privatization of the municipal public sector and collective infrastructures	− Elimination of public monopolies for the provision of standardized municipal services (utilities, sanitation, public safety, mass transit)	− Privatization and competitive contracting of municipal services − Creation of new markets for service delivery and infrastructure maintenance − Creation of privatized, customized and networked urban infrastructures intended to (re)position cities within supranational capital flows
Restructuring urban housing markets	− Razing public housing and other forms of low-rent accommodation − Elimination of rent controls and project-based construction subsidies	− Creation of new opportunities for speculative investment in central-city real estate markets − Emergency shelters become "warehouses" for the homeless − Introduction of market rents and tenant-based vouchers in low-rent niches of urban housing markets
Reworking labor market regulation	− Dismantling of traditional, publicly funded education, skills training and apprenticeship programs for youth, displaced workers and the unemployed	− Creation of a new regulatory environment in which temporary staffing agencies, unregulated "labor corners" and other forms of contingent work can proliferate − Implementation of work-readiness programs aimed at the conscription of workers into low-wage jobs − Expansion of informal economies
Restructuring strategies of territorial development	− Dismantling of autocentric national models of capitalist growth − Destruction of traditional compensatory regional policies − Increasing exposure of local and regional economies to global competitive forces − Fragmentation of national space-economies into discrete urban and regional industrial systems	− Creation of free trade zones, enterprise zones and other deregulated spaces within major urban regions − Creation of new development areas, technopoles and other "new industrial spaces" at subnational scales − Mobilization of new locational policies intended to channel economic capacities and infrastructure investments into globally strategic local/regional agglomerations

Transformations of the built environment and urban form	– Elimination and/or intensified surveillance of urban public spaces – Destruction of traditional working-class neighborhoods in order to make way for speculative redevelopment – Retreat from community-oriented planning initiatives	– Creation of new privatized spaces of elite/corporate consumption – Construction of large-scale mega-projects intended to attract corporate investment and reconfigure local land-use patterns – Creation of gated communities, urban enclaves and other "purified" spaces of social reproduction – "Rolling forward" of the gentrification frontier and the intensification of socio-spatial polarization – Adoption of the principle of "highest and best use" as the basis for major land use planning decisions
Interlocal policy transfer	– Erosion of contextually sensitive approaches to local policy making – Marginalization of "home-grown" solutions to localized market failures and governance failures	– The diffusion of generic, prototypical approaches to "modernizing" reform among policy makers in search of "quick fixes" for local social problems (welfare-to-work programs, place-marketing strategies, zero-tolerance crime policies) – Imposition of decontextualized "best practice" models derived from other institutional contexts upon local policy environments
Reregulation of urban civil society	– Destruction of the "liberal city" in which all inhabitants are entitled to basic civil liberties, social services and political rights	– Mobilization of zero-tolerance crime policies and "broken windows" policing – Introduction of new discriminatory forms of surveillance and social control – Introduction of new policies to combat social "exclusion" by reinserting individuals into the labor market
Re-representing the city	– Postwar image of the industrial, workingclass city is recast through a (re-)emphasis on urban disorder, "dangerous classes" and economic decline	– Mobilization of entrepreneurial discourses and representations focused on the need for revitalization, reinvestment and rejuvenation within major metropolitan areas

For present purposes, two additional aspects of the processes of creative destruction depicted in the figure deserve explication. First, processes of neoliberal localization necessarily unfold in place- and territory-specific forms and combinations. Indeed, in any national or local context, strategies of neoliberal localization can be understood adequately only through an exploration of their uneven, contested interactions with inherited regulatory landscapes at various spatial scales. Consequently, the differential pathways of neoliberal urban restructuring that have crystallized around the world since the 1980s reflect not only the diversity of neoliberal political projects that have been mobilized, but the contextually specific interactions of the latter with inherited frameworks of regulation, both nationally and locally.

Second, since their initial deployment during the late 1970s and early 1980s, neoliberal forms of urban policy have significantly evolved and mutated. Building upon Peck and Tickell's work, we alluded above to the various mutations which neoliberalization processes have undergone in the older industrialized world. We now suggest that these mutations of neoliberalism since the 1980s have unfolded in particularly pronounced forms at subnational scales, and especially within major cities and city-regions.[37] Indeed, each of the broader phases of neoliberalization discussed above has arguably been anchored and fought out within strategic urban-regional spaces.

– During the initial phase of "proto-neoliberalism," cities became flashpoints both for major economic dislocations and for various forms of sociopolitical struggle, particularly in the sphere of social reproduction. During this period, the problem of collective consumption acquired such political prominence that Marxist urban theorist Manuel Castells interpreted it as the sociological essence of the urban phenomenon itself under capitalism.[38] In this context, as the postwar growth regime was being systematically undermined, cities became battlegrounds in which preservationist and modernizing alliances struggled to influence the form and trajectory of economic restructuring. Consequently, local economic initiatives were adopted in many older industrial cities in order to promote renewed growth "from below" while maintaining established sociopolitical settlements and redistributive arrangements.

– During the era of "roll-back" neoliberalism in the 1980s, the dominant form of neoliberal urban policy shifted. In this era of "lean government," municipalities were increasingly constrained to introduce various kinds of cost-cutting measures – including tax abatements, land grants, cutbacks in public services, the privatization of infrastructural facilities and so forth – in order to lower the costs of investment, social reproduction and public administration within their jurisdictions.

Traditional Fordist-Keynesian forms of localized collective consumption were retrenched, as fiscal austerity measures were imposed upon local governments by neoliberalizing national state apparatuses. Under these conditions, enhanced administrative efficiency, coupled with direct and indirect state subsidies to large corporations and an increasing privatization of social reproduction functions, were widely viewed as the "best practices" for promoting a "good business climate" within major local economies. The contradictions of this zero-sum, cost-cutting form of urban entrepreneurialism are now evident throughout the older industrialized world. In addition to its polarizing consequences for major segments of local, regional and national populations, the effectiveness of such strategies for promoting economic rejuvenation has been shown to decline precipitously as they are diffused throughout the world economy.[39]

- The subsequent consolidation of "roll-out" neoliberalism in the early 1990s may be viewed as an evolutionary reconstitution of the neoliberal project in response to its own immanent contradictions and crisis tendencies. Throughout this decade, a marked reconstitution of neoliberal strategies has occurred at the urban and regional scales as well. On the one hand, the basic neoliberal imperative of mobilizing economic space – in this case, urban/regional space – as a purified arena for capitalist growth, commodification and market discipline has remained the dominant political project for municipal governments. Indeed, state institutions have arguably now become even more directly involved in the creative destruction of urban built environments.[40] On the other hand, the conditions for promoting and maintaining economic competitiveness have now been reconceptualized by many urban political and economic elites to include diverse administrative, social and ecological criteria.[41] This suggests that the institutionally destructive neoliberalisms of the 1980s have been superseded by qualitatively new forms of neoliberal localization that actively address the endemic problem of establishing the requisite non-market forms of coordination and cooperation needed to sustain the accumulation process. Under these circumstances, the neoliberal project of institutional "creation" is no longer oriented simply towards promoting market-driven capitalist growth, but has been recalibrated to include new modes of crisis management designed to insulate powerful economic actors from the market failures and governance problems generated during earlier rounds of neoliberal policy reform. These mutations have been expressed through a number of significant institutional realignments at the urban scale, including: (a) the establishment of cooperative business-led networks in local politics; (b) the mobilization of new forms of local economic development policy that foster interfirm cooperation and industrial "clustering"; (c) the deployment of community-based programs to alleviate social exclusion; (d) the promotion of new forms of coordination and interorganizational networking among previously distinct spheres of local state intervention; and (e) the creation of new regional institutions to promote metropolitan-wide place-marketing and intergovernmental coordination.

Clearly, then, the neoliberalization of institutional space at the urban scale has not entailed a linear transition from a generic model of the "welfare city" to a new, encompassing model of the "neoliberal city." Rather, these multifaceted processes of local institutional change have involved an uneven, contested, trial-and-error searching process in which neoliberal strategies have been mobilized in place-specific forms and combinations in relation to the wide-ranging regulatory problems that have afflicted cities around the world during the post-1980s period. Even in the contemporary roll-out phase, neoliberal strategies of localization have tended to exacerbate the regulatory problems they ostensibly aspire to resolve – including economic stagnation, unemployment, sociospatial polarization and uneven development – leading to further mutations of those very strategies and the institutional spaces in which they have been deployed.

Conclusion: From neoliberalized cities to the urbanization of neoliberalism?

It would appear, then, that urban regions are not merely localized arenas in which broader global or national projects of neoliberal restructuring unfold; they have become increasingly central to the ongoing reproduction, mutation and reconstitution of neoliberalism itself during the last four decades. Indeed, it might be argued that an *urbanization of neoliberalism* has been occurring insofar as urban regions have become strategic targets for a broad range of neoliberal policy experiments, institutional innovations and politico-ideological projects. Under these conditions, however, urban regions may also become major forcefields of resistance and opposition to the neoliberal offensive, and as such, strategic arenas in which new rounds of struggle for the "right to the city," and more generally, for alternative forms of urbanization and societal regulation, may be elaborated and fought out.[42]

It remains to be seen, therefore, whether the powerful contradictions inherent in the current urbanized formation of roll-out neoliberalism will provide openings for more progressive, radical-democratic reappropriations of urban space, or whether, by contrast, neoliberal agendas will be entrenched still further within the underlying institutional structures of urban governance. Should this latter outcome occur, we have reason to anticipate the crystallization of still leaner, meaner and more repressive urban geographies in which cities engage aggressively in mutually destructive place-marketing policies, in which transnational capital is permitted to opt out from supporting local social reproduction, and in which the power of urban citizens to influence the basic conditions of their everyday lives is increasingly eroded.

Notes

1   See Pierre Bourdieu, "Neoliberalism, the Utopia (Becoming a Reality) of Unlimited Exploitation," in *Acts of Resistance: Against the Tyranny of the Market,* trans. Richard Nice (New York: Free Press, 1998), 94–105.

2   Kim Moody, *Workers in a Lean World* (New York: Verso, 1997), 119–20.

3   Stephen Gill, "Globalisation, Market Civilisation and Disciplinary Neoliberalism," *Millenium* 24 (1995): 407.

4   Jamie Peck and Adam Tickell, "Searching for a New Institutional Fix: The *After*-Fordist Crisis and Global-Local Disorder," in *Post-Fordism: A Reader,* ed. Ash Amin (Oxford: Blackwell, 1994), 280–315.

5   See, for example, Bourdieu, "Neoliberalism, the Utopia (Becoming a Reality) of Unlimited Exploitation"; Gill, "Globalisation, Market Civilisation and Disciplinary Neoliberalism"; as well as Samir Amin, *Capitalism in the Age of Globalization* (London: Zed, 1997); Naomi Klein, *The Shock Doctrine: The Rise of Disaster Capitalism* (New York: Picador, 2007); Bob Jessop and Rob Stones, "Old City and New Times: Economic and Political Aspects of Deregulation," in *Global Finance and Urban Living,* ed. Leslie Budd and Sam Whimster (London: Routledge, 1992): 171–92; and Engin Isin, "Governing Toronto without Government: Liberalism and Neoliberalism," *Studies in Political Economy* 56 (1998): 169–91.

6   Jamie Peck and Adam Tickell, "Neoliberalizing Space," *Antipode* 34, no. 3 (2002): 380–404.

7   The utopian visions of competitive, self-regulating markets that are propagated within neoliberal ideology are situated, quite literally, "no place": the law of the market is presumed to operate in the same way, and with essentially the same effects, no matter where it is unleashed, leading in turn to economic stability, convergence and equilibrium. In stark contrast, we argue that actually existing neoliberalisms are always embedded within inherited frameworks of institutional organization, political-economic regulation and sociopolitical struggle that decisively shape the forms of restructuring that are subse-

quently induced. For further elaborations on the "variegation" of neoliberalization processes, see Chapter 10 in the present volume, as well as Neil Brenner, Jamie Peck and Nik Theodore, "Variegated Neoliberalization: Geographies, Modalities, Pathways," *Global Networks* 10, no. 2 (2010): 182–222.

8   Alain Lipietz, "Warp, Woof and Regulation: A Tool for Social Science," in *Space and Social Theory,* ed. Georges Benko and Ulf Strohmayer (Cambridge, MA: Blackwell, 1996), 250–83.

9   See also Erik Swyngedouw, "Neither Global nor Local: 'Glocalization' and the Politics of Scale," in *Spaces of Globalization,* ed. Kevin Cox (New York: Guilford, 1997), 137–66; and Pascal Petit, "Structural Forms and Growth Regimes of the Post-Fordist Era," *Review of Social Economy* 57, no. 2 (1999): 220–43.

10 David Harvey, "From Managerialism to Entrepreneurialism: the Transformation of Urban Governance in Late Capitalism," *Geografiska Annaler: Series B Human Geography* 71, no. 1, (1989): 3–17; Doreen Massey, *Spatial Divisions of Labour* (London: Macmillan, 1985); Neil Smith, *Uneven Development* (Oxford: Blackwell, 1984).

11 Erik Swyngedouw, "Territorial Organization and the Space/Technology Nexus," *Transactions of the Institute of British Geographers* 17, no. 4 (1992): 417–33; Michael Storper and Richard Walker, *The Capitalist Imperative: Territory, Technology and Industrial Growth* (London: Blackwell, 1989).

12 Henri Lefebvre, *The Production of Space,* trans. Donald Nicholson-Smith (London: Blackwell, 1991).

13 Ray Hudson, *Producing Places* (New York: Guilford, 2001).

14 Alain Lipietz, "Warp, Woof and Regulation"; David Harvey, "From Managerialism to Entrepreneurialism."

15 Doreen Massey, *Spatial Divisions of Labour;* David Harvey, *The Limits to Capital* (Chicago: University of Chicago Press, 1982).

16 Neil Smith, *Uneven Development.*

17 Neil Brenner, *New State Spaces: Urban Governance and the Rescaling of Statehood* (New York: Oxford University Press, 2004); Simon Duncan and Mark Goodwin, *The Local State and Uneven Development* (London: Polity Press, 1988).

18 Peck and Tickell, "Searching for a New Institutional Fix."

19 Brenner, *New State Spaces.* See also Jamie Peck, "Geographies of Governance: TECs and the Neoliberalisation of 'Local Interests,'" *Space & Polity* 2, no. 1 (1998): 5–31; Danny MacKinnon, "Regulating Regional Spaces: State Agencies and the Production of Governance in the Scottish Highlands," *Environment and Planning* A 33, no. 5 (2001): 823–44.

20 Michel Aglietta, *A Theory of Capitalist Regulation,* trans. David Fernbach (New York: Verso, 1979); Robert Boyer and Yves Saillard, eds., *Théorie de la régulation: l'état des savoirs* (Paris: La Découverte, 1995).

21 Swyngedouw, "Neither Global nor Local"; Brenner, *New State Spaces;* Bob Jessop, "Narrating the Future of the National Economy and the National State," in *State/Culture: State Formation after the Cultural Turn,* ed. George Steinmetz (Ithaca, NY: Cornell University Press, 1999), 278–405.

22 See Bob Jessop, "Fordism and Post-Fordism: A Critical Reformulation," in *Pathways to Industrialization and Regional Development,* ed. Michael Storper and Allen J. Scott (New York: Routledge, 1992), 46–69; Bob Jessop, "The Crisis of the National Spatio-Temporal Fix and the Ecological Dominance of Globalizing Capitalism," *International Journal of Urban and Regional Research* 24, no. 2 (2000): 323–60; Elmar Altvater, "Fordist and Post-Fordist International Division of Labor and Monetary Regimes," in Storper and Scott, *Pathways to Industrialization,* 21–45; and Alain Lipietz, *Mirages and Miracles: The Crisis of Global Fordism* (London: Verso, 1987).

23 On the "reshuffling of the hierarchy of spaces," see Alain Lipietz, "The National and the Regional: Their Autonomy vis-à-vis the Capitalist World Crisis," in *Transcending the State-Global Divide,* ed. Ronen Palan and Barry Gills (Boulder: Lynne Rienner Publishers, 1994), 23–44. See also Erik Swyngedouw, "The Mammon Quest: 'Glocalisation', Interspatial Competition and the Monetary Order: The Con-

struction of New Scales," in *Cities and Regions in the New Europe,* ed. Mick Dunford and Grigoris Kaf-kalas (London: Belhaven Press, 1992), 39–62; as well as Jessop, "The Crisis of the National Spatio-Temporal Fix"; and Brenner, *New State Spaces.*

24 Lipietz, "The National and the Regional," 35.

25 See Alain Lipietz, "Reflections on a Tale: The Marxist Foundations of the Concepts of Regulation and Accumulation," *Studies in Political Economy* 26 (1988): 7–36.

26 Bob Jessop, "Conservative Regimes and the Transition to Post-Fordism: The Cases of Great Britain and West Germany," in *Capitalist Development and Crisis Theory,* ed. Mark Gottdiener and Nicos Komninos (New York: St. Martin's Press, 1989), 269.

27 Lipietz, "The National and the Regional"; Bob Jessop, "Post-Fordism and the State," in Amin, *Post-Fordism,* 251–79.

28 Peck and Tickell, "Searching for a New Institutional Fix."

29 Jessop, "Post-Fordism and the State."

30 See Chapter 10 in the present volume;; as well as Brenner, Peck and Theodore, "Variegated Neoliberalization"; and Peck and Tickell, "Neoliberalizing Space."

31 Martin Rhodes, "'Subversive Liberalism': Market Integration, Globalization and the European Welfare State," *Journal of European Public Policy* 2, no. 3 (1995): 384–406.

32 Peck and Tickell, "Neoliberalizing Space."

33 Alain Lipietz, "A Regulationist Approach to the Future of Urban Ecology," *Capitalism, Nature, Socialism* 3, no. 3 (1992): 101–10.

34 The term "projected spaces" is derived from Lipietz, "The National and the Regional."

35 Swyngedouw, "The Mammon Quest."

36 Helga Leitner and Eric Sheppard, "Economic Uncertainty, Inter-Urban Competition and the Efficacy of Entrepreneurialism," in *The Entrepreneurial City: Geographies of Politics, Regime and Representation,* ed. Tim Hall and Phil Hubbard (Chichester: Wiley, 1998), 285–308.

37 Peck and Tickell, "Neoliberalizing Space."

38 Manuel Castells, *The Urban Question: A Marxist Approach,* trans. Alan Sheridan (Cambridge, MA: MIT Press, 1977).

39 See Chapter 5 in the present volume, as well as Paul Cheshire and Ian Gordon, "Territorial Competition and the Predictability of Collective (In)action," *International Journal of Urban and Regional Research* 20, no. 3 (1996): 383–99.

40 Jason Hackworth and Neil Smith, "The Changing State of Gentrification," *Tijdschrift voor Economische en Sociale Geografie* 92, no. 4 (2001): 46–77.

41 Michael Harloe, "Social Justice and The City: The New 'Liberal' Formulation," *International Journal of Urban and Regional Research* 25, no. 4 (2001): 889–97.

42 See, for example, Helga Leitner, Jamie Peck and Eric Sheppard, eds., *Contesting Neoliberalism: Urban Frontiers* (New York: Guilford, 2006); Jenny Künkel and Margit Mayer, eds., *Neoliberal Urbanism and Its Contestations* (New York: Palgrave, 2011).

4 From Global Cities to Globalized Urbanization

with Roger Keil

Urbanization is rapidly accelerating, and extending ever more densely, if unevenly, across the earth's surface. The combined demographic, economic, sociotechnological, metabolic and sociocultural processes of urbanization have resulted in the formation of a globalized network of spatially concentrated human settlements and infrastructural configurations in which major dimensions of modern capitalism are materialized, reproduced and contested. This pattern of increasingly globalized urbanization starkly contradicts earlier predictions, in the waning decades of the twentieth century, that the era of urbanization was nearing its end due to the diffusion of new information technologies, declining transportation costs and increasingly dispersed patterns of human settlement. Despite these trends, all major indicators suggest that urbanization processes are dramatically intensifying and accelerating.

Over four decades ago, the French philosopher Henri Lefebvre anticipated the "generalization" of capitalist urbanization through the establishment of a planetary "fabric" or "web" of urbanized spaces.[1] Today, Lefebvre's prediction is no longer a futuristic speculation, but provides a realistic starting point for inquiry into our global urban reality. This is not to suggest that the entire world has become a single, densely concentrated city: the patterns and pathways of urbanization are intensely variegated around the world; meanwhile, uneven spatial development, sociospatial polarization and territorial inequality remain pervasive, endemic features of modern capitalism. Rather, Lefebvre's prediction was that the process of urbanization would increasingly come to condition all major aspects of planetary social existence and, in turn, that the fate of human social life – indeed, that of the earth itself – would subsequently hinge upon the discontinuous dynamics and uneven trajectories of urbanization.

The urban revolution of the early twenty-first century poses major challenges for the field of urban studies. The origins of this research field lie in the concern to investigate relatively bounded urban settlements, understood as internally differentiated, self-contained metropolitan "worlds," in isolation from surrounding economic, political and environmental networks – as, for instance, in the concentric ring model developed in the work of Chicago School of urban sociology. Today, however, it is not the internal differentiation of urban worlds within neatly contained ecologies of metropolitan settlement or, for that matter, the extension of urbanized social relations and built environments into rural hinterlands, that constitutes the central focal point for urban studies. Instead, in conjunction with the uneven yet worldwide generalization of capitalist urbanization, we are being confronted with new forms, infrastructures and patterns of global connectivity, along with new geographies of disconnection, peripheralization, exclusion and vulnerability, within, among and beyond the world's major urbanizing regions. How to decipher these transformations, their origins, and their consequences? What categories and models of urbanization are most appropriate for understanding them, and for coming to terms with their wide-ranging implications for social life, political regulation and ecological conditions?

Since the early 1980s, critical urban researchers have devoted intense energies to precisely these questions – on the one hand, by analyzing emergent forms of globalized urbanization and their impacts upon social, political and economic dynamics in major cities; on the other hand, by introducing a host of new conceptualizations and research methods intended to grasp the changing realities of urbanization under late twentieth and early twenty-first century capitalism. The resultant literatures on "world," "global" and "globalizing" cities contain fascinating, provocative and often controversial insights. Meanwhile, ongoing debates on the missing links and open questions within these literatures continue to inspire new generations of researchers as they work to decipher the urbanizing world(s) in which we are living. In this chapter, our goal is to outline some of the methodological foundations for, and major lines of investigation within, research on globalizing cities, while also alluding to several emergent debates and agendas that have reanimated and differentiated this field during the last decade, with specific reference to the conceptualization and investigation of global interurban networks.[2] In so doing, we hope to stimulate readers to contribute their own critical energies to the tasks of understanding and shaping the future dynamics and trajectories of worldwide urbanization, both within and beyond the major urban regions on which we focus our attention here.

Urbanization and global capitalism

Although the notion of a world city has a longer historical legacy, it was consolidated as a core concept for urban studies during the 1980s, in the context of interdisciplinary attempts to decipher the crisis-induced restructuring of global capitalism following the collapse of the postwar political-economic and spatial order. Until this period, the dominant approaches to urban studies tended to presuppose that cities were neatly enclosed within national territories and nationalized central place hierarchies. Thus, for example, postwar regional development theorists viewed the national economy as the basic container of spatial polarization between core urban growth centers and internal peripheries. Similarly, postwar urban geographers generally assumed that the national territory was the primary scale on which rank-size urban hierarchies and city-systems were organized. Indeed, even early uses of the term "world city" by famous twentieth century urbanists such as Patrick Geddes and Peter Hall likewise expressed this set of assumptions.[3] In their work, the cosmopolitan character of world cities was interpreted as an outgrowth of their host states' geopolitical power. The possibility that urban development or the formation of urban hierarchies might be conditioned by supranational or global forces was not systematically explored.

This nationalized vision of the urban process was challenged as of the late 1960s and early 1970s, with the rise of radical approaches to urban political economy. The seminal contributions of neo-Marxist urban theorists such as Henri Lefebvre, David Harvey and Manuel Castells generated a wealth of new categories and methods through which to analyze the specifically capitalist character of modern urbanization processes. From this perspective, contemporary cities were viewed as spatial materializations of the core social processes associated with the capitalist mode of production, including, in particular, capital accumulation and class struggle. While these new approaches did not, at that time, explicitly investigate the global parameters of urbanization, they did suggest that cities had to be understood within a macrogeographical context defined by the ongoing development and restless spatial expansion of capitalism. In this manner, radical urbanists elaborated an explicitly spatialized and reflexively multiscalar understanding of capitalist urbanization. Within this new conceptual framework, the spatial and scalar parameters for urban development could no longer be taken for granted, as if they were pregiven features of the social world. Instead, urbanization was now increasingly viewed as an active moment within the ongoing production and transformation of capitalist sociospatial configurations.

Crucially, these new approaches to urban political economy were consolidated during a period in which, throughout the older industrialized world, cities and regions were undergoing any number of disruptive sociospatial transformations associated with the crisis of North Atlantic Fordism and the consolidation of a new international division of labor dominated by transnational corporations. Extensive research subsequently emerged on topics such as industrial decline, urban property markets, territorial polarization, regionalism, collective consumption, post-Fordism, local state intervention, the politics of place and urban social movements. Among many other, more specific insights, these research initiatives indicated that the sources of contemporary urban transformations could not be understood in purely local, regional or national terms. Rather, the post-1970s restructuring of cities and regions had to be grasped as an expression and outcome of worldwide economic, political and sociospatial transformations. Thus, for instance, plant closings and workers' struggles in older industrial cities such as Chicago, Detroit, Liverpool, Dortmund or Turin could not be explained simply in terms of local, regional or even national developments, but had to be analyzed in relation to broader secular trends within the world economy that were fundamentally reworking the conditions for profitable capital accumulation and reconstituting the global geographies of industrial production. Analogous arguments regarding the significance of global context were meanwhile articulated regarding other major aspects of urban and regional restructuring – for instance, the crystallization of new patterns of intranational spatial inequality, the emergence of new, place- and region-specific forms of economic and social policy, and the activities of new types of territorially based social and political movements.

In opening up their analyses to the global dimensions of urban restructuring, critical urban political economists in the 1970s and early 1980s also began to draw upon several recently consolidated approaches to the political economy of capitalism that likewise underscored its intrinsically globalizing dimensions. Foremost among these was the model of world system analysis developed by Immanuel Wallerstein and others, which explored the worldwide polarization of economic development and living conditions under capitalism among distinct core, semi-peripheral and peripheral zones.[4] World system theorists insisted that capitalism could be understood adequately only on the largest possible spatial scale, that of the world economy as a whole, and over a very long temporal period spanning many centuries. World system theorists thus sharply criticized the methodologically nationalist assumptions of mainstream social science, arguing instead for an explicitly globalist, *longue durée* understanding of modern capitalism. The rise of world system theory during the 1970s resonated with a more general resurgence of neo-Marxian approaches to geopolitical economy during this period. In the context of diverse studies of transnational corporations, underdevelopment, dependency, class formation, crisis theory and the internationalization of capital, these new approaches to radical political economy likewise explored the global parameters of capitalism both in historical and contemporary contexts.

It is against this background that the emergence of a distinct field of research on globalizing cities must be contextualized. Like the other critical analyses of urban restructuring that were being pioneered during the 1980s, global city theorists built extensively upon the analytical foundations that had been established by neo-Marxist urban political economists, world system theorists and other radical analysts of global capitalism during the preceding decade.

Global cities and urban restructuring

According to Peter J. Taylor, "The world city literature as a cumulative and collective enterprise begins only when the economic restructuring of the world-economy makes the idea of a mosaic of separate urban systems appear anachronistic and frankly irrelevant."[5] During the course of the 1980s and 1990s, the latter assumption was widely abandoned among critical urban researchers, leading to a creative outpouring of research on the interplay between urban restructuring and various worldwide economic – and, subsequently, political, cultural and environmental – transformations. Numerous scholars contributed key insights to this emergent research agenda, but the most influential, foundational statements were presented by John Friedmann and Saskia Sassen.[6] The global city concept is most closely associated with the work of these authors, who are appropriately cited as pioneers in exploring the interplay between globalization and urban development, particularly in the contemporary period.

During the course of the late 1980s and well into the 1990s, global city theory was employed extensively in studies of the role of major cities as global financial centers, as headquarters locations for transnational corporations (TNCs) and as agglomerations for advanced producer and financial services industries, particularly in Euro-America and East Asia. During this time, much research was conducted on several broad issues:

– *The formation of a global urban hierarchy.* Global city theory postulates the formation of a worldwide urban hierarchy in and through which transnational corporations coordinate their production and investment activities. The geography, composition and evolutionary tendencies of this hierarchy have been a topic of intensive research and debate since the 1980s. Following the initial interventions of Sassen and Friedmann, subsequent scholarship has explored a variety of methodological strategies and empirical data sources through which to map this hierarchy.[7] However, whatever their differences of interpretation, most studies of the global urban system have conceptualized this grid of cities simultaneously (a) as a key spatial infrastructure for the accelerated and intensified globalization of capital, including finance capital; and (b) as a medium and expression of the new patterns of global sociospatial polarization that have emerged during the post-1970s period.

– *The contested restructuring of urban space.* The consolidation of global cities is understood, in this literature, not only with reference to the global scale, on which new, worldwide linkages among cities are being established. Just as importantly, researchers in this field have suggested that the process of global city formation also entails significant spatial transformations at the urban scale, within cities themselves, as well as within their surrounding metropolitan regions. According to global cities researchers, the globalization of urban development has generated powerful expressions in the built environment. For example, the intensified clustering of transnational corporate headquarters and advanced corporate services firms in the city core overburdens inherited land-use infrastructures, leading to new, often speculative, real estate booms as new office towers and high-end residential, infrastructural, cultural and entertainment spaces are constructed within and beyond established downtown areas. Meanwhile, the rising cost of office space in the global city core may generate massive spillover effects on a regional scale, as small- and medium-sized agglomerations of corporate services and back offices crystallize throughout the urban region. The consolidation of such headquarter economies may also generate significant shifts within local housing markets as developers attempt to transform once-devalorized properties into residential space for corporate elites and other members of the "creative" professional milieux. Consequently, gentrification ensues in formerly working-class neighborhoods and deindustrialized spaces, and considerable residential and employment displacement may be caused in the wake of rising rents and housing costs. Global cities researchers have tracked these and many other spatial transformations at some length: the urban built environment is viewed as an arena of contestation in which competing social forces and interests, from transnational firms and developers to residents and social movements – struggle over issues of urban design, land use and public space. Of course, such issues are intensely contested in cities around the world. Global cities researchers acknowledge this, but were particularly concerned in the 1980s and 1990s to explore their distinctive forms and outcomes in Euro-American and East Asian cities that had come to serve key command-and-control functions in the global capitalist system.

– *The transformation of the urban social fabric.* One of the most provocative, if also highly controversial, aspects of global cities research during its initial phase involved claims regarding the effects of global city formation upon the urban social fabric. Friedmann and Sassen, in particular, suggested that the emergence of a global city hierarchy would generate a "dualized" urban labor market structure dominated, on the one hand, by a high-earning corporate elite and, on the other hand, by a large mass of workers employed in menial, low-paying and/or informalized jobs.[8] For Sassen, this "new class alignment in global cities" emerged in direct conjunction with the downgrading of traditional manufacturing industries and the emergence of the advanced producer and financial services complex.[9] Her work on London, New York and Tokyo suggested that broadly analogous, if place-specific patterns of social polarization were emerging in these otherwise quite different cities, as a direct consequence of their newly consolidated roles as global command-and-control centers. This "polarization thesis" has attracted considerable discussion and debate. Whereas some scholars have attempted to apply the Friedmann/Sassen argument to a range of globalizing cities, other analysts have questioned its logical and/or empirical validity.[10]

In close conjunction with the consolidation of global cities research around the above-mentioned themes, new generations of critical urban scholars began to extend the empirical scope of the theory beyond the major urban command-and-control centers of the world economy – that is, cities such as New York, London, Tokyo; as well as various supraregional centers in East Asia (Singapore, Seoul, Hong Kong, Shanghai), North America (Los Angeles, Chicago, Miami, Toronto) and western Europe (Paris, Frankfurt, Amsterdam, Zurich, Milan). In this important line of research, the basic methodological impulses of global city theory were applied to diverse types of cities around the world, but particularly in the global North, that were likewise undergoing accelerated processes of economic and sociospatial restructuring.[11] Here, the central analytical agenda was to relate the dominant socioeconomic trends within particular cities – for instance, industrial restructuring, changing patterns of capital investment, labor-market segmentation, sociospatial polarization and class and ethnic conflict – to the emergence of a worldwide urban hierarchy and the geoeconomic and geopolitical forces that underlie it. In this manner, analysts demonstrated the usefulness of global city theory in relation to a broad range of urban transformations – now also including urban governance restructuring and the emergence of new forms of urban social protest – that were unfolding during the post-1980s period. They thus signaled a significant reorientation of the literature away from "global cities" as such, to what Peter Marcuse and Ronald van Kempen famously labelled "globalizing cities," a term intended to underscore the diversity of pathways and the place- and region-specific patterns in and through which processes of globalization and urban restructuring were being articulated.[12]

Global interurban networks – debates and horizons

The debate on global city formation thus no longer focuses primarily on the headquarters locations for transnational capital, the associated agglomeration of specialized producer and financial services, and the resultant transformation of urban and regional spaces. Increasingly, work on globalizing cities engages with a broad range of globalized or globalizing vectors – including not only economic flows, but the crystallization of new social, cultural, political, ecological, media and diasporic networks as well. In this context, scholars have begun to reflect more systematically on the nature of the very network connectivities that link cities together across the world economy. Such explorations have animated various strands of empirical research on cities, as well as ongoing interpretive debates about the nature of globalized urbanization itself. As the field expands and advances, the contours of research on globalizing cities are now increasingly differentiated, but certain shared concerns have nonetheless persisted. Accordingly, we summarize here four major dimensions of global interurban connectivity that have, in recent years, inspired significant pathways of research and debate among contemporary urbanists.

— *Types of interurban networks.* In the 1980s and 1990s, scholars tended to assume that a single global urban hierarchy existed; debates focused on how to map it, and on what empirical indicators were most appropriate for doing so. However, the discussion has shifted considerably during the last decade, as researchers now argue that the world system is composed of multiple, interlocking interurban networks. While the question of transnational corporate command-and-control remains central, there is now an equal interest in global cultural flows, political networks, media cities and other modalities of interurban connectivity, including those associated with large-scale infrastructural configurations. For instance, the cases of Washington, DC, Geneva, Brussels, Nairobi and other bureaucratic headquarters of the global diplomatic and NGO communities point towards a network of global political centers. Religious centers such as Mecca, Rome and Jerusalem, among many others, constitute yet another such network. Moreover, in some cases, places that ostensibly lack strategic economic assets nonetheless acquire global significance through their role in the worldwide networks of social movement activism. Porto Alegre, Brazil, where the World Social Forum has been based, and Davos, Switzerland, where the World Economic Forum takes place every January, are cases in point. This line of investigation suggests that, interwoven around the structures of capital which underpin the world urban system, there also exists a complex latticework of interurban linkages that are constituted around many other types of connections.

— *The spatiality of interurban networks.* In contrast to the somewhat simplistic understanding of global cities as neatly bounded, local places or nodal points in which transnational capital could be anchored, several scholars have suggested alternative understandings of the geographies produced through globalized urbanization.

Doreen Massey, for instance, argues against the notion that global cities contain distinct properties that make them inherently "global."[13] Instead, she advances an understanding of the global cities network as a set of dialectical relationships that connect actors in cities, and cities as institutional actors, through a variety of simultaneously globalized and localized streams. Thus, the space of global cities is "*relational*, not a mosaic of simply juxtaposed differences" and the global city "has to be conceptualized not as a simple diversity, but as a meeting place, of jostling, potentially conflicting, trajectories."[14] Other scholars have explored the ways in which processes of global city formation have been connected to rescaling processes insofar as they rework inherited configurations of interscalar relations, often in unpredictable, unexpected ways.[15] More recent research explores the methodological and empirical implications of these interventions with reference to diverse aspects of globalized urbanization, from urban political ecologies and governance realignments to new social movement mobilizations. Each of these research strands breaks in important ways with inherited, place-bound or purely nodal conceptualizations of global cities, pointing instead towards new concepts of relationality, topology and rescaling as alternative bases for understanding the variegated geographies of globalized urbanization.

— *The scope of interurban networks.* Much global cities research in the 1980s and 1990s focused on major cities and city-regions in the global North. More recently, several scholars have questioned this focus, and explored some of its problematic implications for the conceptualization of global city formation itself. For instance, in an influential intervention, Jennifer Robinson criticized the project of classifying cities based on their alleged importance within a single global hierarchy or network, arguing instead for a broader understanding of the diverse, often more mundane or "ordinary" ways in which the globality of cities is constituted and reproduced.[16] While directing attention back towards locally embedded, place-based social relations, Robinson's work also advocated a reconceptualization of transnational flows and interconnectivities themselves, from points of view that are not focused one-sidedly upon the logics of capital investment and finance. An analogous idea is taken up by Ananya Roy in her recent plea for a rethinking of the theoretical geographies of urban studies.[17] In this context, Roy proposed "a rather paradoxical combination of specificity and generalizability: that theories have to be produced *in* place (and it matters *where* they are produced), but that they can then be appropriated, borrowed, and remapped. In this sense, the sort of theory being urged is simultaneously located and dis-located."[18] In practical terms, the dynamic relationships between specificity and generalizability, expounded forcefully by Robinson, Roy and others, underscore a challenge faced by all cities under contemporary capitalism: to manage, simultaneously, their internal contradictions and their external positionality in the world system.[19] More generally, this line of research and theory-building has suggested some productive methodological strategies through which cities throughout the world system – including those located outside of the economic "heartlands" of the global North – may also be investigated through the tools of a critically revised approach to globalized urbanization.[20]

– *The dangers of interurban networks.* Although strongly critical of their socioecological implications, most global city research in the 1980s and 1990s emphasized the newly emergent strategic connectivities of capital, labor and information across the world economy, which were widely viewed as the most essential preconditions for local economic development. In that context, foreign direct investment and thick webs of interfirm relationships were seen as the "stuff" of which global city relationships were made. Of course, as noted above, such geoeconomic connectivities were widely seen as being deeply contradictory, insofar as they intensified sociospatial polarization and undermined local institutional control within and among cities. Yet, aside from this emphasis on the problems of polarization and governance failure in situ, the wide-ranging "downsides" of interurban connectivity, as well as the endemic dysfunctionalities, contradictions and failures in the network itself, have only recently been explored by critical urban researchers.[21] In particular, the political ecologies of globalizing cities are today increasingly structured through rising vulnerabilities in and across the global cities network as a whole – for instance, related to its enhanced capacity to spread economic instability, disease, crime or terrorism through its circuits of connectivity – and by a wide range of governance problems, at various spatial scales, that flow directly from these vulnerabilities. In this way, the core sociospatial and institutional infrastructures of the global city system now increasingly mediate and animate a range of other flows – for instance, of risk, infection, insecurity and violence – that threaten to disrupt the basic socioeconomic operations and circulations on which that system depends.

An invitation to research – and action

What we know now about globalizing cities in a world system has confirmed some of the predictions that were made by urban scholars in the 1980s, and contradicted others. At that time, the Cold War was ongoing, the Internet economy (as well as Facebook, Twitter and the like) did not yet exist, terrorist networks were primarily of local and regional concern, and the "Third World" was little more than an afterthought in significant strands of Euro-American urban social theory. Of course, the world has been dramatically transformed since then: through a cascade of interconnected geoeconomic, geocultural, geomilitary and technological trans-formations, the post–Cold War world has become even more tightly connected than ever before, not least through global urban networks and hierarchies. Moscow is no longer behind an "iron curtain"; Berlin is unified; South Africa has over-thrown apartheid; Brazilian cities are now major nodes in the global economy; China is undergoing a process of hyperurbanization that may be completely unprec-edented in scale, speed and impact; and Shanghai, Dubai, Mumbai and Lagos have become standard reference points in global public discourse, film and the musical imagination.

While geographical proximities among cities and their inhabitants have increased, not least through newly established networks of surveillance in the age of "big data," social distanciation within cities and across interurban networks is also arguably now even greater than ever. Although the much-touted *"Blade Runner* scenario" of unfettered social breakdown and generalized anomie has not materialized in most cities, internal sociospatial divisions have markedly intensified, and are gener-ating new forms of exclusion, division, ghettoization, violence and social suffering. In Mike Davis's famous formulation, "a planet of slums" has been consolidated, and its assemblages of informalized housing, ad hoc collective infrastructure and everyday survival strategies stand in stark contrast to the shining, vertically asser-tive citadels of banking, culture and entertainment that adorn large metropolitan centers around the world.[22] In most parts of the world, the morphology of city settlement space continues to push outwards into ever more distant hinterlands to forge what Deyan Sudjic has termed "100-mile cities." Such galaxies of megapoli-tan expansion may now encompass even more massive territories of agglomeration, infrastructural densification and socioeconomic interdependency that render traditional, nodal conceptions of cityness increasingly obsolete.[23]

Under these conditions, new forms of politics and contestation are also proliferating as globalized, diversified urban communities lay claim to the right to the city in unexpected, often quite radical ways, in a diversity of territorial and ecological settings. As the shockwaves of financial crisis and climate change further disrupt geoeconomic operations, territorial governance, infrastructural ecologies and everyday life in cities from Athens, Madrid and New Orleans to Dubai, Buenos Aires and Jakarta, we can certainly anticipate new alignments of power and struggle to contribute further impetus to the ongoing politics of space, both within and beyond the world's major centers of political-economic power.

All of this (and more) has certainly challenged many of the claims made by the first generation of global cities researchers over four decades ago. For example, one of the more persistent criticisms that has been leveled at global city researchers is that their work serves to glorify the status of particular cities in worldwide inter-urban competition, and thus represents an uncritical affirmation of global neoliberalism. Relatedly, it has been insinuated that research on global cities actively embraces, or at least offers ideological cover for, the policies of municipal boosters in search of local distinction on the world stage. In our view, these criticisms are based upon a mistaken identification of the colloquial notion of the global/world city, which has come to have a "life of its own" in global public discourse, with the critical concept developed in the scholarly literatures we have discussed in this chapter. While the former is a descriptive, affirmative notion often used by municipal power brokers to draw attention to specific places and to advance their political-ideological strategies, the latter is a polysemic analytical term that has been employed by critical urbanists concerned to decipher the power relations, inequalities and injustices associated with contemporary forms of urban restructuring around the world. Whatever their limits and blind spots, critical studies of globalizing cities have arguably helped sensitize scholars to the ways in which networked cities and metropolitan regions continue to serve as strategic basing points for the operations of capitalism, including in the current formation of accelerating geoeconomic integration and intense geopolitical volatility.

Still, at least some of the confusion around the notion of the global(izing) city may, in fact, be attributed to the substantive content of social science research on this topic. In some cases, the "hype" generated through studies of the purported "globality" of a particular place – for instance, Los Angeles, Dubai, Singapore or Shanghai – may have actually permitted certain critical urban researchers to be unwittingly enlisted as ideological "mercenaries" advancing projects of global city boosterism. In this context, it is useful to recall that John Friedmann and Goetz Wolff's first foray into global cities research contained the programmatic subtitle, "an agenda for research and *action*."²⁴ Certainly, for Friedmann and his collaborators, analyzing the global city was intended as a first step towards effecting progressive and even radical social transformation, precisely to counteract the polarizations, exploitations, injustices and irrationalities associated with the growing role of transnational capital in the everyday social life of cities. Thus, data on the formation of global urban hierarchies, on the intensification of sociospatial polarization and on the "hollowing out" of local governance capacity within global cities was clearly understood as a call to arms for progressive planners and policy makers, as well as for social movement activists. Their role, in Friedmann's view, was to mobilize new public policies designed to reduce the suffering of the global city's increasingly impoverished, internationalized working classes and migrant populations and, still more ambitiously, to subject the apparently "deterritorialized" operations of transnational capital to localized, democratic political control. For others, of course, this call to action was interpreted as an imperative to establish the "positive business climate" and general investment conditions that were deemed necessary for world city formation. However, in an incisive intervention into the public policy debate in East Asian city-states craving world city status in the 1990s, Friedmann presented an important reminder to his audience:

> [U]rban outcomes are to a considerable extent the result of public policies. They are, in part, what we choose them to be. The cities of the next century will thus be a result of planning in the broadest sense of that much abused term. This is not to fall into the naïve belief that all we need to do is to draw a pretty picture of the future, such as a master plan, or adopt wildly ambitious regulatory legislation as a template for future city growth. … Instead of waxing enthusiastic about megaprojects – bridges, tunnels, airports, and the cold beauty of glass-enclosed skyscrapers – which so delight the heart of big-city mayors, I am talking about people, their habitat and quality of life, the claims of invisible migrant citizens and now, in yet another turn, the concept of civil society.²⁵

What, then, can critical research on globalizing cities teach us about contemporary capitalism more generally? Beyond its significance to urban specialists, does this research tradition make a more general contribution to our understanding of contemporary global society, and to our ability to shape the latter in progressive, emancipatory ways? From our point of view, critical research on globalizing cities does indeed offer us some useful bearings, some intellectual and political grounding, as we attempt to orient ourselves within a profoundly disjointed, confusing, and in many ways, highly authoritarian, new world order. Whether or not this critical perspective can also help illuminate possibilities for progressive or radical socioecological transformation is, of course, ultimately a political question – one that can only be decided through ongoing, emergent and future social struggles.

Notes

1   Henri Lefebvre, *The Urban Revolution,* trans. Robert Bononno (Minneapolis: University of Minnesota Press, 2003 [1970]).

2   For a detailed overview of previous research on globalizing cities, see Neil Brenner and Roger Keil, eds., *The Global Cities Reader* (New York: Routledge, 2006).

3   Patrick Geddes, "A World League of Cities" *Sociological Review* 26 (1924): 166–67; Peter Hall, *The World Cities* (New York: McGraw-Hill, 1966).

4   Immanuel Wallerstein, *The Modern World-System I* (New York: Academic Publishers, 1974).

5   Peter J. Taylor, *World City Network: A Global Urban Analysis* (New York: Routledge, 2004), 21.

6   John Friedmann, "The World City Hypothesis," *Development and Change* 17, no. 1 (1986): 69–83; Saskia Sassen, *The Global City* (Princeton, NJ: Princeton University Press, 1991).

7   See, in particular, the work of the Globalization and World Cities (GaWC) research team at Lough-borough University: http://www.lboro.ac.uk/gawc/.

8   Friedmann, "The World City Hypothesis"; Sassen, *Global City.*

9   Sassen, *Global City,* 13.

10   Peter Marcuse and Richard van Kempen eds., *Globalizing Cities: A New Spatial Order?* (Oxford: Blackwell, 2000).

11   Michael Peter Smith and Joe Feagin, eds., *The Capitalist City* (Cambridge, MA: Blackwell, 1987).

12   Marcuse and van Kempen, *Globalizing Cities.*

13   Doreen Massey, *World City* (London: Polity, 2007), 22.

14   Ibid, 89.

15   Neil Brenner, "Global Cities, 'Glocal' States: Global City Formation and State Territorial Restructuring in Contemporary Europe," *Review of International Political Economy* 5, no. 1 (1998): 1–37.

16   Jennifer Robinson, "Global and World Cities: A View from off the Map," *International Journal of Urban and Regional Research* 26, no. 3 (2002): 531–54.

17   Ananya Roy, "The 21st Century Metropolis: New Geographies of Theory," *Regional Studies* 43, no. 6 (2009): 819–30.

18 Ibid.

19 Stefan Kipfer and Roger Keil, "Toronto, Inc.? Planning the Competitive City in Toronto," *Antipode* 34, no. 2 (2002): 227–64.

20 For an important critical counterpoint to these positions, which also suggests new lines of research on globalizing cities, see Michiel van Meeteren, Ben Derudder and David Bassens, "Can the Straw Man Speak? An Engagement with Postcolonial Critiques of 'Global Cities Research,'" *Dialogues in Human Geography* (forthcoming, 2016). See also David Bassens and Michiel van Meeteren, "World Cities under Conditions of Financialized Globalization: Towards an Augmented World City Hypothesis," *Progress in Human Geography* 39, no. 6 (2015): 752–75.

21 Stephen Graham, ed., *Disrupted Cities: When Infrastructure Fails* (London: Routledge, 2009); S. Harris Ali and Roger Keil, eds., *Networked Disease: Emerging Infections in the Global City* (London: Blackwell, 2008).

22 Mike Davis, *Planet of Slums* (London: Verso, 2006).

23 See Deyan Sudjic, *The 100-Mile City* (London: Mariner Books, 1993); as well as Edward Soja, "Regional Urbanization and the End of the Metropolis Era," in *The New Blackwell Companion to the City,* ed. Gary Bridge and Sophie Watson (Oxford: Blackwell, 2011), 679–89.

24 John Friedmann and Goetz Wolff, "World City Formation: An Agenda for Research and Action," *International Journal of Urban and Regional Research* 6, no. 3 (1982): 309–44; italics added.

25 John Friedmann, *World City Futures: The Role of Urban and Regional Policies in the Asia-Pacific Region,* Occasional Paper no. 56 (Hong Kong: Chinese University Press, 1997), 2, 26.

5   Territorial Competitiveness: Lineages, Practices, Ideologies

with David Wachsmuth

Since the 1980s, the notion of *territorial competitiveness* has become one of the foundations of mainstream, "entrepreneurial" approaches to local economic development.[1] This concept is premised on the assumption that subnational territories – cities and metropolitan regions, in particular – must compete with one another for economic survival through the attraction of transnationally mobile capital investment. The invocation of territorial competitiveness is generally accompanied by the assertion that various types of (national, regional or local) institutional transformation and policy reorientation are required in order to enhance locationally specific socioeconomic assets. Such assumptions – and, more generally, a widespread sense of panic among local policy makers and urban planners regarding the perceived "threats" of worldwide interlocality competition – have figured crucially in the proliferation of a broad array of political initiatives oriented towards promoting urban territorial competitiveness during the last four decades. Such policies have appeared in diverse forms (neoliberal, centrist and social democratic), at various spatial scales (from the Organization for Economic Cooperation and Development [OECD], the World Bank and national intergovernmental systems to metropolitan regions, municipalities and even neighborhoods), and under a range of labels (industrial districts, clustering, science parks, technopoles, human capital, global cities, creative cities, and so forth). But they have all generally entailed an abandonment of earlier concerns with sociospatial redistribution and "balanced" urbanization, and a concerted emphasis on enhancing the "attractiveness" of a local economy for external capital investment, positioning a city strategically within supranational circuits of capital, bolstering local socioeconomic assets and downsizing the administrative infrastructures of large-scale public agencies. In this sense, the rise of territorial competitiveness as a concept has been intertwined with a major reorientation of urban governance regimes across the world economy.

Against the background of these strategic and institutional realignments, this chapter explores the lineages of territorial competitiveness discourses within and beyond the field of urban planning, their intellectual basis, and their implications for public policies oriented towards promoting local economic development. We argue that, despite its contemporary pervasiveness, the concept of territorial competitiveness is premised upon flawed intellectual assumptions, and serves primarily as a means of ideological mystification in the sphere of local policy development. Rather than offering a basis for viable local economic development policies, it obfuscates the restructuring processes that are under way within and among contemporary cities, and thus contributes to the formulation of ineffective, wasteful and socially polarizing policies. Our somewhat gloomy conclusion is that, because so many localities within the global interurban system have adopted policies oriented towards the promotion of territorial competitiveness, significant strategic disadvantages accrue to those localities that attempt to opt out of such policies, or to adopt alternatives to them. Thus, in the absence of comprehensive global or supranational regulatory reform, escape routes from this apparent "competitiveness trap" presently appear circumscribed.

Our analysis is focused primarily upon North American and western European developments during the last four decades. It is important to note, however, that the concept of territorial competitiveness has been mobilized as a key element of local economic policy and urban planning discourse in cities, regions and states throughout the world economy.[2] More systematic analysis of territorial competitiveness policies in the major cities of the global South awaits further research and debate. We hope that the critical orientation elaborated here might provide a useful reference point for such discussions.

"Compete or die"

Since the early 1980s, one of the foundations of mainstream approaches to local economic development planning in North America and western Europe has been the notion of an intensified global competition among cities for external capital investment and for localized competitive advantages. In this view, global economic restructuring is a ferociously competitive struggle not merely between capitalist firms, but between *economic territories*, generally localities, cities or city-regions. According to one typical formulation, "In the present context of internationalization, the historical competition between cities has acquired a special importance. Every large European city tries to find the right mode to compete with others in an increasingly competitive framework. That competition is played out at two levels: the global and the European."[3] Analogous assumptions regarding the intensification of interurban competition in Europe underpin a special issue of the journal *Urban Studies* devoted to the theme of "Competitive Cities."[4] Countless additional examples of such arguments can be found throughout the recent academic literature on urban development.

These visions of intensified interlocality competition have also been pervasive in local policy and urban planning discourse, beginning in the USA during the 1970s, and soon thereafter diffusing to western Europe, East Asia and beyond. References to the "threat," "problem" or "challenge" of interurban competition abound in policy reports, press releases and glossy brochures published by municipal governments, planning offices, chambers of commerce and urban economic development agencies throughout the world. Various models of the changing global and supranational urban hierarchies, often influenced by politically neutralized versions of world city theory, have come to figure quite prominently in such documents, enabling local boosterists and political entrepreneurs proudly to advertise their own city's ranking while representing as dramatically as possible the ways in which other closely ranked cities are poised to threaten local competitive advantages. Although the structure of world urban hierarchies remains a matter of continued debate among academic urbanists, most city marketing agencies have developed homegrown "benchmarking" techniques for representing their own city's ranking within the hierarchy in the most favorable light possible.[5] Indeed, the assumption that cities compete against one another has become so naturalized among local policy makers that most discussions of the issue accept such competition as a self-evident fact, and turn immediately to the problem of local economic development strategy.

The notion of interlocality competition has played an essential role in the mobilization of what David Harvey famously labeled "entrepreneurial" urban policies, which entail the mobilization of local political institutions to enhance the territorially embedded competitive advantages of cities and city-regions in relation to supranational or global spaces of perceived economic competition.[6] Due to their intensive focus on the need to bolster place-specific, territorially inscribed socioeconomic assets, such strategies of local economic development have also been characterized as urban locational policies.[7] Crucially, then, there is a direct link between the increasingly widespread vision of a worldwide interlocality competition and the growing emphasis in policy and planning circles on localized forms of territorial competitiveness. Policies oriented towards the latter goal are generally justified as strategic responses to the former state of affairs.

Commenting on the European situation in the 1990s, Dutch urbanists Leo van den Berg and Erik Braun explicitly asserted this connection by declaring that "cities and towns are waking up to the fact [*sic*] that an entrepreneurial and anticipatory policy is called for to cope with urban and regional competition."[8] Most academic commentators on entrepreneurial cities have likewise tended to accept uncritically these "declarations of economic war" among local policy makers and boosterists, taking for granted that they represent a relatively transparent reflection of a radically transformed geoeconomic situation, and that territorial competitiveness represents a coherent, justifiable concern in such a context. As Gillian Bristow explains, "Competitiveness is portrayed as the means by which regional economies are externally validated in an era of globalisation, such that there can be no principled objection to policies and strategies deemed to be competitiveness-enhancing, whatever their indirect consequences."[9] In short, urban commentators, planners and policy makers alike appear to have convinced themselves that interlocality competition has become an ineluctable fact of life in an age of "globalization," to which localities have no choice but to adjust or else risk incurring serious economic disadvantages. Both in theory and in practice, contemporary discourses of inter-locality competition and territorial competitiveness suggest a grim categorical imperative: *"compete or die."*[10]

Geoeconomic contexts of territorial competitiveness policy

Whether under the rubric of urban entrepreneurialism, urban locational policy, or territorial competitiveness, policy responses to this new categorical imperative must be contextualized in relation to at least four fundamental geoeconomic transformations: deindustrialization and reindustrialization; the information and logistics revolution; the rise of flexible forms of industrial organization; and the globalization of finance capital.[11]

— *Deindustrialization and reindustrialization.* The post-1970s round of deindustrialization and reindustrialization has generated dramatic decline in older industrial regions and equally dramatic growth within "sunrise" regions specialized, in particular, in producer and financial services, high-technology industries and other advanced forms of revitalized craft production.[12] Confronted with these global sectoral shifts, urban and regional planners have explored new ways of influencing the sectoral composition of their territories – whether through the phasing out, subsidization or modernization of traditional mass production industries; through the nurturing or direct financing of economic development in high-tech or producer and financial service sectors; through the mobilization of property, venture capital and new infrastructural investments to develop entirely new sectoral specializations within a region; or through some combination of these strategies. These policy responses have been closely intertwined with new discourses and practices of competition between particular types of cities – for instance, between cities that are attempting to phase out or modernize traditional industrial sectors, between cities that specialize in similar growth industries, or between cities that are attempting to attract similar types of external capital investment.[13]

– *The information and logistics revolution.* The information revolution, based primarily upon the development of new telecommunications technologies, has dramatically enhanced the capacity of firms to coordinate and recalibrate production networks on a global scale.[14] Meanwhile, the continued deployment of new logistics tech-nologies has caused the cost and time of commodity circulation to decline signi-ficantly. Consequently, as Helga Leitner and Eric Sheppard argue, "locational advantages stemming from accessibility to markets, resources and labour have become less important relative to other site-specific differences between cities (such as labour costs, industrial clusters and local governance systems) in affecting their attractiveness to private investors."[15] Within at least some niches of the spatial division of labor, these new technological capacities have also enabled firms to shift activities more easily among various possible locations as labor costs, taxes or political conditions change within particular places. Under these circumstances, local policy makers and urban planners have experienced extensive pressures to construct place-specific locational advantages for firms within their jurisdictions that secure the profitability of existing industries while also serving as magnets for additional external capital investment. Insofar as the competitive advantages of cities and regions are today technologically, institutionally and politically constructed rather than being based upon pregiven factor endowments or static locational conditions, new regulatory imperatives have arisen above all on the local and regional scales to coordinate, maintain and enhance the place-specific preconditions for economic growth.[16] In most older industrial states, local and regional policy makers have understood these new regulatory dilemmas with reference to a zero-sum competition between locations to attract investment from mobile corporations.[17]

– *New forms of industrial organization.* The erosion of traditional Fordist mass production systems, with their large-scale agglomerations of fixed capital and labor-power, has also had important consequences for urban governance. The shift towards putatively more "flexible" forms of industrial organization in recent decades appears to have significantly reduced the costs of fixed investment in any given location for the simple reason that "smaller plants can be built, which take fewer years to pay for."[18] Insofar as fixed capital investment costs can be paid off more swiftly, the mobility of capital is thereby enhanced, for "it now takes fewer years before a production facility is paid for; at which time the firm will reassess the benefits of continuing production in that city."[19] In this new environment of "flexibilized" industrial organization, local policy makers and planners are confronted with intensified pressures continually to upgrade the infrastructures of transportation, communication and production within their jurisdictional boundaries in order to anticipate the shifting locational requirements of the industrial sectors they wish to attract and cultivate.

– *The globalization of finance.* Under conditions of sustained economic crisis, capital seeks new outlets to protect itself from devalorization. The massive financialization of capital that has occurred on a world scale since the early 1980s can be viewed as one such strategy to this end.[20] Processes of financialization have changed the conditions for urban and regional governance in significant ways, most crucially by altering the regulatory frameworks through which local and regional governments borrow money to finance and sustain fixed capital investments within their jurisdictions.[21] The international range of financial institutions, instruments and mechanisms through which money can be borrowed and lent has massively increased since the 1970s, opening up new financial options for many localities, but also subjecting them more directly to the volatile seas of global financial markets. The bankruptcy of Orange County, California, in 1994 due to its speculative investments in futures markets and the near bankruptcy of Jefferson County, Alabama, in 2009 at the hands of JP Morgan–designed synthetic derivatives represent two typical instances of the major risks to which cities and regions are being subjected in contemporary "casino capitalism."[22] Such bankruptcies, generally followed by politically aggressive, socially regressive local austerity measures, have become far more commonplace, especially in the USA, following the Wall Street crisis of 2008.[23] To the extent that local governments and planning agencies are now being constrained to repay their loans within a strict time frame, pressures to enhance the employment capacity and tax yield of the local economy or to slash local budgets are also significantly increased.[24] In short, as local governments come to rely more extensively upon global financial markets to fund economic development projects, they are also subjected to a range of new fiscal constraints, making a politics of territorial competitiveness appear not only plausible but essential for longer-term urban planning and development.

Taken together, then, these geoeconomic transformations have entailed a variety of new pressures upon cities and regions around the world to (re)activate economic development within their boundaries. According to Harvey, the rise of entrepreneurial forms of urban governance and associated discourses of local territorial competitiveness has entailed nothing less than "a radical reconstruction of central to local state relations and the cutting free of local state activities from the welfare state and the Keynesian compromise."[25] In this sense, the proliferation of territorial competitiveness policy has been inextricably intertwined with a fundamental restructuring of inherited Keynesian state forms and the crystallization of new, post-Keynesian formations of statehood: a rescaled institutional rule-regime oriented towards a neoliberalization of intergovernmental and interscalar relations across the world economy.[26]

Contours of territorial competitiveness policy

Within the field of local and regional economic policy, the new emphasis on territorial competitiveness represents a striking discursive and ideological realignment, not only in specialized industrial districts and global cities, but in traditional centers of manufacturing as well. Whereas priorities such as balanced urbanization, territorial redistribution and sociospatial equalization prevailed across much of the older industrialized and state-socialist world from the 1950s up through the mid-1970s, the worldwide economic crises of the latter decade seriously destabilized the political coalitions and institutional architectures that had been constructed to promote such agendas.[27] In stark contrast, within territorial competitiveness discourses, cities and city-regions are no longer represented as mere transmission belts undergirding national economic regimes or as concentrations of standardized, fixed capital investments and land resources. Instead, they are described as flexible, internationalized milieux endowed with place-specific locational assets, innovation networks and endogenous learning capacities that must be continually upgraded in relation to competing local economies. Internal networks of cooperation, both between firms and between major public and private actors, are increasingly viewed as an optimal basis on which to compete more effectively in an uncertain geoeconomic environment.[28]

At any spatial scale, territorial competitiveness policies hinge upon the assumption that territorial units, like capitalist firms, compete against one another in order to maximize profits and economic growth. In this viewpoint, the competitiveness of a given territory is said to flow from its capacity to achieve these goals effectively and durably, whether by attracting inward investment flows, by lowering investment costs, by increasing productivity levels, by providing a suitably skilled labor force, by creating an innovative environment or by means of other strategies intended to enhance the value of economic activities located within its boundaries.[29] The goal of territorial competitiveness policy, therefore, is to maintain and expand the capacities for profit-making and economic growth that are thought to be embedded within, or potentially attached to, specific political jurisdictions.

For present purposes, it is not necessary to embrace a particular definition of competitiveness, either for firms or for territories. Our point is simply to observe that, since the early 1980s, national, regional and urban policy makers and planners across western Europe, North America, East Asia and elsewhere have become concerned to enhance various attributes of cities and city-regions that are considered to contribute to their "competitiveness" relative to other global investment locations.[30] Given the earlier, Fordist-Keynesian understanding of cities as localized subunits of national economies, this new emphasis on urban territorial competitiveness in relation to supranational circuits of capital represents a striking political, ideological and scalar realignment.[31] The proliferation of territorial competitiveness policies during the last four decades is at once an expression and an outcome of this changing conception of how cities and metropolitan regions contribute to, and function within, economic life.

While such policies are frequently justified with reference to the widely disseminated writings of corporate strategists such as Michael Porter and Kenichi Ohmae, they have been grounded, in practice, upon a diverse range of assumptions regarding the sources of competitive advantage within local economies and the role of state institutions in promoting the latter.[32] We do not attempt here to compare systematically the nationally, regionally and locally specific types of territorial competitiveness policies that have crystallized during the last four decades, though this would undoubtedly be an illuminating exercise. Instead, we proceed on a more abstract, meso-level in order to specify three analytical axes on which such policies may be decoded.

1. *Forms of territorial competition.* According to Michael Storper and Richard Walker's foundational distinction, interfirm competition under capitalism occurs in weak and strong forms.[33] Whereas weak competition is oriented towards the reduction of costs and the redistribution of resources within a given spatial division of labor (static comparative advantages), strong competition is oriented towards the transformation of the conditions of production in order to introduce new technological capacities and a new spatial division of labor (dynamic competitive advantages). Territorial competitiveness policies may likewise be oriented towards weak or strong forms of interfirm competition, depending on the balance of cost cutting, deregulatory state initiatives and those that attempt to enhance firm productivity and innovative milieux within the jurisdiction in question.[34] Neoliberal or defensive approaches to competitiveness policy attempt to capitalize upon weak forms of interfirm competition; they are based upon the assumption that lowering the costs of investment within a given territory will attract mobile capital investment and thus enhance its competitiveness. By contrast, social democratic or offensive approaches to competitiveness policy attempt to capitalize upon strong forms of interfirm competition; they are based on the assumption that territorial competitiveness hinges upon the provision of nonsubstitutable socio-economic assets such as innovative capacities, collaborative interfirm networks, advanced infrastructural facilities and skilled labor power. Within any national or

local context, the precise balance among neoliberal/defensive and social democratic/ offensive approaches to territorial competitiveness policy is an object and outcome of sociopolitical struggles over the form of state intervention into the urban process.[35]

2. *Fields of territorial competition.* Building upon Harvey's study of urban entrepreneurialism, four distinct fields of territorial competitiveness policy may be delineated according to the particular circuits of capital they target.[36] First, territorial competitiveness policies may attempt to enhance a city's advantages within spatial divisions of labor, generally by establishing or strengthening place-specific conditions for the production of particular types of goods and services. Second, territorial competitiveness policies may attempt to enhance a city's advantages within spatial divisions of consumption, generally by creating or strengthening a localized infrastructure for tourism, leisure or retirement functions. Third, territorial competitiveness policies may attempt to enhance a city's command-and-control capacities in the spheres of finance, information processing and government. Finally, territorial competitiveness policies may target governmental subsidies and investments – the spatial divisions of public redistribution – to promote local economic development. These policies may be locally mobilized, as when municipalities compete for infrastructure grants from superordinate levels of government, or they may be carried out in a top-down fashion by national state agencies or, in the European context, by the European Commission. While these fields of territorial competition may be distinguished analytically, most competitiveness policies attempt, in practice, to enhance a city's position simultaneously within multiple fields.

3. *Geographies of territorial competition.* Finally, territorial competitiveness policies entail the delineation of determinate geographical parameters within which the process of economic development is to unfold. These parameters may be defined with reference to three key elements. The first is spaces of competitiveness: the strategic spaces within which place-specific economic capacities are to be mobilized. Central business districts, inner-city enterprise zones, revitalized manufacturing and port areas, and high-technology enclaves are common examples. The second geographical factor is spaces of competition. These are the broader, often global, spaces within which urban economies or their component economic zones are

to be positioned as putatively attractive investment locations. The global cities of New York and London are thus understood to be competing within a different global space from, for example, export processing zones in Manila, Shenzhen and São Paulo, or manufacturing regions such as Detroit, Manchester or Dortmund. The final factor is positioning strategies: scale-attuned political initiatives designed to articulate urban spaces of competitiveness into the supranational spaces of competition.[37] For instance, some territorial competitiveness policies attempt to transform an urban economy into a key articulation point within a nested hierarchy of regional, national and supranational economic spaces. Other such policies may attempt to reorganize inherited urban hierarchies – whether vertically, through the promotion of new forms of cooperation among different tiers of state power; or horizontally, through the promotion of transversal alliances among geographically dispersed cities occupying complementary positions in the global division of labor. In this sense, even though all forms of territorial competitiveness policy strive to position cities and regions favorably within supranational circuits of capital, this goal may be pursued through diverse political-geographical strategies.

Territorial competitiveness policies have an inherently speculative character due to "the inability [of political alliances] to predict exactly which package [of local investments] will succeed and which will not, in a world of considerable economic instability and volatility."[38] Moreover, as we argue below, such policies are often grounded upon untenable assumptions and unrealistic predictions regarding the possible future trajectories of local economic development. Despite these endemic problems, however, the proliferation of territorial competitiveness policies has at once embodied and accelerated a significant transformation in the character of state intervention into the urban process during the last four decades: the spatially redistributive state forms of the Fordist-Keynesian-developmentalist period have been largely superseded by a more fragmented, multiscalar constellation of post-Keynesian state institutions that explicitly promote an intensification of uneven spatial development within and beyond their jurisdictional boundaries.[39]

Measuring competition

As territorial competitiveness has become a key orienting principle of urban policy, various state and nongovernmental bodies have directed more attention to measuring it. Tore Fougner has demonstrated how the "competitiveness indexing" and country "benchmarking" performed by organizations such as the World Economic Forum have helped discursively normalize the competitiveness concept at the national scale.[40] The quantitative, technocratic methodologies used to construct indices and to rank countries are only feasible, though, because of the relative abundance, quality and uniformity of national statistics. In many cases, the relevant data do not exist for cities and urban regions, while methodological differences in defining cities and metropolitan areas makes international comparisons doubly problematic.

It should not be surprising, then, that the last few decades have witnessed a marked increase in efforts to statistically delineate urban regions, to standardize these delineations, and to use them to rank and compare cities with one another. Such initiatives must confront two separate but related questions. First, who is competing? In other words, how is the relevant unit of territorial competition to be defined? Second, what are the stakes and spoils of this competition? In other words, what are the appropriate benchmarks for deciding which territorial units are competing most successfully?

The first question has been by and large answered with reference to the increasingly popular concept of the metropolitan region. This concept was introduced as a statistical measure in the United States around the beginning of the twentieth century, but has become a major keyword in contemporary discussions among planners and policy makers regarding the prospects of local spaces in the global economy.[41] During the last several decades, the concept of the metropolitan region (or some variant thereof) is increasingly being adopted throughout the world as the standard urban measurement concept. In the European Union, for example, the pan-EU statistical agency has been collaborating with national governments to standardize the measurement of the "larger urban zone" (LUZ), which is a close proxy for the metropolitan region, so that LUZs are statistically comparable across nations.[42] Similarly, in 2006, OECD held a conference on standardizing the measurement of metropolitan regions across its member states. A submission to the conference by the Greater London Authority lays out the rationale for doing so:

London, like many cities, requires an international benchmarking standard. It needs to compare itself with other cities for the purpose of identifying best practice for policy… Nor is this need confined to the authorities responsible for London: national and international governments need common standards both to compare the situation of cities and to allocate and implement policy resources […] It is our view that having a common standard is more important than having the right standard since in some senses if there is a common standard which represents city-regions in a reasonably consistent way then that itself is the "right" standard.[43]

There is a marked tension, however, between the varied spaces of competitiveness that are targeted by contemporary urban policy (from metropolitan regions down to individual neighborhoods) and the pervasive statistical standardization of the metropolitan region as the de facto unit of competitiveness. Indeed, in many cases, the territorial unit being benchmarked and the territorial unit being targeted by competitiveness policies are completely different. For example, the recent Toronto Board of Trade competitiveness report compares the Toronto metropolitan region with a host of others, even though the Toronto metropolitan region encompasses four different regional governments (in whole or in part) and fully 24 different municipal governments.[44] Which government or government agency is expected to act on the report's findings? Moreover, most metropolitan areas are simply commuting zones. Even assuming the possibility of policy coordination across the relevant state agencies, a commuting zone is only likely to be a sensible unit of analysis for very specific types of policies (notably labor-market interventions).

The metropolitan region, for better or for worse, has become the primary basis for defining the city as a globally competitive unit. But what are these metropolitan regions competing at? Historically, efforts at quantifying national competitiveness have focused on macroeconomic indicators such as gross domestic product, terms of trade, and productivity. But, beginning in 1979 with the publication of the *Report on the Competitiveness of European Industry* and gaining widespread acceptance in the writings of Michael Porter, academic and governmental bodies began attempting to quantify national competitiveness directly.[45] Each of the two major annual competitiveness reports currently published – *The Global Competitiveness Report* and *The World Competitiveness Yearbook* – constructs multidimensional indices to measure, respectively, "the set of factors, policies and institutions that determine the level of productivity of a country" and "the ability of nations to create and maintain an environment which sustains the competitiveness of enterprises."[46] The substantial difference between these two formulations already demonstrates that "competitiveness," unlike GDP or terms of trade, is an ambiguous term; the challenge is not only to measure it, but to elaborate a definition that is precise enough to enable such measurement.

Urban competitiveness benchmarks began to be produced somewhat after national ones, particularly since the early 1990s. Although the discursive terrain of urban competitiveness benchmarking is still very much in formation, the two most influential concepts for such discussions have been "global cities" and "creative cities." The former notion is loosely derived from the pioneering work of John Friedmann on hierarchies of world cities within the new international division of labor, and Saskia Sassen on the concentration of financial and producer services functions in specific urban regions.[47] However, most benchmarking strategies that invoke such concepts bracket the strongly critical thrust of Friedmann and Sassen's interventions, which emphasized the socially polarizing consequences of financialization and labor market dualization within major metropolitan regions. Instead, those who invoke the global cities concept for benchmarking purposes generally adopt an affirmative, boosterist approach to cities' efforts to position themselves strategically as financial centers within the global division of labor. Richard Florida, who popularized the idea of creative cities, has been focused much more unapologetically on competitiveness, benchmarking and urban policy, and has devoted considerable energies to marketing his own particular formula for local economic development to cities and subnational governments around the world.[48] Florida argues that a new "creative class" is the lynchpin of modern economic success, and that cities must compete to attract these highly mobile creative professionals through supply-side policies to attract technology, talent and tolerance. Despite its dubious methodology, Florida has become quite successful in selling municipal governments on his Creativity Index.[49]

Both approaches to urban benchmarking suggest specific, privileged domains of global urban competition. In this respect, they differ from the general national competitiveness rankings discussed above (although the Creativity Index, for example, is in practice nearly as broad as each of the two major national indices). But the underlying arbitrariness of competitiveness benchmarking makes it a common tool for boards of trade, place-promotion agencies, local chambers of commerce, local economic development corporations and other urban development interests to justify policies that supposedly enhance competitiveness. There are usually two different messages, each aimed at a different target. One is the purported need to promote competitiveness, and is aimed primarily at local government; the other is the city's purported success at promoting competitiveness, and is aimed primarily at mobile capital. The local "competitiveness reports" that are produced by such organizations tend to follow national ones in comparing cities across a broad range of indicators.[50] As long as governmental and nongovernmental organizations remain committed to the idea of urban regions as the key competitive territorial units in the global economy, we should expect further, more elaborate initiatives to increase quantitative measurement and comparison of these regions.[51]

Decoding territorial competitiveness

The premise of competitiveness benchmarking is that it clarifies the process by which cities and city-regions are competing. But the very concept of territorial competitiveness is a cipher: it masks as much as it reveals about urban governance and interlocality interaction in the contemporary age.[52] Consequently, like so many other popular catchphrases in the contemporary globalization debates – such as the "hypermobility" of capital, the "weakening" of the state and the "deterritorialization" of social space – the notion of territorial competition must be systematically decoded.

As a number of commentators have indicated, the notion of territorial competitiveness rests upon an untenable analogy between capitalist firms and urban territories.[53] According to Paul Krugman's now-famous polemic against popular US economists such as Robert Reich and Lester Thurow, competitiveness becomes a "dangerous obsession" when applied to any organizational entities other than capitalist firms. It is logically incoherent, in Krugman's view, to apply the concept of competitiveness to national territories because they "have no well-defined bottom line": "countries […] do not go out of business" and thus cannot be understood appropriately as wealth-creating machines.[54] Insofar as firms must define their "bottom line" in terms of profits, Krugman argues, they are the only organizations to which the attribute of competitiveness can be defensibly ascribed. On this basis, Krugman concludes that the notion of territorial competitiveness should be eradicated entirely both from social-scientific investigation and from political debate, for it contributes to vacuous analyses and wasteful policies.

Given the problematic, highly amorphous character of the notion of competitiveness when applied to territorial units rather than firms, what explains the proliferation of local strategies for achieving this elusive but almost universally endorsed goal during the last three decades?[55] Why, in short, has the "dangerous obsession" of local territorial competitiveness become such a popular indulgence among policy makers and other local boosterists? Unfortunately, Krugman's critique brackets this crucial question by attributing such policies to the supposed intellectual sloppiness and incompetence of their proponents. Yet, as Peter Dicken appropriately cautions:

> Whether Krugman is right or wrong in his analysis, there seems little likelihood of policy makers actually heeding his warnings and refraining from both the rhetoric and the reality of competitive policy measures. As long as the concept of national [or local] competitiveness remains in currency then no single state [or municipality] is likely to opt out.[56]

Critiques by Krugman and others notwithstanding, then, it would be seriously misleading to dismiss the intense policy concern with something called "competitiveness" as a mere conceptual fallacy or ideological fantasy. Rather, we suggest that the rise of territorial competitiveness policies represents a more general realignment of contemporary state institutions towards various forms of transnational economic competition, signaling the formation of what some authors have termed "competition states."[57] Although neoliberalism is a particularly significant manifestation of this multiscalar, productivist reorientation of national state power, it is only one among many political forms in which such competition states have been consolidated.

But here emerges a second major problem with the concept of territorial competitiveness. The concept of interlocality competition attributes to cities agentic properties and posits their competitive interaction as unified territorial collectivities. However, the determinate politico-institutional conditions under which localities might become agentic, and adopt competitive orientations towards other localities, are generally presumed rather than interrogated. As Harvey notes, the reification of cities into "active agents" must be avoided insofar as capitalist urbanization is "a spatially grounded social process in which a wide range of different actors with quite different objectives and agendas interact through a particular configuration of interlocking spatial practices."[58] Cities are localized social structures in which any number of highly antagonistic spatial practices – including class relations, accumulation strategies and diverse politico-ideological projects – arise and are reproduced.[59] Accordingly, as Leslie Budd explains, "To propose cities or regions competing with each other presupposes a unity of purpose between the constituent economic and social interests and that city governance has an autonomy and freedom of manoeuvre."[60]

The point, however, is not to deny that the different actors located within cities may, under certain conditions, organize collectively to promote common interests and agendas, but rather to emphasize that such collective mobilizations cannot be abstractly presupposed. As Kevin Cox and Andrew Mair explain:

> If people interpret localised social structures in explicitly territorial terms, come to view their interests and identities as "local," and then act upon that view by mobilising locally defined organisations to further their interests in a manner that would not be possible were they to act separately, then it seems eminently reasonable to talk about "locality as agent."[61]

The local territorial alliances that result from such mobilizations have played an important role in the historical geography of capitalist urbanization. For instance, urban growth machines – coalitions of land-based elites oriented towards a maximization of local property values – have long played a shaping role in US urban development and represent what is perhaps the paradigmatic example of such alliances.[62] Other forms of local territorial alliances, based upon diverse regimes of public-private collaboration, cross-class coalitions and place-based attachments of various kinds, have likewise emerged at various spatial scales throughout the history of capitalist urbanization in other national contexts.[63]

According to David Harvey's classic analysis of the issue in *Limits to Capital,* the essential basis for the formation of local territorial alliances is the fact that:

> a portion of the total social capital has to be rendered immobile in order to give the remaining capital greater flexibility of movement.

The value of capital, once it is locked into immobile physical and social infrastructures, has to be defended if it is not to be devalued.[64]

Therefore, territorial alliances to promote economic growth within a particular city or city-region are generally (but not necessarily) anchored within those factions of capital and labor whose resources and interests are most closely tied to various large-scale immobile infrastructures and investments within the city, such as real estate, fixed capital outlays, utilities and infrastructural facilities. Harvey's explanation of this fundamental and recurrent tendency towards a "regionalization of class and factional struggle" under capitalism is worth quoting at length:

> Some factions of capital are more committed to immobile investment than others. Land and property owners, developers and builders, the local state and those who hold the mortgage debt have everything to gain from forging a local alliance to protect and promote local interests and to ward off the threat of localized, place-specific devaluation. Production capital which cannot easily move may support the alliance and be tempted to buy local labour peace and skills through compromises over wages and work conditions – thereby gaining the benefits of co-operation from labour and a rising effective demand for wage goods in local markets. Factions of labour that have, through struggle or historical accident, managed to create islands of privilege within a sea of exploitation may also rally to the cause of the alliance. Furthermore, if a local compromise between capital and labour is helpful to local accumulation, then the bourgeoisie as a whole may support it. The basis is laid for the rise of a territorially based alliance between various factions of capital, the local state and even whole classes, in defense of social reproduction processes (both accumulation and the reproduction of labour power) within a particular territory. The basis for the alliance rests, it must be stressed, on the need to make a certain portion of capital immobile in order to give the remainder freedom to move.[65]

The resultant localized territorial alliances are grounded upon formal and informal partnerships among diverse local institutions and actors, including chambers of commerce, trade unions, local planning authorities, the city government itself and, above all, different factions of capital and labor.[66] As Harvey elsewhere notes, the overarching objective of such territorial alliances is "to preserve or enhance achieved models of production and consumption, dominant technological mixes and patterns of social relations, profit and wage levels, the qualities of labor power and entrepreneurial-managerial skills, social and physical infrastructures, and the cultural qualities of living and working."[67] To accomplish these wide-ranging goals, territorial alliances generally mobilize scale-specific accumulation strategies in which certain locally rooted locational assets are selected and actively promoted.[68]

We thus arrive at the following result: cities and city regions can be said to engage in interlocality competition only to the extent that *territorial alliances* are formed – whether at local or supralocal scales – with the explicit goal of promoting a specific locality as a unit within such competition. In the absence of such alliances, it is logically incoherent to speak of the city as an agent; and in the absence of an entire *urban system* permeated by such alliances, it is logically incoherent to speak of interlocality competition. Interlocality or territorial competition is therefore better understood as a horizontal relationship between growth- and investment-oriented territorial alliances, rather than as a vertical relationship between immobile places and mobile flows of capital, or, for that matter, with reference to conventional notions of capital versus communities, flows versus places or the global versus the local. It is a shorthand term, in this view, for describing the *macrogeographical field of strategic interaction* among competing, locally or regionally based territorial alliances.

From this perspective, territorial competitiveness policies cannot be explained simply as a localized response to the supposed constraints imposed by enhanced interlocality competition; they must be seen, first and foremost, as basic animators of that competition which simultaneously naturalize it and make it appear inevitable. And, as we discuss below, as the number of territorial alliances engaged in such competitive interactions expands, powerful incentives to adopt competitiveness-oriented urban policies, and thus to join the competitive fray, are imposed upon those localities that had previously attempted to opt out.[69] Nonetheless, the role of territorial competitiveness policies as a generative force within interlocality competition cannot be grasped adequately if they are interpreted only as a reaction to externally imposed pressures. The shift towards territorial competitiveness policies is, therefore, best conceived not merely as a transition undergone by individual cities, but as a *relational* transformation of a large-scale urban hierarchy due to the intensified competitive interaction of multiple local territorial alliances within it.

Regulatory failures of territorial competitiveness policy

Territorial competitiveness policies are now pervasive in cities and city-regions across the world economy – but their apparent omnipresence tells us little regarding their effectiveness in practice. In fact, despite the claims made on behalf of such policies by their advocates, there is little empirical evidence that they actually serve the major purposes to which they are put. Rather, the bulk of critical social science analysis of such policies suggests that their main effects are regressive, wasteful and dysfunctional, whether in economic, administrative or political terms.[70]

As we have discussed, the perception of intensified interlocality competition enhances competitive pressures upon subnational administrative units to offer favorable terms to potential investors. As territorial competitiveness policies have subsequently been diffused, the potential disadvantages of a failure or refusal to introduce them have escalated. Despite this, there is currently little evidence that territorial competitiveness policies generate positive-sum, supply-side gains for local economies, for instance, by upgrading locally embedded industrial capacities. More frequently, such initiatives have entailed public subsidies to private firms, leading to a zero-sum redistribution of capital investment among competing locations. In this manner, territorial competitiveness policies may induce inefficient allocations of public resources as taxpayer revenues are channeled towards the promotion of private accumulation rather than towards the general conditions of production or social expenditures. Hence, as Paul Cheshire and Ian Gordon conclude, "much territorial competition [among cities] is pure waste."[71]

Additionally, the proliferation of territorial competitiveness policies has encouraged "the search for short-term gains at the expense of more important longer-term investments in the health of cities and the well-being of their residents."[72] Even though some cities have managed to acquire short-term competitive advantages through the early adoption of territorial competitiveness policies, such advantages have generally been eroded as analogous policies have been diffused among similarly positioned cities within wider spatial divisions of labor. In this sense, while territorial competitiveness policies have helped unleash short-term bursts of economic growth within some cities and regions, they have proven far less effective in sustaining that growth over the medium- or long-term.[73]

A further problem concerns the limited geographical reach of territorial competitiveness policies, which generally entail the targeting of strategic, globally connected urban regions, or specific locations therein, as the engines of national economic dynamism. Such policies are premised upon the assumption that enhanced urban territorial competitiveness will benefit the broader regional and national space-economies in which cities are embedded. In practice, however, territorial competitiveness policies have contributed to the establishment of technologically advanced, globally connected urban enclaves that generate only limited spillover effects into their surrounding territories. This tendency towards "glocal enclavization" is being articulated at a local scale, as advanced infrastructural hubs and high-technology production centers are delinked from adjoining neighborhoods, and at supralocal scales, as globally competitive agglomerations are delinked from older industrial regions, contiguous or nearby hinterlands, and other marginalized spaces within the same national territory.[74] The resultant intensification of territorial inequality may undermine macroeconomic stability; it may also breed divisive, disruptive political conflicts.

Particularly in their defensive, neoliberal forms, territorial competitiveness policies have encouraged a race to the bottom in social service provision as national, regional and municipal governments attempt to reduce the costs of capital investment within their territorial jurisdictions. This process of regulatory undercutting is dysfunctional on a number of levels: it aggravates rather than alleviates municipal fiscal and regulatory problems; it worsens life chances for significant segments of local and national populations; and it exacerbates entrenched inequalities within national urban hierarchies.[75]

The aforementioned regulatory problems may assume more moderate forms in conjunction with offensive, social-democratic forms of territorial competitiveness policy. Nonetheless, offensive forms of territorial competitiveness policy are likewise prone to significant crisis tendencies. First, like defensive approaches to territorial competitiveness policy, offensive approaches "operate … as a strategy for strengthening some territories vis-à-vis other territories and other nations"; they thus intensify uneven development beyond the territorial zones in which they are deployed.[76] The macroeconomic instability that subsequently ensues may undermine the very localized socioeconomic assets upon which offensive territorial competitiveness policies depend. Second, even more so than defensive forms of territorial competitiveness policy, offensive approaches to urban economic development suffer from serious problems of politicization. Their effectiveness hinges upon being confined to locally delineated areas; yet the apparent successes of such strategies at a local scale generate intense distributional pressures as other localities and regions within the same national territory strive to replicate the "recipe" or to reap some of its financial benefits.[77]

The proliferation of place-specific strategies of territorial competitiveness exacerbates coordination problems within and among national, regional and local state institutions. First, because territorial competitiveness policies enhance the geographical differentiation of state regulatory activities without embedding subnational competitive strategies within an encompassing national policy framework, they have undermined the organizational coherence and functional integration of state institutions. Second, this lack of supranational or national regulatory coordination in the field of urban policy may exacerbate the economic crisis tendencies discussed above: it enhances the likelihood that identical or analogous growth strategies may be replicated serially across wider urban systems, thus accelerating the diffusion of zero-sum forms of interlocality competition.[78]

Finally, the proliferation of territorial competitiveness policies has frequently generated new conflicts regarding democratic accountability and political legitimation. Many of the new, highly fragmented institutional forms established to implement territorial competitiveness policies are dominated by unelected government bureaucrats, technical experts, property developers and corporate elites who are not accountable to the populations that are most directly affected by their activities.[79] While this lack of political accountability may enable regulatory agencies to implement such policies more efficiently, it systematically undermines their ability to address broader social needs and to maintain territorial cohesion. It may also generate serious legitimation deficits if oppositional social forces are able to politicize the negative socioeconomic consequences of territorial competitiveness policies or their undemocratic character.

These considerations obviously paint a much gloomier picture of territorial competitiveness discourse and practice than that found in the mainstream literature on local economic development or, for that matter, that promoted by boosterist territorial alliances mobilized around specific projects to promote locational policies within cities or city-regions. Our analysis suggests that territorial competitiveness is, at core, an ideological keyword that facilitates regressive institutional, distributive and political shifts; undermines the localized preconditions for economic development; destabilizes the organizational infrastructure for urban and regional governance; and contributes to the further erosion of inherited relays of democratic accountability. To be sure, we do not mean to suggest that either the ideology or the practice of territorial competitiveness is in itself the cause of the developments sketched above, which are obviously intertwined with a complex ensemble of geoeconomic and geopolitical transformations and associated institutional contestations. Our goal here, rather, has been to expose some of the problematic intellectual assumptions that underpin this concept, to outline some of the regressive uses to which it has been put, and to underscore its essentially political-ideological character.

Beyond the competitiveness trap?

Paradoxically, despite the massively dysfunctional consequences outlined above, the widespread adoption of policies oriented towards local territorial competitiveness imposes powerful constraints upon any subnational governance institutions that attempt to forge alternative policy orientations. Insofar as national states, regions and cities that do try to opt out from competitiveness policies or other entrepreneurial strategies may accrue serious economic disadvantages in terms of lost investment, jobs and tax revenues, the "incentive … to try to gain at the expense of other states [and cities]" remains extremely powerful.[80] As David Harvey analogously notes of entrepreneurial urban policies (invoking Marx's famous description of intercapitalist competition as an "external coercive power" over individual capitalists):

> Indeed to the degree that inter-urban competition becomes more potent, it will almost certainly operate as an "external coercive power" over individual cities to bring them closer into line with the discipline and logic of capitalist development.[81]

These arguments thus point towards the urgent question: can an alternative discourse and practice of local economic development be elaborated? Can localities escape from the "competitiveness trap" to which they have apparently been consigned due to the last four decades of worldwide geoeconomic and geopolitical restructuring?

At the present time, various pathways of urban governance restructuring remain possible, but competitiveness-oriented agendas appear to be as entrenched than ever, not least because they have been so broadly naturalized as taken-for-granted priorities for economic policy at all spatial scales.[82] As we contemplate this rather grim scenario, Harvey's analysis of urban entrepreneurialism from the 1980s remains remarkably prescient. As he then explained:

> The problem is to devise a geopolitical strategy of inter-urban linkage that mitigates inter-urban competition and shifts political horizons away from the locality and into a more generalisable challenge to capitalist uneven development [...] [A] critical perspective on urban entrepreneurialism indicates not only its negative impacts but its potentiality for transformation into a progressive urban corporatism, armed with a keen geopolitical sense of how to build alliances and linkages across space in such a way as to mitigate if not challenge the hegemonic dynamic of capitalist accumulation to dominate the historical geography of social life.[83]

How, when and where such a geopolitical strategy might be adopted, and what slogan might be most appropriate to its aspirations – the "right to the city" may provide one especially salient possibility – are questions that remain to be fought out in cities, city-regions and, indeed, at all other spatial scales of governance.

Notes

1 David Harvey, "From Managerialism to Entrepreneurialism: The Transformation of Urban Governance in Late Capitalism," *Geografiska Annaler: Series B Human Geography* 71, no. 1 (1989): 3–17.

2 See, for example, Tore Fougner, "The State, International Competitiveness and Neoliberal Globalisation: Is There a Future beyond the 'Competition State,'" *Review of International Studies* 33 (2006): 165–85; Bob Jessop, "The Crisis of the National Spatio-temporal Fix and the Ecological Dominance of Globalizing Capitalism," *International Journal of Urban and Regional Research* 24, no. 2 (2000): 323–60; and Ann Markusen, ed., *Reigning In the Competition for Capital* (Kalamazoo, MI: W. E. Upjohn Institute for Employment Research, 2007).

3 Joan-Eugeni Sánchez, "Competitive Political and Administrative Systems," in *European Cities in Competition,* ed. Chris Jensen-Butler and Jan van Weesep (Aldershot: Avebury, 1997), 463.

4   See, for example, Iain Begg, "Cities and Competitiveness," *Urban Studies* 36, no. 5–6 (1999): 795–810; Ian Gordon, "Internationalization and Urban Competition," *Urban Studies* 36, no. 5–6 (1999): 1001–16; and William Lever, "Competitive Cities in Europe," *Urban Studies* 36, no. 5–6 (1999): 1029–44.

5   On the structure of world urban hierarchies, see Peter Taylor and Michael Hoyler, "The Spatial Order of European Cities under Conditions of Contemporary Globalization," *Tijdschrift voor Economische en Sociale Geografie* 91, no. 2 (2000): 176–89.

6   Harvey, "From Managerialism to Entrepreneurialism."

7   Neil Brenner, *New State Spaces: Urban Governance and the Rescaling of Statehood* (Oxford: Oxford University Press, 2004).

8   Leo van den Berg and Erik Braun, "Urban Competitiveness, Marketing and the Need for Organising Capacity," *Urban Studies* 36, no. 5–6 (1999): 987.

9   Gillian Bristow, "Everyone's a 'Winner': Problematising the Discourse of Regional Competitiveness," *Journal of Economic Geography* 5, no. 3 (2005): 285–304.

10 Aram Eisenschitz and Jamie Gough, "Theorizing the State in Local Economic Governance," *Regional Studies* 32, no. 8 (1998): 762.

11 This discussion draws extensively upon the analysis elaborated in Helga Leitner and Eric Sheppard, "Economic Uncertainty, Inter-Urban Competition and the Efficacy of Entrepreneurialism," in *The Entrepreneurial City: Geographies of Politics, Regime and Representation,* ed. Tim Hall and Phil Hubbard (Chichester: Wiley, 1998), 286–93.

12 Michael Storper and Allen Scott, "The Geographical Foundations and Social Regulation of Flexible Production Complexes," in *The Power of Geography,* ed. Jennifer Wolch and Michael Dear (Boston: Unwin Hyman, 1989), 19–40.

13 Stefan Krätke, *Stadt, Raum, Ökonomie* (Basel: Birkhäuser Verlag, 1995), 141.

14 Manuel Castells, *The Rise of the Network Society* (Cambridge, MA: Blackwell, 1996).

15 Leitner and Sheppard, "Economic Uncertainty," 288.

16 Allen J. Scott, *Regions and the World Economy* (London: Oxford University Press, 1998).

17 Kevin Cox, "Globalisation, Competition and the Politics of Local Economic Development," *Urban Studies* 32, no. 2 (1995): 213–24.

18 Leitner and Sheppard, "Economic Uncertainty," 290.

19 Ibid.

20 Giovanni Arrighi, *The Long Twentieth Century* (London: Verso, 1994); David Harvey, *The Enigma of Capital and the Crises of Capitalism* (New York: Oxford University Press, 2011).

21 Leitner and Sheppard, "Economic Uncertainty," 291–93.

22 Susan Strange, *The Retreat of the State* (New York: Cambridge University Press, 1996).

23 Jamie Peck, "Pushing Austerity: State Failure, Municipal Bankruptcy and the Crises of Fiscal Federalism in the USA," *Cambridge Journal of Regions, Economy and Society* 7 (2014): 17–44.

24 Leitner and Sheppard, "Economic Uncertainty," 292.

25 Harvey, "From Managerialism to Entrepreneurialism," 15.

26 See Chapters 3, 6, and 10 in the present volume; as well as Brenner, *New State Spaces.*

27 Ibid.

28 See, among other works, Michael Storper, *The Regional World* (New York: Guilford, 1996); Philip Cooke and Kevin Morgan, *The Associational Economy* (New York: Oxford University Press, 1998); and Aram Eisenschitz and Jamie Gough, *The Politics of Local Economic Development* (New York: Macmillan, 1993).

29 Begg, "Cities and Competitiveness."

30 Gordon, "Internationalization and Urban Competition."

31 John Lovering, "Creating Discourses rather than Jobs: The Crisis in the Cities and the Transition Fantasies of Intellectuals and Policy Makers," in *Managing Cities: The New Urban Context,* ed. Patsy Healey (London: Wiley, 1995), 109–26; Pierre Veltz, "The Dynamics of Production Systems, Territories and Cities," in *Cities, Enterprises and Society on the Eve of the 21st Century,* ed. Frank Moulaert and Allen Scott (London: Pinter, 1997), 78–96.

32 Michael Porter, *The Competitive Advantage of Nations* (London: Macmillan, 1990); Kenichi Ohmae, *The End of the Nation State: The Rise of Regional Economies* (New York: Free Press, 1990).

33 Michael Storper and Richard Walker, *The Capitalist Imperative: Territory, Technology and Industrial Growth* (London: Blackwell, 1989).

34 Danièle Leborgne and Alain Lipietz, "Two Social Strategies in the Production of New Industrial Spaces," in *Industrial Change and Regional Development: The Transformation of New Industrial Spaces,* ed. Georges Benko and Mick Dunford (London: Belhaven, 1991), 27–49.

35 Aram Eisenschitz and Jamie Gough, "The Contradictions of Neo-Keynesian Local Economic Strategy," *Review of International Political Economy* 3, no. 3 (1996): 434–58.

36 Harvey, "From Managerialism to Entrepreneurialism."

37 Jessop, "The Crisis of the National Spatio-Temporal Fix."

38 Harvey, "From Managerialism to Entrepreneurialism," 10–11.

39 Brenner, *New State Spaces.*

40 Fougner, "The State, International Competitiveness and Neoliberal Globalisation."

41 Scott, *Regions and the World Economy.*

42 Torbiörn Carlquist, "Revision of the Larger Urban Zones in the Urban Audit Data Collection" (paper on behalf of Eurostat, Defining and Measuring Metropolitan Regions, Paris, November 27, 2006).

43 Alan Freeman and Paul Cheshire, "Defining and Measuring Metropolitan Regions: A Rationale" (paper on behalf of the City of London, Defining and Measuring Metropolitan Regions, Paris, November 27, 2006), 2.

44 Toronto Board of Trade, "Toronto as a Global City: Scorecard on Prosperity" (policy report, Toronto, March 2009).

45 Porter, *The Competitive Advantage of Nations.*

46 Fougner, "The State, International Competitiveness and Neoliberal Globalisation," 313.

47 See Chapter 4 in the present volume, as well as John Friedmann and Goetz Wolff, "World City Formation: An Agenda for Research and Action," *International Journal of Urban and Regional Research* 6, no. 3 (1982): 309–44, and Saskia Sassen, *The Global City: New York, London, Tokyo,* 2nd ed. (Princeton, NJ: Princeton University Press, 2001).

48 Richard Florida, *The Rise of the Creative Class: And How It's Transforming Work, Leisure, Community, and Everyday Life* (New York: Basic Books, 2002).

49 For a detailed critique and analysis, see Jamie Peck, "Struggling with the Creative Class," *International Journal of Urban and Regional Research* 29, no. 4 (2005): 740–70.

50 See, for example, Europe Economics, "The Competitiveness of London: Future Challenges from Emerging Cities" (policy report, London Chamber of Commerce and Industry, London, April 2008); Toronto Board of Trade, "Toronto as a Global City."

51 See, for example, Henry Puderer, "Defining and Measuring Metropolitan Areas: A Comparison Between Canada and the United States" (paper on behalf of Statistics Canada, Defining and Measuring Metropolitan Regions Conference, Paris, November 27, 2006).

52 Leslie Budd, "Territorial Competition and Globalisation: Scylla and Charybdis of European Cities," *Urban Studies* 35, no. 4 (1998): 663–85. See also Bristow, "Everyone's a 'Winner.'"

53 Leitner and Sheppard, "Economic Uncertainty," 301.

54 Paul Krugman, "Competitiveness: A Dangerous Obsession," *Foreign Affairs,* March/April 1994, 31.

55 See also Begg, "Cities and Competitiveness"; Budd, "Territorial Competition and Globalisation"; Bristow, "Everyone's a 'Winner.'"

56 Peter Dicken, *Global Shift: The Internationalization of Economic Activity,* 3rd ed. (New York: Guilford, 1998), 88.

57 Philip Cerny, *The Changing Architecture of Politics* (London: Sage Publications, 1990); Bob Jessop, *The Future of the Capitalist State* (London: Polity, 2005).

58 Harvey, "From Managerialism to Entrepreneurialism," 5.

59 Cox, "Globalisation, Competition and the Politics of Local Economic Development."

60 Budd, "Territorial Competition and Globalisation," 670.

61 Kevin Cox and Andrew Mair, "From Localised Social Structures to Localities as Agents," *Environment and Planning* A 23, no. 2 (1991): 198.

62 John Logan and Harry Molotch, *Urban Fortunes: The Political Economy of Place* (Berkeley: University of California Press, 1987).

63 See, for example, David Harvey, *The Urban Experience* (Baltimore: Johns Hopkins University Press, 1989); Ann Markusen, *Regions: The Economics and Politics of Territory* (Totawa, NJ: Rowman & Littlefield, 1987); Clarence Stone and Heywood Sanders, eds., *The Politics of Urban Development* (Lawrence, KS: University Press of Kansas, 1987); and Bae-Gyoon Park, Richard Child Hill and Asato Saito, eds., *Locating Neoliberalism in East Asia: Neoliberalizing Spaces in Developmental States* (Oxford: Blackwell, 2013).

64 David Harvey, *The Limits to Capital* (Chicago: University of Chicago Press, 1982), 419–20.

65 Ibid., 420.

66 Paul Cheshire and Ian Gordon, "Territorial Competition and the Predictability of Collective (In)Action," *International Journal of Urban and Regional Resarch* 20, no. 3 (1996): 383–99.; Stone and Sanders, eds., *The Politics of Urban Development.*

67 Harvey, *The Urban Experience,* 148–55.

68 Bob Jessop, "The Narrative of Enterprise and the Enterprise of Narrative: Place-marketing and the Entrepreneurial City," in *The Entrepreneurial City: Geographies of Politics, Regime and Representation,* ed. Tim Hall and Phil Hubbard (Chichester: Wiley, 1998), 77–102.

69 Leitner and Sheppard, "Economic Uncertainty."

70 Ibid.; see also Cheshire and Gordon, "Territorial Competition"; Bristow, "Everyone's a 'Winner.'"

71 Paul Cheshire and Ian Gordon, eds., *Territorial Competition in an Integrating Europe* (Aldershot: Avebury, 1995), 122. See also Cheshire and Gordon, "Territorial Competition"; and Bristow, "Everyone's a 'Winner.'"

72 Leitner and Sheppard, "Economic Uncertainty," 305.

73 Jamie Peck and Adam Tickell, "Searching for a New Institutional Fix: The After-Fordist Crisis and Global-Local Disorder," in *Post-Fordism: A Reader,* ed. Ash Amin (Oxford: Blackwell, 1994), 280–315.

74 Stephen Graham and Simon Martin, *Splintering Urbanism* (New York: Routledge, 2001).

75 Eisenschitz and Gough, "Theorizing the State in Local Economic Governance."

76 Leborgne and Lipietz, "Two Social Strategies," 47.

77 Eisenschitz and Gough, "The Contradictions of Neo-Keynesian Local Economic Strategy."

78 Ash Amin and Anders Malmberg, "Competing Structural and Institutional Influences on the Geography of Production in Europe," in Amin, *Post-Fordism,* 227–48.

79 Erik Swyngedouw, "The Heart of the Place: The Resurrection of Locality in an Age of Hyperspace," *Geografiska Annaler: Series B Human Geography* 71, no. 1 (1989): 31–42.

80 Dicken, *Global Shift,* 88.

81 Harvey, "From Managerialism to Entrepreneurialism," 10.

82 For further discussion of various scenarios, see Markusen, *Reigning In the Competition for Capital.*

83 Harvey, "From Managerialism to Entrepreneurialism," 16.

6   Good Governance: Ideology of Sustainable Neoliberalism?

In the early 2000s, in conjunction with a world's fair held in Hanover, Germany, several national governments (Germany, Brazil, South Africa and Singapore) organized a conference in Berlin, "URBAN 21," to explore the interplay between globalization and urban restructuring. In that context, a ministry of the German government appointed a rather audaciously titled "World Commission" to produce a *World Report on the Urban Future* that would stimulate discussion among conference participants during the Berlin proceedings.[1] The World Commission was mainly composed of career politicians (including mayors and national ministers), international policy makers from the United Nations and the World Bank, several prominent architects, and a few academics. Looking back on this document with over fifteen years' hindsight, we find a fascinating perspective on how, at the turn of the present century, global political-economic elites were narrating the governance problems associated with cities, and the role of cities in broader regulatory transformations, both global and national. While such issues had previously been thematized in global perspective by international policy-making organizations such as the World Bank and UN Habitat, they had largely been understood as crystallizing in regionally and nationally specific forms, requiring sector-specific policy responses (especially, for instance, in relation to the problem of housing the urban poor). In contrast, anticipating more recent discussions under the rubric of the UN's Habitat III conference, the World Commission emphasized the globalization of the urban question, and the need for an integrated, cross-sectoral approach to the "millennial challenge" of promoting sustainable urban governance.[2] Indeed, within a few years of the publication of the *World Report* under the official title *Urban Future 21: A Global Agenda for Twenty-First Century Cities,* debates on the "urban age" and sustainable urban development were in full swing among policy makers, planners and designers around the world. The assertion that cities were important to global governance, which had a certain aura of boldness at the turn of the twenty-first century, would very quickly become commonplace – one of the key spatial ideologies of our time.[3]

Shortly before the Berlin conference, in collaboration with a local tenants' organization, several German urban activists organized a series of brief replies to the *World Report* by critical academics from Europe and North America, which were subsequently published in a pamphlet that was circulated at the event.[4] The essay below was produced in that context, as a contribution to the analysis and critique of the processes of roll-out neoliberalization that were then being consolidated and naturalized in urban governance systems around the world.[5] I argue that, rather than offering a basis for establishing more democratic, progressive or ecological forms of urbanism, the discourse of "good governance" serves as an ideological weapon for justifying regressive institutional reforms that enhance commodification, social polarization and uneven spatial development within and among cities, while simultaneously undermining the capacities of state institutions to manage accelerated processes of urban restructuring in ways that serve the public interest. Insofar as such popular discursive tropes obfuscate the power relations, conflicts and contradictions associated with urban restructuring, while also legitimating market-disciplinary, technoscientific, exclusionary and/or repressive responses to contemporary urban governance challenges, they urgently require systematic deconstruction by critical urban thinkers.

The authors of the *Urban Future 21 World Report* purport to articulate an agenda for "reinventing the city" in the new millennium. The ideological lynchpin of their project is the notion of "good governance," which is said to provide a means to reconcile such diverse sociopolitical goals as economic growth, democracy, social solidarity, livability and ecological sustainability.

This chapter explores what I take to be the central paradox of this thoroughly contradictory document. On the one hand, many of the goals mentioned in the *World Report* – most obviously, enhanced democracy, social solidarity and ecological sustainability – surely remain key components of Left political agendas, both progressive and radical. On the other hand, it can be argued that the main political thrust of the *World Report* is to defend a neoliberal agenda of urban institutional restructuring and social reform, oriented towards intensified market discipline, profit maximization, unfettered economic growth and enhanced capitalist power over major aspects of everyday life. Despite the references to issues such as social reproduction, poverty alleviation and ecological sustainability contained in the *World Report*, such priorities are justified primarily as a means to achieve the overarching goal of maintaining urban economic competitiveness under contemporary geoeconomic conditions.

Much of the *World Report* amounts to an exercise in naturalizing the US-dominated, neoliberal form of globalization that still prevailed, albeit in a deteriorating form, around the turn of the twenty-first century. The concept of capitalism is never mentioned in the *World Report,* but is referenced repeatedly through its fetishized forms of appearance – population growth and technological development – which are together described as the "basic driving forces" underlying contemporary urban change. The putative "necessity" for cities to compete within global circuits of production, finance and exchange is represented as a brute fact of nature that is beyond human design or political deliberation, a quasi-ontological condition to which policy makers and citizens alike must simply conform, or else risk marginalization or even extinction in a ruthless global survival of the fittest. Cities, the *World Report* argues, must be transformed into maximally self-reliant, efficient, service-oriented, entrepreneurial units within a world economy increasingly dominated by hypermobile transnational corporations and placeless financial flows. National and central governments are seen primarily as hindrances to local economic development, and thus as bureaucratic encumbrances whose contribution to, and influence upon, urban policy should be minimized. In short, the city is to be "reinvented" to serve as a space for "locational policies" (*Standortpolitik*) – that is, as an institutional arena for boosterist, business-friendly political strategies intended to attract inward capital investment.[6] Under these conditions, the discourse of "good governance" – defined as an "integrated effort on the part of local government, civil society and the private sector" – can be decoded as an ideological frame through which, in Marco Revelli's apt formulation, to promote the "real subsumption of territory under capital."[7]

Good governance is a mind-numbingly vacuous concept that could easily exemplify the principles of "doublethink" that are grimly satirized in George Orwell's dystopian novel *1984.* The *World Report'*s authors present this "all-embracing" concept in a chapter that left me rubbing my eyes in disbelief, wondering how such a blatantly fanciful model of urban governance could be taken seriously. Following an abstract, completely decontextualized presentation of various ideal-typical normative goals that are claimed to be associated with "sustainable" economic, social, ecological, political and cultural modes of life, the notion of good governance is introduced as a kind of magic wand through which all could supposedly be attained simultaneously.[8] As with so many of the stale ideological terms deployed in contemporary "Third Way" political discourse, the key to good governance is its pure formalism: the contradictory class, political and institutional interests that underpin any effort to govern a city only become evident when generic notions such as "work and wealth," "empowering the citizenry" and "stable ecosystems" are concretized with reference to particular socioeconomic conditions, political alliances, governance arrangements, societal forces and social movements. Once this is accomplished on even the most rudimentary level, it becomes readily obvious that massive trade-offs are involved in all forms of urban policy implementation, that the prioritization of some political goals necessarily entails the marginalization or suppression of others, and that the power to influence such processes is distributed asymmetrically within contemporary cities by criteria such as class, race/ethnicity, gender and national citizenship. And once such basic elements of modern capitalist cities are taken into consideration, the discourse of "good governance" is immediately revealed as an expression of *pure ideology* in Ernst Bloch's classic sense of promoting "the premature harmonization of social contradictions within existing social relations."[9]

Despite its substantive vacuity, however, the notion of good governance deserves closer critical scrutiny due to its ideological function in contemporary political discourse and practice, across diverse places, scales and territories. Indeed, the dissemination of the notion of good governance among both neoliberal and centrist policy makers, politicians and technocrats arguably marks a significant ideological shift on the institutional landscape of contemporary capitalism.

The project of good governance was first promoted by the World Bank in the late 1980s to implement "market-friendly" forms of state intervention in developing and newly industrialized countries. In that context, good governance represented a notable drift of World Bank policy away from the traditional neoliberal approach to structural adjustment that had prevailed during the early 1980s, which privileged orthodox, free-market goals such as minimal state interference, minimal price distortion and the aggressive promotion of export-oriented growth. The World Bank's shift to the discourse of "market-friendly" intervention and good governance by the early 1990s thus signaled the consolidation of a revised global development project based upon an intensified mobilization of state institutions to subsidize private capital investment and to guide market relationships. In this project, states are increasingly seen to play a key role in maintaining the sociopolitical, legal-constitutional and financial conditions for the imposition of market rule: states must thus not be dismantled, but restructured, in order to promote capitalist control, labor discipline and market exchange relations within national territories.[10]

More generally, as Stephen Gill argues, the 1990s was a decade in which a number of unaccountable global institutions – including the World Bank, the International Monetary Fund (IMF), the World Trade Organization (WTO) and the World Economic Forum (WEF) – attempted to "lock in" new forms of market discipline and capitalist power on a global scale, in significant part through the imposition of measures to reconfigure national state power itself. The large-scale, bureaucratized, democratic-constitutional national states that were consolidated during the preceding century of world capitalist development were now increasingly seen as an impediment to economic growth; hence state institutions were to be reorganized at all spatial scales, to promote what Gill has termed the "three Cs" of capitalist power:

> … public policy has been redefined so that governments seek to prove their *credibility,* and the *consistency* of their policies according to the criterion of the *confidence* of investors. In this way, new political and constitutional initiatives in the sphere of money and finance are linked to the imposition of macro-economic and micro-economic discipline in ways that are intended to underpin the power of capital in the state and civil society.[11]

In this context, national states across the world economy were reconfigured in order to promote, extend and intensify market discipline not only within domestic civil societies, but directly *within* the state apparatus itself. Hierarchical state bureaucracies were to be transformed into "flexible," "lean" and increasingly unaccountable agencies for fast policy transfer, business-friendly policy initiatives and public-private collaboration, based upon the ideology of "best practice" and oriented towards the goal of extending commodity relations throughout the social fabric. In short, the radically antistatist, aggressively free-market neoliberalisms that prevailed during the 1980s, which privileged short- and medium-term goals such as trade liberalization, the deregulation of capital markets and the smashing of the postwar class compromise, were tendentially superseded in the 1990s by a potentially more far-reaching form of "disciplinary neoliberalism" that sought "to provide political anchorage for the power of capital *in the long term.*"[12] It was in this context that the discourse and practice of good governance gained global currency, where it came to serve as an ideological frame for legitimating the reconstitution of neoliberal strategies under the rapidly changing geopolitical and geoeconomic conditions of that decade.

It is against this background that we can begin to decipher the internally contradictory political agendas that are articulated in *Urban Future 21*. As the document demonstrates, the project of good governance – with its barely disguised subtexts of extending market discipline and accelerating state retrenchment – is now also being mobilized at the *urban* scale as well. Here, too, it is useful to situate the turn towards good governance in relation to the earlier, relatively antistatist modes of neoliberalization that were promoted during the preceding decade. Throughout the 1980s, the dominant form of urban economic policy in major city-regions involved various kinds of cost-cutting measures – for instance, tax abatements, land grants, cutbacks in public services, the privatization of infrastructural facilities and so forth – through which municipalities attempted to lower the costs of administration, production and reproduction within their jurisdictions, and thereby, to accelerate external capital investment. Enhanced administrative efficiency, coupled with direct and indirect public subsidies to transnational corporations and an increasing privatization of social reproduction, were widely assumed to be the "best practices" for promoting a "good business climate." The contradictions of this zero-sum, cost-cutting form of urban entrepreneurialism and roll-back neoliberalism are now well known. In addition to their polarizing, disruptive consequences for major segments of local, regional and national populations, the relative effectivity of such strategies has been shown to decline quite dramatically as they are diffused throughout the global urban system.[13]

Under these circumstances, especially since the mid-1990s, a significant reconstitution of neoliberal economic strategy began to be pursued in major metropolitan regions around the world. On the one hand, the basic neoliberal imperative of mobilizing economic space as a purified arena for capitalist growth, commodification and market discipline was further entrenched as a taken-for-granted political priority for municipal governments. On the other hand, however, the conditions for promoting economic competitiveness were now reconceptualized by urban political-economic elites to include diverse "extra-economic" criteria, such as those discussed in the *World Report*.[14] The discourse of good governance exemplifies this expanded conceptualization of urban territorial competitiveness, in which all aspects of city space, including its "social capital," innovative capacities, cultural milieu and ecological conditions, are viewed as potential economic assets for attracting further capital investment. In this way, by representing one of the major *causes* of contemporary urban crises – unfettered commodification and market competition – as the basis for their potential *resolution,* the notion of good governance became an increasingly central ideological basis for the further entrenchment, reconstitution and extension of neoliberal political strategy during the course of the 1990s. On both supraurban and urban scales, then, the fetishized discourse of good governance was grafted onto the classical liberal ideology of free markets and open competition in order to justify the long-term institutionalization of neoliberal-productivist policy agendas.

At this juncture, a further question presents itself: why did *cities* become such important arenas for this type of reconstituted, roll-out neoliberal political project? The answer, I believe, lies less in the nature of urban agglomeration economies or urban civil societies as such, than in the changing positions of municipal governments within the restructured and rescaled national states of the post-Keynesian epoch. One of the overarching agendas of the *World Report* is to demand a new approach to subnational political organization and intervention. First, drawing upon the notion of subsidiarity, the *World Report* advocates a radical decentralization of powers and responsibilities from the national to the regional and local levels of the state: it is argued that cities should become increasingly self-reliant, revenue-generating machines, rather than depending upon fiscal subsidies and transfers from higher levels of government. Second, the *World Report* advocates intensified cooperation between the local state and private capital in the formulation, financing and implementation of municipal policies. Whereas the *World Report* concedes that various tasks will continue to be fulfilled by national governments, maximal fiscal and administrative decentralization is said to provide the optimal basis for efficient, effective municipal policy.[15]

We thus arrive at what is, arguably, the core political agenda of the *World Report* – to promote a new form of *national* political regime in which intense competition between municipalities for external capital investment, as well as for tax revenues and intergovernmental fiscal transfers, is permanently institutionalized. The *World Report* proposes the construction of a radically new framework of intergovernmental relations in which municipalities would secure local revenues for local expenditures only by taxing local economic and social activities (whether in the form of business taxes, property taxes, sales taxes and so forth). Such a national political framework would force local governments to compete aggressively against one another to entrap both capital and labor, and particularly those activities that might yield maximal tax revenues, within their territorial jurisdictions. In postunification Germany, neoliberal politicians from some of the wealthiest *Länder* aggressively promoted such a structure under the rubric of so-called "competition federalism" (*Wettbewerbsföderalismus*), which was claimed to provide a more efficient framework for intergovernmental fiscal policy than the existing Fiscal Equalization Mechanism (*Finanzausgleich*), with its elaborate machinery of horizontal fiscal transfers.[16] In the USA, intense intermunicipal competition for corporate and property tax revenues, coupled with nimbyist suburban secessionist movements based upon the principle of "home rule," have long been institutionalized, and were significantly intensified in the wake of Reagan's New Federalism.[17] The *World Report* can thus be viewed as a manifesto in favor of new, intensely polarized national political geographies in which all localities would be forced to rely more directly than ever upon their own socioeconomic assets in order to secure the revenues required to provide basic governmental operations and public services.

Whether this enhanced level of urban political autonomy represents a blessing or a curse is a matter for political debate, but such a discussion is foreclosed by the *World Report*'s confident technocratic dogmatism. This issue points, in turn, towards one of the central contradictions within the *World Report*'s proposed agenda for good governance: on the one hand, values such as local social solidarity and democracy are embraced; at the same time, through its aggressive promotion of endogenous growth potentials and intermunicipal competition, the *World Report* contains a thinly veiled attack on all forms of supralocal solidarity and national redistributive policy, whether those associated with the Keynesian welfare state compromise in Euro-America, or any others that might be proposed. In this sense, the agenda of good governance is premised upon a distinctively geographical inside/outside ontology: cooperation, solidarity and democracy may be permitted within an urban territory; but beyond it, a logic of market anarchy, profit maximization and cut-throat inter-spatial competition is to reign supreme. While the authors of the *World Report* enthusiastically affirm Tiebout-style interlocality competition as a means to allocate resources most efficiently, such competition operates in practice primarily as a redistributive political mechanism through which, in aggregate, municipal governments constrain one another to transfer local resources to transnational capital in the form of investment incentives and other public subsidies.[18] The result is a deeply polarized, fragmented vision of global and national political space, characterized by intensified uneven development and territorial competition among subnational entities such as regional and local governments, both within and beyond national borders.

I am extremely doubtful, therefore, that the discourse of good governance articulated in the *World Report* and elsewhere signals the emergence of a softer, milder or more moderate form of urban economic policy. The issue, rather, is the attempted construction of what Joachim Hirsch has termed a "sustainable neoliberalism" – that is, a form of neoliberal politics that can more effectively manage or displace its internal social contradictions beyond the short-term temporal horizons of early, roll-back forms of neoliberalism. As Hirsch notes, the mainstream social-democratic project of the so-called Third Way is focused above all upon "strengthening the national-competition state for global competition in a somewhat longer time-frame."[19] Within this only superficially "reformist" vision, the neoliberal politics of aggressive productivism, labor discipline and market fetishism remain essentially unchallenged. The main qualitative modification of this putatively "sustainable" form of neoliberalism consists in the effort to superimpose new, politically mediated mechanisms of crisis displacement upon the traditional neoliberal cocktail of market-friendly regulation, enhanced commodification and intensified inter-spatial competition. The discourse of good governance amounts to little more than ideological embellishment for this cynically instrumental strategy of crisis management: it is, at core, a means of perpetuating the neoliberal politics of market discipline while rolling out new politico-institutional buffers for canalizing the crisis tendencies induced through earlier rounds of roll-back neoliberal policy reform, market liberalization and deregulation. Metropolitan regions are increasingly the sites and targets for such policy experiments and institutional mutations, and for the intensifying political-ideological struggles that surround them.

Notes

1   The document was subsequently published in the form of a book by Peter Hall and Ulrich Pfeiffer, *Urban Future 21: A Global Agenda for Twenty-First Century Cities* (London: E & FN Spon/Federal Ministry of Transport, Building and Housing of the Republic of Germany, 2000).

2   Ibid., 1–40. On earlier rounds of debate on international urban policy, see Susan Parnell, "Defining a Global Urban Development Agenda," *World Development* 78 (2016): 529–40; Nikos Katsikis, "Two Approaches to 'World Management': C. A. Doxiadis and R. B. Fuller," in *Implosions/Explosions: Towards a Study of Planetary Urbanization*, ed. Neil Brenner (Berlin: Jovis, 2014), 480–504.

3 See Neil Brenner and Christian Schmid, "The 'Urban Age' in Question," *International Journal of Urban and Regional Research* 38, no. 3 (2014): 731–55.

4 The project was organized by Volker Eick and Renate Berg, working with the Berliner MieterGemeinschaft. Contributors included, among others, Ulrich Brand, Susan Ruddick, John Friedmann, Maria Mies, Roger Keil, Bob Jessop and Neil Smith. The texts are available in German at: http://www.bmgev.de/politik/archiv/urban21.html?sword_list%5B0%5D=urban&sword_list%5B1%5D=21. For further reflections on the *World Report,* and its broader significance in struggles over urban governance, see John Friedmann's subsequent discussion in "Introduction: Urban Futures as Ideology," in his book *The Prospect of Cities* (Minneapolis: University of Minnesota Press, 2002), xi–xxvi.

5 On roll-out neoliberalism, see Chapter 3 in the present volume. The terminology is from Jamie Peck and Adam Tickell, "Neoliberalizing Space," *Antipode* 34, no. 3 (2002): 380–404.

6 For further elaborations on the concept of locational policy in the German context, see Neil Brenner, "Building 'Euro-regions': Locational Politics and the Political Geography of Neoliberalism in Post-Unification Germany," *European Journal of Urban and Regional Studies* 7, no. 4 (2000): 317–43. For a more analytical treatment, see also Neil Brenner, *New State Spaces: Urban Governance and the Rescaling of Statehood* (New York: Oxford University Press, 2004).

7 Hall and Pfeiffer, *Urban Future 21,* 164. See Marco Revelli, *Die gesellschaftliche Linke* (Münster: Westfälisches Dampfboot, 1997), 114.

8 Hall and Pfeiffer, *Urban Future 21,* 165.

9 Leo Panitch, "The New Imperial State," *New Left Review,* 2 (March/April 2000): 7.

10 Ray Kiely, "Neoliberalism Revised? A Critical Account of World Bank Concepts of Good Governance and Market Friendly Intervention," *Capital & Class* 64 (Spring 1998): 63–88.

11 Stephen Gill, "The Constitution of Global Capitalism," paper presented to panel on "The Capitalist World, Past and Present," International Studies Association Annual Convention, Los Angeles, 2000, manuscript, p. 5. See also Stephen Gill, "Globalisation, Market Civilisation and Disciplinary Neoliberalism," *Millenium* 24 (1995): 407; Gill, "New Constitutionalism, Democratisation and Global Political Economy," *Pacifica Review* 10, no. 1 (1998): 23–38; as well as Stephen Gill and A. Claire Cutler, eds., *New Constitutionalism and World Order* (New York: Cambridge University Press, 2014).

12 Gill, "Constitution," 2.

13 For discussion and elaboration, see Chapter 5 in the present volume.

14 Even the more progressive strands within the so-called "new regionalist" discourse on learning economies and untraded interdependencies have certain affinities with the more cynical, neoliberal versions of this argument. For an illuminating polemic on this issue, see John Lovering, "Theory Led by Policy: The Inadequacies of the 'New Regionalism,'" *International Journal of Urban and Regional Research* 23, no. 2 (1999).

15 Hall and Pfeiffer, *Urban Future 21,* 311–30.

16 Brenner, "Building 'Euro-regions.'"

17 For an overview, see, among other works, Neil Brenner, "Is There a Politics of 'Urban' Development? Reflections on the US Case," in *The City in American Political Development,* ed. Richardson Dilworth (New York: Routledge, 2009), 121–40; Neil Brenner, "Decoding the Newest 'Metropolitan Regionalism' in the US: A Critical Overview," *Cities* 19, no. 1 (2002): 3–21.

18 Helga Leitner and Eric Sheppard, "Economic Uncertainty, Inter-Urban Competition and the Efficacy of Entrepreneurialism," in *The Entrepreneurial City: Geographies of Politics,* Regime and Representation, ed. Tim Hall and Phil Hubbard (Chichester: Wiley, 1998), 286–93.

19 Joachim Hirsch, "Tote leben manchmal länger. Auf dem Weg zu einem nachhaltigen Neoliberalismus," in *Das Ende des Neoliberalismus?,* ed. Joachim Bischoff et. al. (Hamburg: VSA, 1998), 218.

7 Open City or the Right to the City?

Around the world, progressive, critically minded architects, landscape architects and urban designers are engaged in place-making projects that propose to create a more "open city" – one that would, in Gerald Frug's succinct formulation, enable "every resident and visitor to feel that he or she belongs [...] regardless not just of wealth, race, religion or sexual orientation, but of any other way of dividing people into categories."[1] While such initiatives are generally steered by state institutions, as well as by property developers and corporate patrons, they have also often emerged in response to local struggles against the forms of privatization, gentrification, displacement, enclosure and sociospatial exclusion that have been unleashed under post-Keynesian, neoliberalizing capitalism. In the context of an ongoing global financial crisis, in which market fundamentalism remains the dominant political ideology of most national and local governments, proposals to counteract the deep social and spatial divisions of early twenty-first-century cities are surely to be welcomed by all those committed to promoting more just, egalitarian, democratic, diverse, cosmopolitan and tolerant forms of urban life.[2]

But how can relatively small-scale design interventions confront the monstrously difficult task of – as Richard Sennett poses the question–"heal[ing] society's divisions of race, class, and ethnicity"?[3] Even the most radical designers are seriously constrained by the politico-institutional contexts in which they work, and today these are generally defined by the naturalized imperatives of growth-first, market-oriented urban economic policy and by approaches to urban governance in which corporate and property-development interests maintain hegemonic control over local land-use regimes. In practice, moreover, the interventions of designers concerned with "opening up" the city via project-based initiatives have often intensified the very forms of spatial injustice which, at least in rhetorical terms, they aspire to contravene. This is because the conditions associated with "urbanism" – the effervescence of dense zones of centrality, interaction, exchange, diversity and spontaneous encounters – also frequently generate major economic payoffs, in the form of privately appropriated profits, for those who own the properties surrounding the project site. While many places have provisionally experimented with instruments of community reinvestment, local land trusts and profit-sharing mechanisms in relation to such newly created arenas of urbanism, the predominant global trend is for growth machine interests – often linked to speculative, predatory investments in global financial markets – to reap the major financial rewards derived from them. Consequently, early twenty-first-century initiatives to construct an "urban commons" through site-based public design interventions all-too-frequently yield the opposite: a city in which the ruling classes reinforce tight control over the production and appropriation of urban space. As socially vibrant and aesthetically attractive as such newly constructed sites of urbanism may often be, they offer no more than a fleeting glimpse of the genuinely democratic, socially egalitarian urbanism that is consistently precluded at a larger, city-wide or metropolitan scale, often by the very politico-institutional forces and coalitions that brought such sites into being at a microspatial scale. The "open city" thus becomes an ideology which masks, or perhaps merely softens, the forms of top-down planning, market-dominated governance, sociospatial exclusion and displacement that are at play both within and beyond these redesigned spaces of putative urban "renaissance."

The case of the High Line in Chelsea, Manhattan, exemplifies this quagmire. A brilliant, far-sighted design intervention, initially spearheaded through a community-based initiative, opens up a long-inaccessible, derelict industrial space for public appropriation, to great popular acclaim. In so doing, it intensifies earlier, more sporadic forms of gentrification through a wave of new investment oriented primarily towards elite consumers in surrounding blocks – luxury hotels and housing; high-end restaurants, cafes and shops – that can only be accessed by the wealthiest residents and tourists. In this way, a design intervention that is putatively oriented towards expanding and activating the urban public sphere accelerates processes of gentrification, displacement, segregation and exclusion at the neighborhood and urban scales.[4] The construction of a supposedly "open" urban space thereby creates new barriers to a genuinely public, democratic, diverse and egalitarian urbanism, not only within the site of intervention, but across the surrounding fabric of buildings, blocks and neighborhoods. In major cities around the world, across otherwise distinct national and local contexts, some version of this narrative could, alas, be elaborated with reference to a long list of prominent project-based design interventions, including many of those in which quite imaginative, skillful and ostensibly progressive design schemes have been implemented.[5]

To what degree, and in what ways, is the practice of design implicated in such retrograde outcomes? At first glance, such problems may appear to result less from the intricacies of the design scheme itself, than from the broader system of rules – for instance, regarding land-use, property ownership, financing, taxation, investment and public goods – that govern the city, region and territory in which the project-based design intervention happens to be situated. Surely the designers cannot be faulted for working as imaginatively as possible within the constraints imposed by such rule-regimes. After all, what other options might they have, since they generally lack control or influence over investment flows, property ownership structures and political decisions? And even if the conditions imposed by the client are less than ideal, isn't it far better to see a good, creative, imaginative design implemented than a bad, derivative, boring one?

From my point of view, the above formulations offer an insufficiently critical perspective on the role of the designers, and the design professions, whose expertise, creative capacities and labor-power are recurrently harnessed to mask, naturalize, manage or soften the sociospatial contradictions of neoliberal urbanism. The position outlined above implies, rather naively, that design is insulated, both as a professional practice and as a form of social engagement, from the broader political-economic contexts in which it is embedded, and which actively fuel and frame its everyday operations. Such assumptions are untenable – empirically, politically and ethically; they involve, as Edward Soja observes, a myopic "scalar warp" in which the *problematique* of reshaping urban life is reduced to a microspatial "examination of the organization and appearances of bunches of buildings divorced from their larger urban and regional context."[6] Designers concerned with social justice – the open city in a genuinely democratic, egalitarian sense – can and must push beyond the formal, spatially reductionist vision of the city as "bunches of buildings set in floating pods," to grapple with, as Soja proposes, "the nesting of regional worlds that extends from the spaces of the individual body and building through multiple levels of human activity and identity to metropolitan, regional, subnational, national and global scales."[7] Only by doing so, I believe, can designers also begin to devise strategies to push back, with their full technical expertise, creative capacities, professional influence and political imagination, against the rules, constraints and ideologies imposed by neoliberal, market-oriented systems of urban governance and the forms of sociospatial injustice they produce at various spatial scales. A genuinely open city would be one in which investment is channeled to serve social need rather than private gain; in which public institutions secure and protect shared, common resources from private appropriation; and in which all inhabitants have secured equal capacities to influence decisions that affect the spaces, institutions and resources shared by all. Any design intervention that claims to promote the open city without pursing these core goals will be seriously incomplete, if not delusionary.

The fatal flaw of the interventions discussed above is thus not the exclusionary, undemocratic "external" context of design, but rather that the *design vision is itself too narrow,* both spatially and operationally. Spatially, there is a danger of circumscribing the site too modestly, and thus of stimulating urbanism only within a bounded "pocket" or "pod" of activity that does not interrupt broader systems of market-based land use, investment and displacement at larger spatial scales, across multiple sites, places and territories. Operationally, there is a danger of programming the design intervention using an epistemology that is fixated upon consumerism, "quality of life" and the provision of urban amenities, rather than opening up spaces for appropriation, self-management and ongoing transformation "from below," through the users themselves.[8] To the degree that design interventions for an open city are restricted to formal, aesthetic elements or fetishize a narrowly consumerist vision of the public realm, their main impact may be to offer ideological cover for the urbanisms of injustice, displacement and exclusion that continue to be rolled forward aggressively in neoliberalizing cities and city-regions around the world.[9]

Writing in 1968, amidst the tumultuous events of May in Paris, French theorist Henri Lefebvre introduced a concept that continues to challenge such mystifications – *the right to the city.*[10] This concept powerfully resonates with contemporary debates among designers on the open city, because it likewise envisions a city that is appropriated by and accessible to all inhabitants. But Lefebvre's concept pushes much further than this. It is not only a call for popular access to what already exists within cities – the radically inclusionary sense of "belonging" outlined by Gerald Frug in the formulation quoted above. More radically still, Lefebvre's notion of the right to the city is also a militant, persistent demand for the democratization of control over the collective means of producing urban space. An open city, in this sense, is not merely a space that can be accessed and enjoyed equally by all, and where all types of people feel they belong equally; it would also be a realm in which *the institutional capacity to produce and transform space* has itself been radically democratized, such that it becomes equally available to all who inhabit urban space – to repeat Frug's precise formulation – "regardless not just of wealth, race, religion or sexual orientation, but of any other way of dividing people into categories."[11]

Lefebvre referred to this capacity as *autogestion* – grassroots self-management – and he insisted that, "far from being established once and for all, [it] is itself the site and the stake of struggle."[12]

The design of the right to the city, therefore, requires us not only to produce spaces of open access, whether within specific project sites or at larger spatial scales. More importantly, the pursuit of this right requires us to find ways of transforming the rules of urban governance so as to open up urban space to democratic redesign, through an ongoing process of grassroots appropriation and reappropriation. By integrating questions of institutional form, regulatory process, democratic empowerment, collective use and sociospatial transformation into their vision of the site, the intervention and the program, designers can play a strategically and politically essential role in the ongoing struggle for the right to the city.

Notes

1 Gerald Frug, "Legalizing Openness," in *Open City: Designing Coexistence,* ed. Tim Rieniets, Jennifer Sigler and Kees Christiaanse (Zurich and Rotterdam: Sun Publishers and International Architecture Biennial Rotterdam, 2009), 167.

2 See Susan Fainstein, *The Just City* (Ithaca, NY: Cornell University Press, 2009); Edward W. Soja, *Seeking Spatial Justice* (Minneapolis: University of Minnesota Press, 2010).

3 Richard Sennett, "The Open City," accessed November 10, 2013, http://www.richardsennett.com/site/SENN/UploadedResources/The%20Open%20City.pdf.

4 Kevin Loughran, "Parks for Profit: The High Line, Growth Machines and the Uneven Development of Public Spaces," *City & Community* 13, no. 1 (2014): 49–68; Alexander J. Reichl, "The High Line and the Ideal of Democratic Public Space," *Urban Geography* (2016). DOI: 10.1080/02723638.2016.1152843.

5 For more general discussion of such tendencies, see Michael Sorkin, "The Ends of Design," in *Urban Design,* ed. Alex Krieger (Minneapolis: University of Minnesota Press, 2009), 155–82; and Fainstein, *The Just City.*

6 Edward W. Soja, "Designing the Postmetropolis," in *Urban Design,* 258.

7 Soja, "Designing the Postmetropolis," 258, 259.

8 For a productive engagement with "counterprojects" produced by the "users" of space, see the contributions to Kenny Cupers ed., *Use Matters: An Alternative History of Architecture* (New York: Routledge, 2013).

9 On which, see Chapters 3 and 10 in the present volume, as well as Jamie Peck, "Austerity Urbanism," *CITY* 16, no. 6 (2012): 626–55.

10 Henri Lefebvre, "The Right to the City," in *Writings on Cities,* ed. and trans. Eleonore Kofman and Elizabeth Lebas (Cambridge, MA: Blackwell, 1996). See also David Harvey, "The Right to the City," *New Left Review,* 53 (September/October 2008): 23–40; and Neil Brenner, Peter Marcuse and Margit Mayer, eds., *Cities for People, Not for Profit: Critical Urban Theory and the Right to the City* (New York: Routledge, 2011).

11 Frug, "Legalizing Openness," 167.
12 Henri Lefebvre, "Comments on a New State Form," in *State, Space, World: Selected Writings,* ed. Neil Brenner and Stuart Elden, trans. Gerald Moore, Neil Brenner, and Stuart Elden (Minneapolis: University of Minnesota Press, 2009), 134.

8 Is Tactical Urbanism an Alternative to Neoliberal Urbanism?

What can "tactical urbanism" offer cities under extreme stress from rapid population growth, intensifying industrial restructuring, inadequate social and physical infrastructures, rising levels of class polarization, insufficiently resourced public institutions, proliferating environmental disasters, and growing popular alienation, dispossession and social unrest? An exhibition on *Uneven Growth* at the Museum of Modern Art (MoMA) aims to explore this question through speculative interventions by teams of architects whose remit was to make design proposals for six of the world's "megacities" – Hong Kong, Istanbul, Lagos, Mumbai, New York, and Rio.[1] The exhibition has provoked considerable debate about our contemporary planetary urban condition and, more specifically, about the capacities of architects, urban designers and planners to influence the latter in progressive, productive ways.

Such a debate is timely, not least because inherited paradigms of urban intervention – from the modernist-statist programs of the postwar epoch to the neoliber-

Figure 8.1: Installation view of *Uneven Growth: Tactical Urbanisms for Expanding Megacities,* November 22, 2014–May 10, 2015

Figure 8.2: Installation view of *Uneven Growth: Tactical Urbanisms for Expanding Megacities,*
November 22, 2014–May 10, 2015

alizing, market-fundamentalist agendas of the post-1980s period – no longer appear
viable. Meanwhile, as David Harvey notes in his comment on the MoMA exhibition, "the crisis of planetary urbanization" is intensifying. Megacities, and the
broader territorial economies on which they depend, appear to be poorly equipped,
in both operational and political terms, to resolve the monstrous governance problems and social conflicts that confront them. Under these conditions, Harvey grimly
declares: "We are […] in the midst of a huge crisis – ecological, social, and political – of planetary urbanization without, it seems, knowing or even marking it."[2]

   Against this foreboding background, can "tactical urbanisms" provide tractable
solutions, or at least open up some productive perspectives for actualizing alternative urban futures? It would be unrealistic to expect any single approach to urban
intervention to resolve the "wicked problems" that confront contemporary urbanizing territories, especially in an era in which inherited templates for shaping urban
conditions are so widely being called into question.[3] And yet, despite the cautiously
exploratory tone of its curators' framing texts in the exhibition catalogue, the
MoMA project on *Uneven Growth* articulates a strong set of claims regarding the
potentials of tactical urbanism.[4] Indeed, the very decision to dedicate the public

platforms of MoMA's Department of Architecture and Design to a set of proposals framed around "tactical urbanism" suggests an affirmation of the concept. In the various documents and texts associated with the exhibition, the notion of tactical urbanism is presented as a robust interpretive frame for understanding a variety of emergent urban design experiments in contemporary megacities. MoMA curator Pedro Gadanho explains his choice of the concept as a basis for stimulating debate and practical experimentation regarding possible future pathways of urban design intervention, and above all, as a means to promote "social justice in the conception and appropriation of urban space."[5] As the search for new approaches to organizing our collective planetary urban future gains increasing urgency, these broadly affirmative discourses around tactical urbanism demand critical scrutiny.[6]

Urban crises, tactical responses

In the exhibition catalogue, Gadanho and several other internationally influential curators and urban thinkers (including Barry Bergdoll, Ricky Burdett, Teddy Cruz, Saskia Sassen and Nader Tehrani) frame the understanding of tactical urbanism that grounds the exhibition. They offer a variety of contextual reflections and interpretative formulations to explicate its essential elements. Amidst disparate orientations and concerns, several points of convergence emerge:

– Tactical urbanism arises in the context of a broader governance crisis in contemporary cities in which both states and markets have failed systematically to deliver basic public goods (such as housing, transportation and public space) to rapidly expanding urban populations.
– Tactical urbanism is not a unified movement or technique, but a general rubric through which to capture a broad range of emergent, provisional, experimental and ad hoc urban projects.
– Tactical urbanism is mobilized "from below," through organizationally, culturally and ideologically diverse interventions to confront emergent urban issues. Professional designers, as well as governments, developers and corporations, may participate in and actively stimulate tactical urbanism. But its generative sources lie outside the control of any clique of experts or any specific institution, social class or political coalition.

- Tactical urbanism proposes immediate, "acupunctural" modes of intervention in relation to local issues that are viewed as extremely urgent by its proponents. Its time-horizon is thus relatively short, even "impulsive" and "spontaneous." Its spatial scale likewise tends to be relatively circumscribed – for instance, to the park, the building, the street or the neighborhood.
- Specific projects of tactical urbanism are said to evolve fluidly in relation to broader shifts in political-economic conditions, institutional arrangements or coalitional dynamics. These qualities of malleability and open-endedness are widely praised in discussions of tactical urbanism, generally in contrast to the comprehensive plans, formal-legal codes and rigid blueprints that were characteristic of modernist-statist projects of urban intervention.
- Tactical urbanism generally promotes a grassroots, participatory, hands-on, "do-it-yourself" vision of urban restructuring in which those who are most directly affected by an issue actively mobilize to address it, and may continually mobilize to influence the evolution of methods and goals. For this reason, tactical urbanism is often presented as an "open-source" model of action and as a form of "reappropriation" of urban space by its users.

Most of the commentators involved in *Uneven Growth* present tactical urbanist projects as an alternative to both modernist-statist and neoliberal paradigms of urban intervention – for instance, because they are grounded upon participatory democracy; because they aim to promote social cohesion; and because they are not formally preprogrammed in advance or "from above." However, it is the opposition of tactical urbanism to modernist, comprehensive forms of urban planning that is most cogently demarcated in the wide-ranging narratives associated with the exhibition. Modernist-statist modes of urban intervention, it is argued, have receded due to the ideological ascendancy of neoliberalism and the associated "disassembling of nation-states" (Saskia Sassen) since the 1980s.[7] To the degree that some elements and offshoots of that tradition are still being mobilized in the megacities of the developing world via holistic, comprehensive planning and "top-down action," they are often "entangled in inefficient politics, corrupt bureaucracy, and economic insufficiency" (Pedro Gadanho).[8] Tactical urbanism is thus presented as a potential palliative for urban problems that state institutions and formal urban planning procedures, in particular, have failed to address adequately.

Subverting neoliberal urbanism?

However, despite the confident affirmations of many of the contributors to *Uneven Growth*, it is considerably less obvious as to how the projects associated with tactical urbanism could effectively counteract neoliberal urbanism. Indeed, especially in light of the stridently anti-planning rhetoric that pervades many tactical urban interventions and their tendency to privilege informal, incremental and ad hoc mobilizations over larger-scale, longer term, publicly financed reform programs, it seems reasonable to ask in what ways they do, in actuality, engender any serious friction against the neoliberal order, much less subvert it.[9] In some cases, tactical urbanisms appear more likely to *bolster* neoliberal urbanisms by temporarily alleviating, or perhaps merely displacing, some of their disruptive social and spatial effects, but without interrupting the basic rule-regimes associated with market-oriented, growth-first urban development, and without challenging the foundational mistrust of governmental institutions that underpins the neoliberal project.

The relation between tactical and neoliberal forms of urbanism is thus considerably more complex, contentious and confusing than is generally acknowledged in the contributions to the debate in *Uneven Growth,* and in other contemporary affirmations of tactical approaches. It cannot be simply assumed that, because of their operational logics or normative-political orientations, tactical interventions will in fact counteract neoliberal urbanism. On the contrary, as the list of scenarios below illustrates, no less than five specific types of relation between these projects can be readily imagined, only two of which (scenarios 4 and 5 in the list) *might* involve some kind of challenge to market-fundamentalist urban policy. There are at least three highly plausible scenarios in which tactical urbanism will have either negligible or actively beneficial impacts upon a neoliberalized urban rule-regime:

- *Scenario 1: reinforcement.* Tactical urbanism alleviates some of the governance failures and disruptive sociospatial consequences of neoliberal urbanism, but without threatening its grip on the regulatory framework governing urban development.
- *Scenario 2: entrenchment.* Tactical urbanism internalizes a neoliberal agenda (for instance, related to a diminished role for public institutions and/or an extension of market forces) and thus contributes to the further entrenchment, consolidation and extension of neoliberal urbanism.

- *Scenario 3: neutrality.* Tactical urbanism emerges in interstitial spaces that are neither functional to, nor disruptive of, the neoliberal project. It thus coexists with neoliberal urbanism in a relationship that is neither symbiotic, parasitic nor destructive.
- *Scenario 4: contingency.* Tactical urbanism opens up a space of regulatory experimentation that, under certain conditions, contributes to the subversion of neoliberal programs. But, in other contexts, with many of the same conditions present, this does not occur. The impacts of tactical urbanism on neoliberal urbanism are thus contingent; they hinge upon factors extrinsic to it.
- *Scenario 5: subversion.* Tactical urbanism interrupts the basic logics of growth-first, market-oriented urban governance and points towards alternative urban futures based on deepening forms of inclusion, social equity, grassroots democracy and spatial justice.

Tactical urbanism may be *narrated* as a self-evident alternative to neoliberal urbanism, but we must ask: is this really the case, and if so, how, where, under what conditions, via what methods, with what consequences, and for whom? Clarification of these (undeniably tricky) issues is essential to any serious consideration of the potentials and limits of tactical urbanism under contemporary conditions.

Vicissitudes and variegations of neoliberal urbanism

Neoliberal urbanism, it should be emphasized, is not a unified, homogenous formation of urban governance, but represents a broad *syndrome* of market-disciplinary institutions, policies and regulatory strategies.[10] While certainly connected to the ideology of free-market capitalism, this syndrome has assumed deeply variegated political, organizational and spatial forms in different places and territories around the world, and its politico-institutional expressions have evolved considerably since the global economic crises and accompanying geopolitical shocks of the 1970s. Across all the contextual diversity and evolutionary mutation, however, the common denominator of neoliberal urbanisms is the market-fundamentalist project of activating local public institutions and empowering private actors to extend commodification across the urban social fabric, to coordinate a city's collective life through market relations, and to promote the enclosure of noncommodified, self-managed urban spaces.

As Teddy Cruz succinctly notes, all this has promoted the "shift from urbanizations benefitting the many into models of urban profit for the few."[11] Whereas the idea of "urbanizations benefitting the many" broadly corresponds to the now-discredited megaprojects and programming techniques of statist-modernism, the promotion of "urban profit for the few" has been the predominant tendency since the 1980s, at once in the older capitalist world, the former state socialist world and across most of the postcolonial and developing world. Despite plenty of inter-territorial variegation, societal resistance, political contestation and reregulatory pushback, this tendency has persisted, and even intensified, through the many waves of industrial restructuring and financial crisis that have ricocheted across every zone of the world economy since that period, including since the most recent "Great Recession" of the last half-decade. The patterns of "uneven growth" that are under scrutiny in the MoMA exhibition must be understood as its direct expressions and outgrowths. Nader Tehrani productively underscores this fundamental point in his contribution to the exhibition catalogue, asking whether conditions in contemporary megacities result less from earlier design mishaps, explosive population growth or brute physical expansion, than from "the lack of policies that are the preconditions for social welfare: access to education, health, and shelter."[12]

It is, then, neither the contemporary urban condition as such, nor the inefficiencies of postwar, modernist-statist urban planning, that have most directly triggered the situations and problems to which contemporary forms of tactical urbanism are responding. Rather, contemporary tactical urbanisms are emerging in contexts that have been powerfully ruptured and reshaped by historically and geographically specific forms of neoliberal urbanization, based on the class project of restricting "the right to the city" (Henri Lefebvre) to the wealthy, the elite and the powerful, and reorienting major public investments and policy regimes in ways that prioritize that project above all others.[13] Despite its pervasive governance failures, its powerfully destructive socioenvironmental consequences and its increasingly evident ideological vulnerabilities, neoliberalism continues to represent the taken-for-granted "common sense" on which basis urban development practice around the world is still being forged. The question of how designers might contribute to alternative urban futures must thus be framed most directly – and, from my perspective, a lot more combatively – in relation to the apparent resilience and elasticity of neoliberal forms of urban governance.

One important consequence of these observations is the proposition that the architectural and design disciplines could significantly enhance their capacity to make durable, progressive urban interventions by engaging more systematically with questions of *institutional* (re)design – that is, with the systems of collectively binding rules that govern the production, use, occupation and appropriation of space.[14] The latter are arguably even more essential to the ambitious visions for future megacities proposed in *Uneven Growth* than the tactical, acupunctural projects of infrastructural and physical reorganization with which the bulk of the exhibition is concerned. Indeed, in the absence of an aggressively reasserted role for governmental institutions – publicly funded through an equitable and fair tax regime; democratically legitimated and publicly accountable; legally regulated and transparently monitored; and oriented towards the public interest – it is difficult to imagine how the tactical urbanist proposals put forward in *Uneven Growth* could ever attain the larger-scale, longer-term impacts with which the exhibition's contributors are concerned.

Herein lies a potentially serious contradiction. The anti-statist, anti-planning rhetoric of many tactical urbanist interventions may, in practice, significantly erode their capacity to confront the challenges of upscaling their impacts. To the degree that advocates of tactical urbanism frame their agenda as an alternative to an activist role for public institutions in the production of urban space, they are at risk of reinforcing the very neoliberal rule-regimes they ostensibly oppose. This is in no way to suggest that tactical urbanist projects should ignore the serious deficits of state action in contemporary megacities. On the contrary, the critique of how market-oriented state policies (including privatization, deregulation and liberalization) erode public institutions in favor of privatized forms of urban appropriation is essential to any counter-neoliberal, reregulatory project. But just as important, in this context, is the collective demand for more extensive public support for key dimensions of social reproduction – the basic infrastructures associated with housing, transportation, education, public space, health care, recreation, cultural expression and so forth.[15] The point here, then, is simply that there are deep tensions between the project of finding viable alternatives to neoliberal urbanism and any tradition of urban intervention, tactical or otherwise, that seeks to distance itself from state institutions, capacities and responsibilities.

In his contribution to the *Uneven Growth* catalogue, Teddy Cruz offers a hard-hitting, precise formulation of the major challenges associated with this state of affairs, especially among architects and designers:

Without altering the exclusionary policies that have decimated a civic imagination in the first place, architecture will remain a decorative tool to camouflage the neoconservative politics and economics of urban development that have eroded the primacy of public infrastructure worldwide [...] the major problems of urbanization today [...] are grounded in the inability of institutions of urban development to more meaningfully engage urban informality, socioeconomic inequity, environmental degradation, lack of affordable housing, inclusive public infrastructure, and civil participation.[16]

This is precisely the dilemma: how can tactical urbanisms do more than serve as "camouflage" for the vicissitudes, dislocations and crisis tendencies of neoliberal urbanism? Cruz's formulation underscores one of the key conditions under which it might begin to do so: through the reimagination of design, not simply as a "decorative tool" or formal set of techniques-for-hire by the ruling classes, but as a basis for asking critical questions about contemporary urbanism, and as a set of collectively shared, creative capacities through which to "coproduce the city as well as new models of cohabitation and coexistence to advance agendas of socioeconomic inclusion."[17] These goals cannot be realized simply through the redesign and reappropriation of specific physical sites within the city; they also require the creation of "a new role for progressive policy, [and] a more efficient, transparent, inclusive and collaborative form of government."[18] In other words, the pursuit of alternative urbanisms requires the creation not only of new urban spaces, but of new state spaces as well.

Detour, retreat, regression …

These considerations yield a critical perspective from which to examine some of the design proposals for contemporary megacities that are on display in MoMA's *Uneven Growth*. MoMA curator Gadanho's remit to the six design teams was not only to propose a tactical intervention for a specific megacity – "acupunctural outlooks on how change for the better could be induced in diverse urban contexts" – but, in so doing, to offer a new perspective on what a socially engaged architecture might look like, today and in the future. We must thus consider the exhibition materials at once as possible scenarios for a future urbanism, and as visions of how the design disciplines might use tactical approaches to contribute to their realization. Gadanho emphasizes that the exhibition's goal is not to offer immediate solutions to current urban problems, but to put forward broader, speculative visions that might "fuel the public debate on those issues." At the same time, he quite appropriately emphasizes the need for scalability, that is, the prospect of a translocal application of progressive, tactical ideas – "solutions that could be replicated in different contexts." Even if they harness the speculative capacities of design, then, the proposals on display in the exhibition are clearly not meant to be pure fictions – they are presented as critical tools "to reflect upon the problems of today." [19]

My own impression is that only some of the design proposals featured in the exhibition respond effectively to this remit. While the exhibition's theorists broadly agree on the contours of a tactical urbanism, there is evidently considerable confusion, or perhaps simply divergence, regarding the meaning and implications of this notion among the designers themselves. Although all of the design scenarios are presented under the shared rubric of tactical urbanism, some bear little resemblance to an acupunctural, participatory, open-sourced intervention. Indeed, several of the design proposals presented in *Uneven Growth* involve large-scale megaprojects and landscape transformations that could probably only be implemented through a powerful, well-resourced state apparatus; they are difficult to envision as more than partial outgrowths of tactical methods. Meanwhile, other design proposals are consistently framed within tactical parameters, but yield a vision of the urban future that is entirely compatible with neoliberal priorities. Such interventions may respond effectively to the speculative questions about the future of megacities that were posed to the design teams, but they bypass the intricacies of exploring real alternatives to the currently dominant system of market rule.

A number of the proposals circumvent questions of implementation entirely. Building upon local research endeavors and associated visualizations, they put forward relatively decontextualized design "solutions" to the pressing problems of megacity development – for instance, regarding water scarcity, insufficient land for housing, transportation bottlenecks or issues of energy supply. Indeed, several of the proposals may be more readily classified within the rather familiar genre of dystopian design fantasies and technological prophecies in relation to which curator Gadanho proposes to distinguish the more socially oriented, ethically motivated MoMA project. Because they bracket the formidable constraints associated with implementation under a neoliberalized rule-regime, these design scenarios remain at a purely hypothetical level – visions of an alternative universe that are utopian in the literal sense of that word; they are located nowhere. They put the capacities of design thinking on display, often with striking visual flourishes, but with considerably less traction than if the conditions for their potential actualization were more seriously interrogated. Such proposals may well have other merits – for instance, as creative engagements with specific megacity environments and as contributions to global architectural culture. However, viewers who seek in *Uneven Growth* some intellectual and practical resources for elaborating alternatives to neoliberal urbanism are unlikely to find these offerings particularly salient to their concerns.

Strategic openings?

Among the contributions to *Uneven Growth* that most directly attempt to mobilize tactical interventions as part of a broader assault on neoliberal urbanism, the scenarios elaborated by the Mumbai design team (URBZ/Ensamble-POP lab), the Istanbul design team (Atelier d'Architecture Autogérée/Superpool) and one of the New York City teams (Cohabitation Strategies – CohStra) are particularly generative. Notably, each does so through an engagement with the housing question, which has been a fundamental terrain of design intervention and political struggle throughout the history of capitalist urbanization, and which certainly remains so in the age of the "planet of slums." In confronting this well-trodden terrain, the teams illustrate how an expanded vision of design – as a set of combined capacities for spatial intervention, social empowerment and political critique – can contribute to the ongoing struggle for alternative urbanisms.

The Mumbai proposals by URBZ/Ensamble-POP lab mobilize tactical interventions to protect so-called "slum" neighborhoods such as Dharavi and Shivaji Nagar from the massive land development pressures associated with Mumbai's extensively neoliberalized, financialized economy. This is a multifaceted proposal, perhaps reflecting the different positionalities of the project teams in relation to the slum itself (URBZ is a group of activist designers with strong roots in Mumbai's poor neighborhoods, whereas the POP lab is based at MIT). At core, the project presents a series of incremental design strategies to promote an alternative vision of the "slum" as a space of productivity, creativity and ingenuity – a *"tabula pronta,"* in the team's formulation, rather than a *tabula rasa* that can be readily razed to make room for new zones of single-function mass housing. Instead of imposing a new prototype from outside, the designers propose to enhance spatial practices that already animate those neighborhoods – specifically, the integration of residential spaces with work spaces or "tool houses." By supplying a model of up-building that enables residents to construct new platforms for work and everyday life above their homes, and by creating a network of "supraextructures" on a plane stretched like a "magic carpet" above the rooflines, new possibilities for endogenous local economic development and social interaction are envisioned. The developmental potentials thus unleashed would, the designers propose, serve as strong counterpoints to dominant ideologies of the slum as a space of backwardness and pathology, while also stimulating the elaboration of a less polarized growth pattern across the metropolitan fabric.

Figure 8.3: Ensamble Studio/MIT POPlab and URBZ; Mumbai, Reclaiming Growth, 2014

Thorny questions remain, of course, regarding the degree to which the proposed tactical interventions could, in themselves, protect the most strategically located neighborhoods from land development pressures, especially in the absence of a broader political movement that questions the model of market-driven urban growth to which Mumbai's growth coalition committed itself following the liberalization of the Indian economy in the 1990s. Through what institutional mechanisms and political coalitions could tenure security be attained by slum dwellers living in zones of the city that are considered attractive by growth machine interests? As radical geographer Neil Smith pointed out some time ago, when local government institutions align with development interests to exploit such a "rent gap" in the urban land market, organized resistance is likely to be met with considerable vilification, if not outright repression.[20] There is no doubt, however, that design has a fundamental role to play in defending vulnerable populations and neighborhoods against further disempowerment, dispossession and spatial displacement. The proposal for Mumbai by URBZ/Ensamble-POP lab very productively puts this issue on the exhibition's agenda. It will hopefully inspire other designers to take up this project in other megacities, in collaboration with local inhabitants, local social movements and nongovernmental organizations that share their concerns.[21]

While the design proposals presented by the Istanbul and New York teams contain important architectural/morphological elements (pertaining, for instance, to buildings, infrastructures and neighborhood districts), their creative radicalism is strongly rooted in models for new institutional arrangements that would empower each city's low- or middle-income inhabitants to occupy, appropriate and regenerate spaces that are currently abandoned, degraded or being subjected to new forms of vulnerability. In the New York context, the CohStra team focuses on a variety of interstitial or underutilized spaces in the city core – from vacant lots and abandoned buildings to various kinds of lower-density housing provision – in order to propose an alternative framework for land ownership (community land trusts), housing provision (mutual housing associations), building management (cooperative housing trusts) and household financing (community credit unions). In the case of Istanbul, the Atelier d'Architecture Autogérée's design proposal targets the mass housing complexes that were constructed for the burgeoning middle classes during the post-1990s period by Turkey's Housing Development Agency, known as TOKI, which are predominantly located in more peripheral districts within Istanbul's rapidly urbanizing metropolitan territory. Here, the designers propose to retrofit

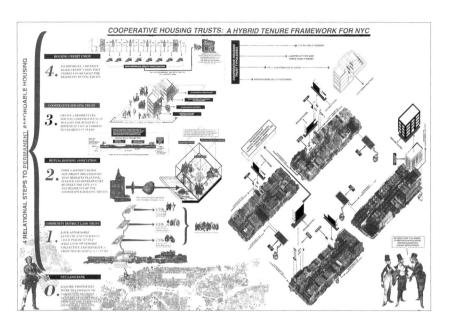

Figure 8.4: CohStra; The Other New York, 2014

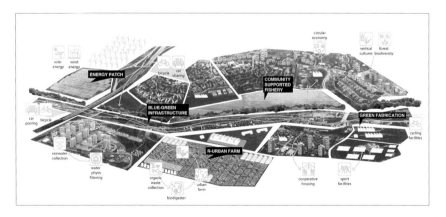

Figure 8.5: Atelier d'Architecture Autogéréé Istanbul, Tactics for Resilient Post-urban Development, 2014

existing TOKI housing ensembles and their immediate landscapes in ways that facilitate new forms of communal self-management by the inhabitants – including, as with CohStra's proposal for New York, community land trusts and local credit unions, along with other forms of collectively managed infrastructure such as community farming and gardens, fisheries, workshops, green energy sources and repair facilities.

As with the Mumbai team's proposal, each of these tactical interventions is framed as a response to a specific, immediate set of threats to urban life that have been imposed by the neoliberal growth model in the city under consideration – the "crisis of affordability" for working New Yorkers; and the destabilization of the model of middle-class consumerism that had been promoted in Istanbul through TOKI mass housing. Notably, however, CohStra and the Atelier d'Architecture Autogérée move beyond a defensive posture in relation to such issues, offering instead a vision of how the spaces that are being degraded under neoliberalized urbanism could become the anchors for an alternative vision of the city as a space of common life and collective self-management. In both projects, the site of design intervention is viewed as a *commons*, a space of continuous, collective appropriation and transformation by its users. Both teams offer a vision of this commons as a *process* to which designers can contribute in fundamental ways, not only by elaborating spatial proposals for the reorganization of housing functions or other dimensions of social reproduction, but by reimagining how such basic institutions as private property, profit-oriented real estate investment, urban land markets, and municipal bureaucracy might be transformed and even superseded to serve social needs, to empower urban inhabitants and to contribute to the creation of a genuine urban public sphere.

Although the Istanbul and New York projects are presented in tactical terms, they are clearly intended as more than fleeting, acupunctural interventions. Part of their appeal, from my point of view, is precisely that they offer a model of tactical urbanism that may be aggressively upscaled and converted into a city-wide or metropolitan counterforce to the neoliberal model. Initially offering a kind of protected enclave for a vulnerable population, each project is then meant to be transformed into a generalizable alternative to the specific forms of housing commodification and accumulation by dispossession that have underpinned and exacerbated "uneven growth" in their respective megacities. To my mind, it is this reflexive attempt to connect the methods of tactical urbanism to a double-edged redesign of urban spaces *and* institutions that makes these teams' proposals effective as tools for envisioning alternatives to the neoliberal city. In thus proceeding, however, the proposals by the Atelier d'Architecture Autogérée and CohStra rather quickly move beyond the realm of tactical urbanism: rather than being a focal point for investigation as such, the latter becomes a kind of launching pad for envisioning and enacting a "politics of space" (Henri Lefebvre) – that is, a political strategy of large-scale sociospatial transformation.

Here, too, of course, the inevitable questions of implementation loom on the immediate horizon. How can this vision of the commons (and of commoning practices) be realized when the dominant class interests and political alliances in each megacity continue to promote a profit-oriented, speculation-driven growth model? Where are the social forces and political coalitions that could counteract that model, and would they really opt for the level of collective coordination and communal sharing proposed by these design teams? How can local alternative economies be protected from incursions by profit-oriented producers, who may (for instance, through economies of scale, or more rationalized forms of labor exploitation) be able to offer more affordable or desirable products to cash-strapped consumers? Designers cannot answer these questions, at least, not among themselves; they can only be decided through political deliberation, public debate and ongoing struggle, at both local and supralocal scales. But, because CohStra and the Atelier d'Architecture Autogérée took the fundamental step of integrating such political-institutional considerations and multiscalar horizons into their spatial proposals, they productively contribute to that process. Just as importantly, given the remit of the MoMA curatorial team, their proposals also articulate a more socially engaged, politically combative vision of what the design disciplines have to offer the urban public sphere in an era of deepening inequality and alarmingly polarized visions of our global urban future.

Back to planning?

Given the difficulties that some of the design teams appear to have had with the tactical urbanism framework, one cannot help but wonder whether it offered them too narrow a terrain, or too limited a toolkit, for confronting the vast, variegated challenges that are currently emerging in the world's megacities. In his "Preface" to the exhibition catalogue, MoMA curator Barry Bergdoll anticipates this conundrum, noting the gap between the "modest scale of some [tactical] interventions" and the "dimensions of the worldwide urban and economic crisis that so urgently needs to be addressed."[22] In the face of these challenges, one can hardly reproach the teams that opted to venture forth with big, ambitious proposals rather than restricting themselves to mere "tactics."

But here arises a further contradiction of the *Uneven Growth* project. A pure form of tactical urbanism would have to be systematically *anti*-programmatic; it could only maintain a consistently tactical approach by resisting and rejecting any movement towards institutionalization.[23] Yet, to the degree that the tactical design experiments on display in *Uneven Growth* articulate a broader vision of urbanism and urban transformation, they necessarily hinge upon the (eventual) articulation of a comprehensive vision of the whole. The generalization of tactical urbanism will thus entail its self-dissolution or, more precisely, its transformation into a project that requires longer-term coordination; stabilized, enforceable, collectively binding rules; and some kind of personnel assigned to the tasks of territorial management – in other words, *planning*. We thus return to the supposedly discredited, outmoded terrain of statist-modernism, the realm of big ambitions, large-scale blueprints, elaborate bureaucratic procedures and comprehensive plans, in opposition to which the precepts of tactical urbanism are recurrently framed. Even if one prefers tactical methods over those of top-down bureaucracies (or, for that matter, those of profit-hungry developers and transnational corporations), it would seem that a serious discussion of large-scale territorial plans, institutional (re)organization, legal codes and political strategies of implementation is unavoidable, at least if the goal is realistically to envision a future for megacities that is more socially and spatially just, democratic, livable and environmentally sane than our present global urban condition.

For anyone sympathetic to tactical urbanism *and* the project of large-scale, progressive urban transformation, this contradiction is probably unavoidable. Can it be made productive, and even affirmed? Perhaps the radical potential of tactical urbanism lies less in its role as an all-purpose method for designing urban futures than as a radically democratic counterweight to any and all institutional systems, whether state-driven, market-dominated or otherwise. Some of the most valuable contributions in MoMA's *Uneven Growth* serve precisely this purpose: they point towards the possibility that, rather than being instrumentalized for social engineering, political control, private enjoyment or corporate profit-making, the capacities of design might be remobilized as tools of empowerment for the users of space, enabling them to occupy and appropriate the urban, continually to transform it, and thus to produce a different city than anyone could have programmed in advance.

But even in this maximally optimistic framing of tactical urbanism, the big questions regarding how to (re)design the city of the future – its economy, its rules of property development and labor relations, its spaces of circulation, social reproduction and everyday life, its modes of governance, its articulations to worldwide capital flows, its interfaces with environmental/biophysical processes, and so forth – remain completely unresolved. As MoMA's Department of Architecture and Design continues its productive engagement with urbanism, let us hope that such questions will stay on the agenda, and that the creative capacities of designers can be harnessed to confront them with all the critical force, political imagination and systematic vision they require.

Notes

1   The exhibition was held at the MoMA, New York City, from November 22, 2014, until May 25, 2015. It is documented in Pedro Gadanho, ed., *Uneven Growth: Tactical Urbanisms for Expanding Megacities* (New York: The Museum of Modern Art, 2014). For a review, see Mimi Zeiger, "Bottom-up, in-between and beyond: On the Initial Process of Uneven Growth," *post: Notes on Modern & Contemporary Art around the Globe,* February 4, 2014, http://post.at.moma.org/content_items/390-bottom-up-in-between-and-beyond-on-the-initial-process-of-uneven-growth. I am grateful to the exhibition's curator, Pedro Gadanho, for inviting me to contribute a version of this essay to the MoMA's online magazine, *post,* and for his exemplary intellectual integrity in agreeing to publish it there despite its critical assessment of the project.

2   David Harvey, "The Crisis of Planetary Urbanization," in Gadanho, *Uneven Growth,* 29.

3   On "wicked problems" in urban planning, see Horst Rittel and Melvin Webber, "Dilemmas in a General Theory of Planning," *Policy Sciences* 4 (1973): 155–69.

4   See Barry Bergdoll, "Preface," and Pedro Gadanho, "Mirroring Uneven Growth: A Speculation on Tomorrow's Cities Today," in Gadanho, *Uneven Growth,* 11–25.

5   Gadanho, "Mirroring Uneven Growth," 23.

6   While this chapter focuses primarily on the agendas and visions presented in the MoMA exhibit, the notion of tactical urbanism has attracted broader interest, engagement and debate across the design disciplines and beyond. For overviews and affirmations from some of its proponents, see Mike Lydon and Anthony Garcia, *Tactical Urbanism: Short-Term Action for Long-Term Change* (Washington, DC: Island Press, 2015); Jaime Lerner, *Urban Acupuncture* (Washington, DC: Island Press, 2014); and Karen Franck and Quentin Stevens, eds., *Loose Space: Possibility and Diversity in Urban Life* (New York: Routledge, 2007).

7   Saskia Sassen, "Complex and Incomplete: Spaces for Tactical Urbanism," in Gadanho, *Uneven Growth,* 41.

8   Gadanho, "Mirroring Uneven Growth," 18.

9   The key text on neoliberal forms of urban governance remains David Harvey's classic essay, "From Managerialism to Entrepreneurialism: The Tranformation of Urban Governance in Late Capitalism," *Geografiska Annaler: Series B Human Geography* 71, no. 1, (1989): 3–17. See also Chapters 3 and 10 in the present volume.

10   See Chapter 10 in the present volume, as well as Neil Brenner, Jamie Peck and Nik Theodore, *The Afterlives of Neoliberalism.* Civic City Cahiers (CCC) (London: Bedford Press/Architectural Association, 2012); Neil Brenner, Jamie Peck and Nik Theodore, "Variegated Neoliberalization: Geographies, Modalities, Pathways," *Global Networks* 10, no. 2 (2010): 182–222; and Jamie Peck, Nik Theodore and Neil Brenner, "Neoliberalism Resurgent? Market Rule after the Great Recession," *South Atlantic Quarterly* 111, no. 2 (2012): 265–88.

11   Teddy Cruz, "Rethinking Uneven Growth: It's about Inequality, Stupid," in Gadanho, *Uneven Growth,* 51.

12   Nader Tehrani, "Urban Challenges: Specifications of Form and the Indeterminacy of Public Reception," in Gadanho, *Uneven Growth,* 60.

13   See Chapters 3 and 10 in the present volume, as well as David Harvey, *A Brief History of Neoliberalism* (Oxford: Oxford University Press, 2005).

14   For a parallel argument, see Jerold Kayden, "Why Implementation Matters," *Harvard Design Magazine* 37 (2014): 57–59. Further elaborations are productively assembled in Simin Davoudi and Ali Madanipour, eds., *Reconsidering Localism* (London: Routledge, 2015).

15   Highly salient on such issues is Robert Lake, "Bring Back Big Government," *International Journal of Urban and Regional Research* 26, no. 4 (2002): 815–22.

16   Cruz, "Rethinking Uneven Growth," 51.

17   Ibid.

18   Ibid., 55.

19   Gadanho, "Mirroring Uneven Growth." All quotes in the preceding paragraph drawn variously from 23, 16.

20   Neil Smith, *The New Urban Frontier: Gentrification and the Revanchist City* (New York: Routledge, 1996).

21   For further details on the URBZ team's ongoing work in Dharavi and their powerful critique of the various developmentalist ideologies associated with what they term "the slum narrative," see Matias Echanove and Rahul Srivastava of URBZ, *The Slum Outside: Elusive Dharavi* (Moscow: Strelka Press, 2014).

22   Bergdoll, "Preface," 12. In his "Introduction" to a closely related MoMA exhibition, *Small Scale, Big Change: New Architectures of Social Engagement* (New York: Museum of Modern Art, 2010), Bergdoll offers a similar assessment, suggesting that a "potential middle ground" must today be found between the heroic visions of modernism and the radical aestheticism of postmodernism.

23   In his writings on the right to the city and *autogestion* in the 1970s, radical urban theorist Henri Lefebvre wrestled repeatedly with an earlier version of this dilemma. See, among other texts, "The Right to the City," in *Writings on Cities,* ed. and trans. Eleonore Kofman and Elizabeth Lebas (Cambridge, MA: Blackwell, 1996). See also Henri Lefebvre, *State, Space, World: Selected Writings,* ed. Neil Brenner and Stuart Elden, trans. Gerald Moore, Neil Brenner and Stuart Elden (Minneapolis: University of Minnesota Press, 2009).

9   Cities for People, Not for Profit?

with Peter Marcuse and Margit Mayer

The unfolding effects of the post-2009 global economic recession are dramatically intensifying the contradictions around which urban social movements have been rallying, suddenly validating their claims regarding the unsustainability and destructiveness of neoliberal forms of urbanization. Cities across Europe, from London, Copenhagen, Paris and Rome to Athens, Reykjavik, Riga and Kiev, have erupted in demonstrations, strikes and protests, often accompanied by violence. Youthful activists are not alone in their outrage that public money is being doled out to the large banks, even as the destabilization of economic life and the intensification of generalized social insecurity continues. In 2009 the Economist Intelligence Unit observed: "A spate of incidents in recent months shows that the global economic downturn is already having political repercussions […] There is growing concern about a possible global pandemic of unrest […] Our central forecast includes a high risk of regime-threatening social unrest."[1] Around the same time, the US director of national intelligence presented the global economic crisis as the biggest contemporary security threat, outpacing terrorism.[2] Preparations to control and crush potential civil unrest are well under way.[3]

In light of these trends, it appears increasingly urgent to understand how different types of cities and metropolitan regions across the world system are being repositioned within increasingly volatile, financialized circuits of capital accumulation and shifting formations of geopolitical power. Equally important is the question of how this crisis has provoked or constrained alternative visions of urban life that point beyond capitalism as a structuring principle of political-economic and spatial organization. Capitalist cities are not only sites for strategies of capital accumulation; they are also arenas in which the conflicts and contradictions associated with historically and geographically specific accumulation strategies are expressed and fought out. As such, capitalist cities have long served as spaces for envisioning, and indeed mobilizing towards, alternatives to capitalism itself, its associated process of profit-driven urbanization and its relentless commodification of social life.

It is this constellation of issues that we wish to emphasize with our title, "Cities for people, not for profit." Through this formulation, we mean to underscore the urgent political priority of constructing cities that correspond to social needs rather than to the capitalist imperative of private profit-making and spatial enclosure. The demand for "cities for people, not for profit" has been articulated recurrently throughout much of the history of capitalism. It was, for instance, expressed paradigmatically by Friedrich Engels as he analyzed the miserable condition of the English working class in the dilapidated housing districts of nineteenth-century Manchester.[4] It was articulated in yet another form by writers as diverse as Jane Jacobs, Lewis Mumford and Henri Lefebvre as they polemicized against the homogenizing, destructive and anti-social consequences of postwar Fordist-modernist urban renewal projects.[5] It has been explicitly politicized and, in some cases, partially institutionalized by municipal socialist movements in diverse contexts and conjunctures during the course of the twentieth century.[6] Of course, both negative and positive lessons can also be drawn from the experience of cities under state socialism, in which hypercentralized forms of state planning replaced commodification as the structuring principle of territorial organization. And finally, the limits of profitbased forms of urbanism have also been emphasized in the contemporary geoeconomic context by critics of neoliberal models of urban development, with its hypercommodification of urban land and other basic social amenities (housing, transportation, utilities, public space, health care, education, even water and sewage disposal) in cities around the world.[7]

It seems particularly urgent to extend and deepen reflection on this *problematique* in the current moment, in which the worldwide financial crisis starting around 2009 and its consequences continue to send shock waves of instability, social suffering and conflict throughout the global urban system. New intellectual resources are particularly important for those institutions, movements and actors that aim to roll back the contemporary hypercommodification of urban life, and on this basis, to promote alternative, radically democratic, socially just and sustainable forms of urbanism. Writing over four decades ago, David Harvey succinctly characterized this challenge as follows:

> Patterns in the circulation of surplus value are changing but they have not altered the fact that cities […] are founded on the exploitation of the many by the few. An urbanism founded on exploitation is a legacy of history. A genuinely humanizing urbanism has yet to be brought into being. It remains for revolutionary theory to chart the path from

an urbanism based in exploitation to an urbanism appropriate for the human species. And it remains for revolutionary practice to accomplish such a transformation.[8]

Harvey's political injunction certainly remains as urgent as ever in the early twenty-first century. In Harvey's view, a key task for critical or "revolutionary" urban theory is to "chart the path" towards alternative, postcapitalist forms of urbanization. How can this task be confronted today, as a new wave of accumulation by dispossession and capitalist enclosure washes destructively across the world economy?[9]

The need for critical urban theory

Mapping the possible pathways of sociospatial transformation – in Harvey's terms, "charting the path" – involves, first and foremost, *understanding* the nature of contemporary patterns of urban restructuring, and then, on that basis, analyzing their implications for action.[10] A key challenge for radical intellectuals and activists, therefore, is to decipher the origins and consequences of the contemporary global financial crisis and the possibility for alternative, progressive, radical or revolutionary responses to it, at once within, among, and beyond cities. Such understandings will have considerable implications for the character, intensity, direction, duration and potential results of resistance.

The field of critical urban studies can make important contributions to ongoing efforts to confront such questions. This intellectual field was consolidated in the late 1960s and early 1970s through the pioneering interventions of radical scholars such as Henri Lefebvre, Manuel Castells and David Harvey, among many others.[11] Despite their theoretical, methodological and political differences, these authors shared a common concern to understand the ways in which, under capitalism, cities operate as strategic sites for commodification processes. Cities, they argued, are major basing points for the production, circulation and consumption of commodities, and their evolving internal sociospatial organization, governance systems and patterns of sociopolitical conflict must be understood in relation to this role. These authors suggested, moreover, that capitalist cities are not only arenas in which commodification occurs; they are themselves intensively commodified insofar as their constitutive sociospatial forms – from buildings and configurations of the built environment to land-use systems, networks of production and exchange, and metropolitan-wide infrastructural arrangements – are sculpted and continually reorganized in order to enhance the profit-making capacities of capital.

Of course, profit-oriented strategies of urban restructuring are intensely contested among dominant, subordinate and marginalized social forces; their outcomes are never predetermined through the logic of capital. Urban space under capitalism is therefore never permanently fixed; it is continually shaped and reshaped through a relentless clash of opposed social forces oriented, respectively, towards the exchange-value (profit-oriented) and use-value (everyday life) dimensions of capitalist property relations.[12] Moreover, strategies to commodify urban space often fail dismally, producing devalorized, crisis-riven urban and regional landscapes in which labor and capital cannot be combined productively to satisfy social needs, and in which inherited sociospatial configurations are severely destabilized, generally at the cost of massive human suffering and environmental degradation. And, even when such profit-making strategies do appear to open up new frontiers for surplus-value extraction, whether within, among or beyond cities, these apparent "successes" are inevitably precarious, temporary ones – overaccumulation, devalorization and systemic crisis remain constant threats. Paradoxically, however, the conflicts, failures, instabilities and crisis tendencies associated with the capitalist form of urbanization have led not to its dissolution or transcendence, but to its continual reinvention through a dynamic process of "implosion-explosion" and "creative destruction."[13] Consequently, despite its destructive, destabilizing social and environmental consequences, capital's relentless drive to enhance profitability has long played, and continues to play, a powerful role in producing and transforming urban sociospatial configurations.[14]

These analytical and political starting points have, since the 1970s, facilitated an extraordinary outpouring of concrete, critically oriented research on the various dimensions and consequences of capitalist forms of urbanization – including patterns of industrial agglomeration and interfirm relations; the evolution of urban labor markets; the political economy of real estate and urban property relations; problems of social reproduction, including housing, transportation, education and infrastructure investment; the evolution of class struggles and other social conflicts in the spheres of production, reproduction and urban governance; the role of state institutions, at various spatial scales, in mediating processes of urban restructuring; the reorganization of urban governance regimes; the evolution of urbanized socionatures; and the consolidation of diverse forms of urban social mobilization, conflict and struggle.[15] Such analyses have in turn contributed to the elaboration of several distinct strands of critical urban research that have inspired generations of intellectual and political engagement with urban questions. These research strands include, at various levels of abstraction: (a) *periodizations* of capitalist urban development that have linked (world-scale) regimes of capital accumulation to changing (national and local) configurations of urban space; (b) *comparative* approaches to urban studies that have explored the place- and territory-specific forms of urban sociospatial organization and regulatory strategy that have crystallized within each of the latter configurations; and (c) *conjunctural* analyses that attempt to decipher ongoing, site-specific processes of urban restructuring, their sources within the underlying crisis tendencies of world capitalism, their ramifications for the future trajectory of urban development, and the possibility of subjecting the latter to some form of popular-democratic control.

This is not, however, to suggest that critical urban studies represents a homogeneous research field based on a rigidly orthodox or paradigmatic foundation. On the contrary, the development of critical approaches to the study of capitalist urbanization has been, and certainly remains, fraught with wide-ranging disagreements about any number of core theoretical, epistemological, methodological and political issues.[16] Even though their form, content and stakes have evolved considerably in relation to the continued forward-movement of worldwide capitalist urbanization, such controversies remain as intense now as they were in the early 1970s.

Nonetheless, against the background of the last four decades of vibrant theorizing, research, debate and disagreement on urban questions under capitalism, we believe it is plausible to speak of a broadly coherent, "critical" branch of urban studies. This critical branch can be usefully counterposed to "mainstream" or "traditional" approaches to urban questions. Aside from their distinctive epistemological foundations,[17] critical approaches to urban studies are generally concerned: (a) to analyze the systemic yet historically specific intersections between capitalism and urbanization processes; (b) to examine the changing balance of social forces, power relations, sociospatial inequalities and political-institutional arrangements that shape, and are in turn shaped by, the evolution of capitalist urbanization; (c) to expose the marginalizations, exclusions and injustices (whether of class, ethnicity, race, gender, sexuality, nationality or otherwise) that are inscribed, naturalized and also contested within existing urban configurations, at once through spatial practices and spatial ideologies; (d) to decipher the contradictions, crisis tendencies and lines of potential or actual conflict within contemporary cities, and on this basis, (e) to demarcate and to politicize the strategically essential possibilities for more progressive, socially just, emancipatory and sustainable formations of urban life.

Cities in crisis: theory ... and practice

We insist on the centrality of commodification as an intellectual and political reference point for any critical account of the contemporary urban condition. But this *problematique* can be explored through various theoretical and methodological lenses. One fruitful avenue is offered by Henri Lefebvre's classic concept of the "right to the city," which has recently been rediscovered by radical academics and activists alike.[18] This slogan represents one important rallying cry and basis for transformative political mobilization in many contemporary cities and metropolitan regions, and it also resonates with earlier calls to create "cities for citizens" through the reinvigoration of participatory urban civil societies.[19] However, this potentially radical political slogan, much like that of "social capital," is also being used ideologically by state institutions, which have co-opted it into a basis for legitimating existing, only weakly participatory forms of urban governance, or for exaggerating the systemic implications of newly introduced forms of citizen participation in municipal affairs.[20] Lefebvre himself grappled with an analogous problem in the 1960s and 1970s, when the Eurocommunist concept of *autogestion* – literally, "self-management," but perhaps more accurately translated as "grassroots democracy" – was being pervasively misappropriated by various interests to legitimate new forms of state bureaucratic planning.[21] In contrast to such tendencies, Lefebvre insisted that "limiting the world of commodities" was essential to any project of radical democracy, urban or otherwise, for this would "give content to the projects of democratic planning, prioritizing the social needs that are formulated, controlled and managed by those who have a stake in them."[22] While several recent studies have explored the challenges and dilemmas associated with such an urban politics of grassroots participation, others have also advocated its construction, extension or reinvention in the wake of restructuring processes that are intensifying the marginalization, exclusion, displacement, disempowerment or oppression of urban inhabitants.[23]

Clearly, since the Fordist-Keynesian period, urban social movements have articulated new hopes and visions, but have also confronted new pressures and constraints. On occasion, they have succeeded in producing major changes, but in other cases their radical promise has been abandoned, co-opted or "mainstreamed." And, of course, not all such movements actually sought systemic change, whether in relation to capitalism, modern state power or other hegemonic institutions, practices and ideologies. But, from the perspective of critical urban theory, one may venture the following conjecture: the transformative potential of emergent social movement mobilizations will depend on two basic factors – the objective position, power and strategies of those currently established in positions of domination; and the objective position, power and strategies of those who are mobilizing in opposition to established forms of neoliberal urbanism.

At present, the objective position in which both elements currently find themselves is *crisis*. Initially, that crisis appears to be rooted in the economic structure, but it has also been extended to forms of governance, regulation and political subjectivity. The strategy of those in power is quite clear, and can be summarized under the rubric of neoliberalism (and its various politico-ideological permutations): its core goal, across diverse politico-institutional contexts and scales, is the promotion of market rule and aggressive commodification. This situation forms the backdrop for the endeavors of contemporary approaches to critical urban theory, which examine various ways in which the social power relations of capitalism – along with imperialism, colonialism, racism and other modalities of social disempowerment – are inscribed within urban landscapes around the world. But what about the forces of resistance to domination, those suffering due to the current crisis and, indeed, the longer-term relations of exploitation of which the current situation is a consequence and part? What is their future, and what kind of change, if any, will they produce?

The nature of the social forces that are adversely affected by existing arrangements and contemporary restructuring processes requires careful investigation and theorization. One productive approach to this analytical task entails distinguishing the *deprived* – those who are immediately exploited, unemployed, impoverished, discriminated against in jobs and education, in ill health and uncared for, or incarcerated; and the *discontented* – those who are disrespected, treated unequally because of sexual, political, or religious orientation, censored in speech, writing, research, or artistic expression, forced into alienating jobs, or otherwise constrained in their capacity to explore the possibilities of life.[24] Members of these partially overlapping groups have considerable cause to oppose the existing system of capitalism and contemporary forms of neoliberal urbanism. But, they are an extremely heterogeneous assemblage of social forces; their common interests are not always obvious; and nor is concerted strategic action a simple matter. The possibility for such action is further constrained by the potent ideological influence of the corporate media, the daily, routinized language of politics, and the perceived need to deal with everyday crises before longer-term, systemic issues can be addressed. And, above all, transformative action is constrained by the propaganda of market fundamentalism, the induced appeal of mass consumerism and authoritarian populism, the technically instrumentalized educational system, the oppressive weight of bureaucracy, and, through it all, the overwhelming force of dominant ideologies of supremacy and exclusion – for instance, nationalism, racism (especially white supremacy), Eurocentrism, Orientalism, heteronormativity, speciesism and so forth.

Several different approaches to resistance and change are, however, possible. The overwhelming reaction to the collapse of the prevailing, speculation-oriented global financial order of "casino capitalism," whose trivial public regulation is itself in the hands of the dominant institutions of corporate capital, is popular outrage. That outrage could well be directed against the system as a whole; it could take a radical turn, in the spirit of Lefebvre. Indeed, an argument could easily be made that the present crisis exposes the vices of the capitalist system as a whole, and that the realization of a genuine right to the city requires the abolition of the rule of private capital over the urban economy, and indeed, that of the world economy as a whole. That would be a radical response, one oriented precisely towards the construction of an "urbanism appropriate for the human species," as envisioned by Harvey.[25]

A liberal-progressive or reformist response, on the other hand, would focus on individual and "excessive" greed, whether of bankers, financiers or politicians, as the villains that have produced the current crisis. Such a response would, accordingly, focus on regulating the activities of such power-brokers more thoroughly than existing neoliberal regulations permit. It would direct outrage not at the system as a whole, but at the bonuses which executives extract from it, the Ponzi schemes which some have perpetrated, or the abuses of political power that have likewise been implicated in the current crisis. To the extent that this response thematizes public ownership at all, it sees this as a step towards restoring the banks to "health," that is, renewed profitability, and then returning them to their private, corporate owners, perhaps now sheltered from excessive "risk" through "good governance." In this reformist strategy, then, the outrage is eviscerated, and the right to the city shrivels to a claim to unemployment benefits and public investment in urban infrastructure (needed in any case to keep businesses "competitive"), with massive bail-outs for banks being offset by some minimal protections for middle-class borrowers of "viable" mortgages.

Will contemporary urban social movements be thus co-opted, as they were during the austerity, roll-out phase of neoliberal restructuring in the 1980s? Will they be content with reforms that merely reboot the system, or will they attempt to address the problem of systemic change, as did the militant student and labor movements of 1968? As of this writing (March 2011), both increased militancy, as in the squatting of foreclosed homes, and co-optation, as in the endless debates about mortgage regulation, appear possible. Prediction is hazardous, not least because urban space continues to serve simultaneously as the arena, the medium and the stake of ongoing struggles regarding the future of capitalism. It is, in Harvey's formulation, the "point of collision" between the mobilizations of the deprived, the discontented and the dispossessed, on the one side, and on the other, ruling class strategies to instrumentalize, control and colonize common social and ecological resources, including the right to the city itself, for the benefit of the few.[26] As such struggles over the present and future shape of our cities intensify, we hope that critical urban theorists will continue to contribute to clarifying what needs to be understood and what needs to be done in order to forge a radical, if not revolutionary, alternative to the dismal, socially and environmentally destructive *status quo* of worldwide neoliberal urbanization. The slogan, "Cities for people, not for profit" is thus intended to set into stark relief what we view as a central political objective for ongoing efforts, at once theoretical and practical, to address the crises of our time.

Notes

1   Economist Intelligence Unit, "Governments under Pressure: How Sustained Economic Upheaval Could Put Political Regimes at Risk," *The Economist,* March 19, 2009, http://viewswire.eiu.com/index. asp?layout=VWArticleVW3&article_id=954360280&rf=0How sustained economic upheaval could put political regimes at risk.

2   Nelson Schwartz, "Rise in Jobless Poses Threat to Stability Worldwide," *New York Times,* February 15, 2009.

3   Nathan Freier, "Known Unknowns: Unconventional 'Strategic Shocks' in Defense Strategy Development,," *Strategic Studies Institute U.S. Army War College,* November 4, 2008: http://www.strategicstudiesinstitute.army.mil/pubs/display.cfm?pubID=890.

4   Friedrich Engels, *The Condition of the Working Class in England,* trans. Victor Kiernan (New York: Penguin, 1987 [1845]).

5   Jane Jacobs, *The Death and Life of Great American Cities* (New York: Vintage, 1962); Lewis Mumford, *The City in History* (New York: Harcourt, Brace, 1961); Henri Lefebvre, "The Right to the City," *Writings on Cities,* ed. and trans. Eleonore Kofman and Elizabeth Lebas (Cambridge, MA: Blackwell, 1996), 63–184.

6   Eve Blau, *The Architecture of Red Vienna, 1919–1934* (Cambridge, MA: MIT Press, 1999); Martin Boddy and Colin Fudge, eds., *Local Socialism?* (London: Macmillan, 1984); Maureen Mackintosh and Hilary Wainwright, eds., *A Taste of Power: The Politics of Local Economics* (London: Verso, 1987).

7   See, for instance, Neil Smith, *The New Urban Frontier: Gentrification and the Revanchist City* (New York: Routledge, 1996); David Harvey, *The Urban Experience* (Baltimore: Johns Hopkins University Press, 1989); and Neil Brenner and Nik Theodore, eds., *Spaces of Neoliberalism* (Cambridge, MA: Blackwell, 2003).

8   David Harvey, *Social Justice and the City* (Baltimore: Johns Hopkins University Press, 1973), 314.

9   David Harvey, "The Right to the City," *New Left Review,* n.s., 53 (September/October 2008): 23–40; Massimo de Angelis, *The Beginning of History: Value Struggles and Global Capital* (London: Pluto, 2007).

10   Harvey, *Social Justice and the City,* 314.

11   Henri Lefebvre, *The Urban Revolution,* trans. Robert Bononno (Minneapolis: University of Minnesota Press, 2003); Lefebvre, "Right to the City"; Manuel Castells, *The Urban Question: A Marxist Approach,* trans. Alan Sheridan (Cambridge, MA: MIT Press, 1977); Harvey, *Social Justice and the City.*

12   Lefebvre, "Right to the City"; Harvey, *Social Justice and the City;* John Logan and Harvey Molotch, *Urban Fortunes: The Political Economy of Place* (Berkeley: University of California Press, 1987).

13   Lefebvre, *Urban Revolution;* Harvey, *Urban Experience.*

14   Exploration of the nexus between cities and commodification had, of course, already been initiated in the mid-nineteenth century by Engels in his classic study of industrial Manchester. However, this constellation of issues was subsequently neglected by most mainstream twentieth-century urbanists, who opted instead for some combination of transhistorical, technocratic or instrumentalist approaches and tended to interpret cities as the spatial expressions of purportedly universal principles of human ecology or civilizational order. For an important midcentury exception, see Lewis Mumford's account of "Coketown" in *The City in History,* 446–81.

15   For useful overviews and paradigmatic interventions, see Michael Dear and Allen Scott, eds., *Urbanization and Urban Planning in Capitalist Society* (London: Methuen, 1980); Edward Soja, *Postmetropolis* (Cambridge, MA: Blackwell, 2000); Nik Heynen, Maria Kaika and Erik Swyngedouw, eds., *In the Nature of Cities: Urban Political Ecology and the Politics of Urban Metabolism* (New York: Routledge, 2006).

16 For useful overviews, see Ira Katznelson, *Marxism and the City* (New York: Oxford University Press, 1993); Peter Saunders, *Social Theory and the Urban Question,* 2nd ed. (New York: Routledge, 1986); and Soja, *Postmetropolis.*

17 See Chapter 2 in the present volume.

18 Lefebvre, "Right to the City."

19 Mike Douglass and John Friedmann, eds., *Cities for Citizens* (New York: Wiley, 1998).

20 Margit Mayer, "The 'Right to the City' in the Context of Shifting Mottos of Urban Social Movements," in *Cities for People, not for Profit,* ed. Neil Brenner, Peter Marcuse and Margit Mayer (New York: Routledge, 2011), 63–85. See also Margit Mayer, "The Onward Sweep of Social Capital," *International Journal of Urban and Regional Research* 27, no. 1 (2003): 110–32.

21 Henri Lefebvre, "Theoretical Problems of Autogestion," in *State, Space, World: Selected Writings,* ed. Neil Brenner and Stuart Elden (Minneapolis: University of Minnesota Press, 2009), 138–52.

22 Ibid., 148.

23 Mark Purcell, *Recapturing Democracy* (New York: Routledge, 2008).

24 Peter Marcuse, "Whose Right(s) to What City?," in Brenner, Marcuse and Mayer, *Cities for People, not for Profit,* 24–41.

25 Harvey, *Social Justice and the City,* 314.

26 Harvey, "Right to the City," 39.

10 After Neoliberalization?

with Jamie Peck and Nik Theodore

In the wake of the global economic crisis of 2008–2009, many prominent commentators have claimed that the ideologies and practices of free-market capitalism, or "neoliberalism," have been discredited, and that a new era of regulatory reform, based on aggressive state interventionism to restrain market forces, is dawning.[1] However, such accounts are generally grounded on untenably monolithic assumptions regarding the inherited regulatory system that is purportedly now in crisis, leading to interpretations of the current crisis as a systemic collapse, analogous to the dismantling of the Berlin Wall.[2] More generally, whatever their interpretation of contemporary crisis tendencies, all major accounts of the 2008–2009 financial meltdown hinge on determinate, yet often unexamined, assumptions regarding the regulatory formation(s) that existed prior to this latest round of crisis-induced restructuring. For this reason, it is an opportune moment for reflection on the processes of regulatory restructuring that have been unfolding since the collapse of North Atlantic Fordism over forty years ago. Such reflection is essential, we believe, to ongoing attempts to decipher emergent patterns of crisis formation under post-2008 capitalism. It also has considerable implications for the understanding of contemporary urban landscapes, which are being profoundly reshaped through contemporary regulatory transformations and contestations.

Debates on regulatory transformation have animated the fields of heterodox political economy and critical urban and regional studies for several decades, and have played a significant role in the literatures on, among other topics, post-Fordism, globalization, triadization, multilevel governance, financialization, state rescaling, the new regionalism, urban entrepreneurialism, and, more recently, neoliberalism/ neoliberalization. For present purposes, we build on discussions of the latter issue – *neoliberalization* – in order to conceptualize processes of regulatory restructuring under post-1970s *and* post-2008 capitalism. From our point of view, the increasingly widespread use of the concepts of neoliberalism and neoliberalization has been accompanied by considerable imprecision, confusion and controversy – in effect, they have become "rascal concepts."[3] Despite these dangers, we argue that a rigorously defined concept of neoliberalization can help illuminate the regulatory transformations of our time, and their multiscalar, variegated and rapidly mutating geographies.

We begin with a series of definitional clarifications that underpin our conceptualization of neoliberalization. On this basis, we distinguish its three major dimensions – (1) regulatory experimentation; (2) inter-jurisdictional policy transfer; and (3) the formation of transnational rule-regimes. Such distinctions form the basis for a schematic periodization of how neoliberalization processes have been extended and entrenched across the world economy. These considerations generate an analytical perspective from which to explore several scenarios for counter-neoliberalizing forms of regulatory restructuring within contemporary and future configurations of capitalism. For purposes of this discussion, we do not offer a detailed account of the contemporary global economic crisis or its medium- or long-term implications. Instead, this analysis is intended to serve a *meta*-theoretical purpose – namely, to stimulate further debate regarding the appropriate analytical framework through which to approach the regulatory dimensions of such questions.

While our analysis here does not consider the effects of these regulatory transformations on particular urban landscapes, we suggest that our approach has major implications for ongoing efforts to decipher them. As we argue below, neoliberalization processes do assume place-specific forms within cities and metropolitan regions, but this increasingly occurs within a georegulatory context defined by systemic tendencies towards market-disciplinary institutional reform, the formation of transnational webs of market-oriented policy transfer, deepening patterns of crisis formation and accelerating cycles of crisis-driven policy experimentation. Against this background, the macrospatial analysis presented here may serve as a useful reference point not only for locally embedded, contextually sensitive analyses, but also for emergent, counter-neoliberalizing political strategies, whether at urban or supraurban scales.

Neoliberalism in question

Since the late 1980s, debates on neoliberalism have figured centrally in heterodox political economy. Inspired by various strands of neo-Marxian, neo-Gramscian, neo-Polanyian, neoinstitutionalist and poststructuralist thought, these concepts have been central to discussions of the crisis of the postwar capitalist order –

variously labeled North Atlantic Fordism, embedded liberalism or national developmentalism – and of post-1970s patterns of institutional and spatial reorganization. Whatever the differences among them, however, all prevalent uses of the notion of neoliberalism involve references to the tendential extension of market-based competition and commodification processes into previously relatively insulated realms of political-economic life. The evolving scholarly and practical-political uses of the term "neoliberalism" would thus appear to provide an initial evidentiary basis for the proposition that processes of marketization and commodification have indeed been extended, accelerated and intensified in recent decades, roughly since the global recession of the mid-1970s.

We cannot attempt here to review the diverse epistemological, methodological, substantive and political positions that have been articulated through these discussions of post-1970s regulatory restructuring.[4] Instead we move directly into an overview of our own theoretical orientation, which will then be further elaborated in relation to the problem of periodization and with reference to the challenges of deciphering contemporary developments.[5]

On the most general level, we conceptualize neoliberalization as one among several tendencies of regulatory change that have been unleashed across the global capitalist system since the 1970s: it prioritizes market-based, market-oriented or market-disciplinary responses to regulatory problems; it strives to intensify commodification in all realms of social life; and it often mobilizes speculative financial instruments to open up new arenas for capitalist profit-making. In our previous work, we have raised critical questions about structuralist accounts of neoliberalization as an all-encompassing hegemonic bloc, and about those poststructuralist arguments that emphasize the radical contextual particularity of neoliberalizing regulatory practices and forms of subjectification. By contrast, we view neoliberalization as a *variegated* form of regulatory restructuring: it produces geoinstitutional differentiation across places, territories and scales; but it does this systemically, as a pervasive, endemic feature of its basic operational logic. Concomitantly, we emphasize the profound *path-dependency* of neoliberalization processes: insofar as they necessarily collide with diverse regulatory landscapes inherited from earlier rounds of regulatory formation and contestation (including Fordist-Keynesianism, national-developmentalism and state socialism), their forms of articulation and institutionalization are quite heterogeneous. Thus, rather than expecting some pure, prototypical form of neoliberalization to be generalized across divergent contexts, we view variegation – systemic geoinstitutional differentiation – as one of its essential, enduring features.

According to international political economist James Mittelman, globalization represents "not a single, unified phenomenon, but a *syndrome* of processes and activities [italics in original]."[6] We suggest that neoliberalization may be conceptualized in analogous terms: it is likewise better understood as a syndrome than as a singular entity, essence or totality. From this point of view, a key task for any analyst of neoliberalization is to specify the "pattern of related activities […] within the global political economy" that constitute and reproduce this syndrome across otherwise diverse sites, places, territories and scales.[7]

Neoliberalization defined

As a first cut into this task, we propose the following formulation: neoliberalization represents *an historically specific, unevenly developed, hybrid, patterned tendency of market-disciplinary regulatory restructuring.* Each element of this statement requires more precise specification.

– *Market-disciplinary regulatory restructuring.* As economic sociologist Karl Polanyi ironically observed, "the road to a free market was opened and kept open by an enormous increase in continuous, centrally organized and controlled interventionism."[8] Correspondingly, we maintain that processes of marketization and commodification under capitalism (efforts to extend "market discipline") are always mediated through state institutions in a variety of policy arenas (for instance, labor, money, capital, social protection, education, housing, land, environment, and so forth). For this reason, we conceive neoliberalization as a particular form of *regulatory* reorganization: it involves the recalibration of institutionalized, collectively binding modes of governance and, more generally, state-economy relations, to impose, extend or consolidate marketized, commodified forms of social life. As such, neoliberalization may be analytically opposed to regulatory processes that either counteract marketization and commodification, or to those that entail qualitatively different agendas – for instance, normatively based forms of collective resource allocation and socioinstitutional coordination.

– *Historically specific.* The ideological and doctrinal roots of neoliberalization can be traced to the classical liberal project of constructing "self-regulating" markets during the *belle époque* of late nineteenth and early twentieth-century British imperialism, as well as to subsequent, postwar interventions by then-renegade free market economists such as Friedrich Hayek and Milton Friedman.[9] The process of *neo*liberalization began to unfold in the early 1970s, following a relatively *longue durée* phase of embedded liberalism in which processes of marketization and commodification had been tendentially restrained through various global and national regulatory arrangements – for instance, the Bretton Woods system and various types of national-developmentalist and welfarist state intervention. Thus understood, specifically neoliberalizing forms of regulatory restructuring began to unfold in conjunction with what some have termed the "second great transformation," the process of worldwide capitalist restructuring that has ensued since the collapse of the post–World War II geoeconomic order.[10] In the aftermath of that crisis, neoliberalization has emerged as a dominant, if not hegemonic, process of regulatory restructuring across the world economy. It would not be entirely inappropriate to refer to this process of market-oriented regulatory change simply as "marketization" or "commodification," since as we have already suggested, one of its features is the project of extending market-based, commodified social relations. We nonetheless opt for the term *neoliberalization* in order to underscore the homologies between post-1970s patterns of market-oriented regulatory restructuring and the earlier project of classical liberalization that was associated with nineteenth and early twentieth-century British imperialism. Parallels to that epoch should not be overdrawn, however. The process of neoliberalization does not represent a return to an earlier framework of capitalist development, or a contemporary reinvention of classical liberal institutional forms, regulatory arrangements or political compromises.[11] Neoliberalization has emerged under qualitatively different geopolitical and geoeconomic conditions, in reaction to historically specific regulatory failures and political struggles, and across entrenched institutional landscapes.

– *Unevenly developed.* Neoliberalization is generally associated with certain paradigmatic regulatory experiments – for instance, privatization, deregulation, trade liberalization, financialization, structural adjustment, welfare reform, and monetarist shock therapy. But as prototypical as these projects of regulatory reorganization have become, their proliferation under post-1970s capitalism cannot be understood through simple diffusion models. Rather than entailing the construction of some fully formed, coherently functioning, regime-like state of neoliberal*ism* that has progressively expanded to encompass global regulatory space, the *process* of neoliberalization has been articulated unevenly across places, territories and scales. The uneven development of neoliberalization results, on the one hand, from the continuous collision between contextually specific, constantly evolving neoliberalization projects and inherited politico-institutional arrangements, whether at global, national or local scales. At the same time, through this collision, neoliberalization processes rework inherited forms of regulatory and spatial organization, including those of state institutions themselves, to produce new forms of geoinstitutional differentiation. Consequently, at each juncture of its evolution, the "moving map" of neoliberalization processes has been variegated, and has been continuously redifferentiated through a rapid succession of regulatory projects and counterprojects, neoliberalizing and otherwise.[12] The uneven development of neoliberalization is therefore not a temporary condition, a product of its "incomplete" institutionalization, but one of its constitutive features. Geoinstitutional differentiation is at once a medium and an outcome of neoliberalization processes.

– *Tendency.* Even as neoliberalization processes systematically rework inherited regulatory landscapes, they should not be viewed as representing a totality encompassing all aspects of regulatory restructuring in any context, site or scale. Rather, neoliberalization is one among several competing processes of regulatory restructuring that have been articulated under post-1970s capitalism – albeit one that has had particularly enduring, multiscalar politico-institutional consequences.[13]

– *Hybrid.* Neoliberalization is never manifested in a pure form, as a comprehensive or encompassing regulatory whole. Instead, neoliberalization tendencies can *only* be articulated in incomplete, hybrid modalities, which may crystallize in certain regulatory formations, but which are nevertheless continually and eclectically reworked in context-specific ways. Consequently, empirical evidence underscoring the stalled, incomplete, discontinuous or differentiated character of projects to impose market rule, or their coexistence alongside potentially antagonistic projects (for instance, social democracy) does not provide a sufficient basis for questioning their neoliberalized, neoliberalizing dimensions.

– *Patterned.* Neoliberalization processes initially gained leverage and momentum in response to a range of crisis tendencies inherited from the postwar political-economic order. During the course of the 1970s, neoliberalization processes reworked Keynesian, national-developmentalist landscapes through a series of collisions between inherited institutional frameworks and newly mobilized projects of regulatory reorganization. Such collisions, and their enduring, if unpredictable, politico-institutional consequences, have long animated the uneven development of neoliberalization processes. Crucially, however, as unevenly as neoliberalization processes have been articulated, they have not entailed a haphazard "piling up" of disconnected, contextually contained regulatory experiments. Rather, processes of neoliberalization have generated significant, markedly patterned, cumulative effects upon the georegulatory configuration of capitalism. From this point of view, the trajectory of neoliberalization processes since the 1970s may be better understood as a wave-like articulation, in which each successive round of neoliberalizing projects transforms the institutional and political-ideological configurations in which subsequent rounds of regulatory restructuring unfold.

Four methodological implications

This conceptualization of neoliberalization has several methodological implications that stand in sharp contrast to certain prevalent assumptions and interpretative orientations that have pervaded recent scholarly discussions:[14]

1. Contrary to prevalent equations of neoliberalization with a worldwide homogenization of regulatory systems, our conceptualization is intended to illuminate the ways in which market-disciplinary forms of regulatory restructuring have actually intensified geoinstitutional difference. It follows that not even the most hypertrophied politico-institutional expressions of neoliberalization – such as those explored in Naomi Klein's analysis of the neoliberal "shock doctrine" in post-coup Chile and occupied Iraq – should be equated with expectations of simple

convergence on a unified and singular market order, in the fashion of Thomas Friedman's journalistic formulation of flat-earth globalization.[15]

2. The conceptualization of neoliberalization proposed here provides a basis on which to grasp the medium- and long-term evolutionary trajectories of market-disciplinary regulatory projects themselves, with particular reference to their erratic, often contradictory cumulative impacts on the political, institutional and discursive landscapes they aspire to reorganize. Neoliberalization processes derive much of their impetus and rationale precisely from the uneven regulatory landscapes that they combatively encounter, and subsequently remake, in a path-dependent, if experimental, fashion. This means, in turn, that the spatial differentiation and evolutionary pathways of neoliberalization processes cannot be grasped as a simple territorial diffusion in which a pregiven regulatory template is installed, extended and/or replicated across an ever-widening area.

3. Given our emphasis on the path dependency of neoliberalization processes, our approach underscores the need for context-sensitive inquiries into patterns of regulatory experimentation. Nonetheless, our conceptualization can be distinguished from the purely "ground-up," inductive or self-consciously "low-flying" approaches to studies of neoliberalization that are sometimes associated with poststructuralist modes of analysis. As understood here, the spaces of regulatory change – jurisdictional units encompassing neighborhoods, cities, regions, national states and multinational zones – are relationally interconnected within a transnational, if not global, governance system. Processes of neoliberalization necessarily assume contextually specific, path-dependent forms, but their sources can rarely be traced to a single site; their politico-institutional consequences generally transcend any one context; and there are significant family resemblances among them.

4. Finally, we conceive neoliberalization processes as being intrinsically contradictory – that is, they entail regulatory strategies that frequently undermine the very socioinstitutional and political-economic conditions needed for their successful implementation.[16] Consequently, policy failure is not only central to the exploratory *modus operandi* of neoliberalization processes; it provides a further powerful impetus for their accelerating proliferation and continual reinvention across sites

and scales. Crucially, then, endemic policy failure has actually tended to spur further rounds of reform within broadly neoliberalized political and institutional parameters: it triggers the continuous reinvention of neoliberal policy repertoires rather than their abandonment.

Towards a 'moving map' of neoliberalization

David Harvey has underscored the difficulties of constructing a "moving map of the progress of neoliberalization on the world stage since 1970."[17] In particular, he emphasizes the partial, unevenly developed character of neoliberal policy realignments within individual national states; the frequency of "slow reversals" and counteracting political mobilizations following initial, more radical, crisis-induced neoliberal assaults; and the vicissitudes of political power struggles that unfold in conjunction with neoliberalizing policy shifts, institutional transformations and their associated crisis tendencies. The challenge, Harvey proposes, is "to understand how local transformations relate to broader trends" by tracking the "turbulent currents of uneven geographical development" that are produced through neoliberalization processes.[18]

How to confront this challenge? What would a "moving map" of neoliberalization processes during the last thirty-plus years look like? With a few notable exceptions, the extant literatures on neoliberalization have spawned no more than partial responses to this challenge, not least due to their underdeveloped conceptualizations of regulatory uneven development.[19] While they have identified any number of key features within the perpetually morphing landscapes of post-1970s market-disciplinary regulatory change, most accounts have been less concerned with relating these elements to one another, and to the broader "currents of uneven geographical development" to which Harvey refers.

For instance, the lion's share of work on neoliberalization is still focused on national-level policy realignments. Such state-centric accounts allude frequently to geoeconomic and geopolitical contexts, but they have tended to presuppose the methodologically nationalist assumption that national states represent the natural or primary unit of regulatory transformation.[20] These methodologically nationalist tendencies have been fruitfully counteracted in treatments of neoliberalization as a globally hegemonic bloc, as well as in more recent work on the neoliberalization of urban and regional governance. Yet, as valuable as such engagements have been, neither strand of discussion has fully grappled with the *constitutively* uneven character of neoliberalization processes, as sketched above. Whereas globalist accounts have productively emphasized the capacity of hegemonic actors and institutions to impose market-disciplinary parameters upon subordinate institutions and regulatory configurations, locally and regionally attuned accounts generally have focused on regulatory transformations that appear to be circumscribed within particular subnational territories or scalar niches. The concept of neoliberalization has enabled researchers in both strands of this discussion to link their analyses to broader metanarratives regarding post-1970s forms of crisis-induced restructuring and regulatory reorganization. Nonetheless, this concept is too often deployed unreflexively or imprecisely, as if it were a self-evident *explanans*, when the processes to which it refers themselves require sustained interrogation and rigorous explanation.

The recent work of Beth Simmons, Frank Dobbin and Geoffrey Garrett confronts much more explicitly the question of how neoliberalization processes have evolved over time and across space.[21] Their analysis usefully examines the differential impacts of four distinct causal mechanisms – coercion, competition, learning and emulation – in explaining what they characterize as the "diffusion" of economic liberalism in the late twentieth century. However, the authors' concern to adjudicate among these causal mechanisms is accompanied by an underdeveloped theorization of the process of neoliberalization itself, which is depicted simply as a "spreading" of market-oriented policy prototypes across national territories within an interdependent international system.[22] Alongside the methodologically nationalist tendencies within this approach, the metaphor of diffusion contains serious limitations as a basis for understanding the uneven geographies of neoliberalization processes during the last forty years. Neoliberalization was not simply invented in one (national) site and then projected – whether through coercion, competition, learning, imitation or any other mechanism – into progressively larger circles of territorial influence. Rather, as Jamie Peck explains, "it more closely resembles a multipolar regime of continuous (re)mobilization, which is animated and reanimated as much by the failures of earlier waves of misintervention and malregulation as it is by 'blue-sky' strategic visions."[23]

Thus understood, the geographies of neoliberalization do not emanate outwards from a point of origin to "fill" other, geographically dispersed zones of regulation. Instead, as emphasized in our definitional sketch, we are dealing with a path-dependent, multicentric process whose evolutionary dynamics and politico-institutional consequences continually transform the global, national *and* local conditions under which subsequent strategies of regulatory restructuring emerge and unfold at all spatial scales. Just as crucially, processes of neoliberalization are spatially uneven, temporally discontinuous and permeated with experimental, hybrid and often self-undermining tendencies. Such considerations, we submit, must lie at the heart of any effort to construct the "moving map" of neoliberalization envisioned by Harvey.[24]

Three analytical dimensions

In order to confront these tasks, we distinguish three core analytical dimensions of neoliberalization processes:[25]

1. *Regulatory experiments:* place-, territory- and scale-specific projects designed to impose, intensify or reproduce market-disciplinary modalities of governance. Such projects are necessarily path-dependent, and generally entail both a destructive moment (efforts to roll back nonmarket, anti-market or market-restraining regulatory arrangements) *and* a creative moment (strategies to roll forward a new politico-institutional infrastructure for marketized regulatory forms).[26] This aspect of neoliberalization has been investigated comprehensively in the vast, case study-based literature on national, regional and local instances of neoliberal regulatory reform.

2. *Systems of inter-jurisdictional policy transfer:* institutional mechanisms and networks of knowledge sharing through which neoliberal policy prototypes are circulated across places, territories and scales, generally transnationally, for redeployment elsewhere. By establishing certain types of regulatory strategies as "prototypical," such networks enhance the ideological legitimacy of neoliberal policy templates while extending their availability as readily accessible, all-purpose "solutions" to contextually specific regulatory problems and crises. At the same time, however, even the most apparently prototypical forms of neoliberal policy are qualitatively transformed through their circulation in such networks. Even though they may appear to be readily available for smooth transfer within a fast-moving circulatory

network, and thus able to promote a homogenization of regulatory space, such policy mobilities remain embedded within politico-institutional contexts that shape their form, content, reception and evolution, generally leading to unpredictable, unintended and intensely variegated outcomes.[27] In the context of neoliberalization processes, therefore, inter-jurisdictional policy transfer is an important mechanism not only of spatial consolidation, but also of institutional differentiation. One of the earliest inquiries into neoliberalizing forms of policy transfer was William Tabb's classic study of fiscal austerity policies in New York City during the 1970s, which outlines paradigmatically how a locally specific response to administrative crisis was transformed into a more general reform template, and subsequently "exported" to other crisis-stricken municipalities across the USA.[28] Jamie Peck's subsequent research charts out a formally analogous but transnational narrative with reference to the geographies of fast workfare policy transfer across regions and national states since the 1980s.[29] At national and transnational scales, this aspect of neoliberalization has also been investigated in the Eastern European context, in the Latin American context and, on a more general level, within the literature on "fast policy" transfer.[30]

3. *Transnational rule-regimes:* large-scale institutional arrangements, regulatory frameworks, legal systems and policy relays that impose determinate "rules of the game" on contextually specific forms of policy experimentation and regulatory reorganization, thereby enframing the activities of actors and institutions within specific politico-institutional parameters. This "parameterizing" aspect of neoliberalization has been analyzed by Stephen Gill in his influential account of the new constitutionalism.[31] For Gill, the new constitutionalism represents a project to institutionalize neoliberal policy precepts over the long term, and globally, through various supranational legal devices. It has operated as a geopolitical and geoeconomic project designed to constrain national states and all other subordinate political institutions to adopt neoliberalized policy precepts in key regulatory spheres (for instance, trade, capital investment, labor, property rights).[32] A variety of other recent works by radical international political economists have likewise underscored the role of multilevel governance arrangements in the construction, imposition and reproduction of neoliberalized, market-disciplinary regulatory arrangements within national and subnational arenas.[33] Such multilevel rule-regimes serve to promote "institutional lock-in mechanisms to separate the

economic and the political under conditions of democracy."[34] In this way, they serve to create and maintain determinate, market-disciplinary parameters around subordinate forms of policy contestation and institutional development.

Restless landscapes of neoliberalization

Any mapping of neoliberalization processes derived from these distinctions would contrast sharply with the diffusionist models that prevail in the orthodox literature, which are closely aligned with the anticipation of policy convergence and various forms of methodological nationalism. But such a mapping could not, in itself, illuminate every concrete feature on the landscapes of neoliberalization, across differential spatiotemporal contexts. Nonetheless, on a more abstract level, such an approach can serve as an analytical basis on which to interpret the creatively destructive trajectories and uneven development of neoliberalization processes since the early 1970s. And, as we suggest below, it also has productive implications for exploring possible alternatives to neoliberalized regulatory forms in the wake of the global economic crisis of 2008–09. Here, we outline these interpretive maneuvers in relatively broad strokes; their concrete elaboration and refinement awaits more detailed research and analysis.

Figure 10.1 outlines a stylized periodization of neoliberalization processes that is derived from the distinctions introduced above. In this figure, the three dimensions of regulatory restructuring no longer serve as ideal-typical categories, but are now mobilized to illuminate the historical-geographical evolution of neoliberalization processes themselves. The top row of the figure delineates each of the three distinctions specified above, understood as interlinked dimensions of regulatory restructuring under conditions of ongoing neoliberalization. The first column specifies a generic, decade-based timeline, from the 1970s through the 2000s. The shaded cells denote the dimensions of regulatory restructuring in which, on our reading, neoliberalization has been most pronounced since its initial institutional elaboration in the 1970s. Concomitantly, the white cells in the upper quadrants of the figure denote zones of regulatory activity that, during the corresponding decade(s) specified in the first column, were largely configured according to market-restraining principles (Keynesianism, "progressive constitutionalism").[35] With each successive decade, the shaded zones in the figure are widened to include

	Dimensions of regulatory restructuring		
	Context-specific forms of regulatory experimentation	Systems of inter-jurisdictional policy transfer	Rule-regimes and parameterization processes
1970s	**Disarticulated neoliberalization** Neoliberalization projects assume place-, territory- and scale-specific forms in a "hostile" geoeconomic context still defined by late Keynesian regulatory arrangements and emergent crisis tendencies	Intensification of neo-Keynesian forms of cross-jurisdictional policy transfer in response to pervasive geoeconomic volatility, especially within the OECD zone Tendential emergence of neoliberalizing forms of policy transfer across interstitial geopolitical vectors (e.g., Chicago to Santiago) Accelerating ideological critiques of Keynesian economic doctrines; increasing signs of systemic crisis within the international rule-regime of postwar embedded liberalism	
1980s	Continued intensification of market-driven forms of regulatory experimentation and institutional reform at various spatial scales and in strategic zones (e.g., USA, UK, Latin America) Tendential weakening / exhaustion of neo-Keynesian networks of policy transfer coupled with ongoing, intensely contested searches for new "institutional fixes" to resolve persistent georegulatory crises Tendential thickening, transnationalization, mutual recursion, programmatic integration and coevolution of policy networks oriented towards market-driven regulatory experiments and institutional reforms (e.g., monetarism, liberalization, privatization, urban entrepreneurialism, reinvented governance, etc.)		Tendential destruction of "progressive constitutionalism" at global, supranational and national scales Tendential consolidation of a "new constitutionalism" through the market-driven redefinition of various global, supranational and national regulatory institutions
1990s	**Deep(ening) neoliberalization** Whether or not they are explicitly market-driven or market-constraining, contextually specific forms of regulatory experimentation and institutional reform are increasingly framed within broadly neoliberalized parameters or "rules of the game" Neoliberalized systems of policy transfer are increasingly mobilized to address the crisis tendencies and contradictions engendered through earlier rounds of market-driven regulatory restructuring Macrospatial institutional frameworks are now recast in neoliberalized terms – market-based parameters are thus increasingly imposed upon subordinate scales of regulatory experimentation		

Figure 10.1 From disarticulated to deep(ening) neoliberalization: a stylized outline

Note: Shaded cells denote the dimensions of regulatory restructuring in which neoliberalization tendencies have been most pronounced. Even in the shaded cells, however, other forms of regulatory restructuring coexist alongside neoliberalization tendencies.

an additional column. This signifies what we view as a tendential, macrospatial shift from *disarticulated* to *deepening* forms of neoliberalization.[36] For purposes of simplicity, we delineate this series of transformations on a decade-by-decade basis, but here too, a more precise specification is required.

As depicted in the first main row of Figure 10.1, disarticulated neoliberalization crystallized during the 1970s, and was based predominantly on place-, territory- and scale-specific forms of market-disciplinary regulatory experimentation. Of course, neoliberal doctrine had emerged during the 1930s and 1940s, when it was mobilized predominantly as a critique of the consolidating Keynesian political-economic order.[37] However, it was not until the early 1970s that real-time experiments in neoliberalization were elaborated, albeit within a largely hostile geoeconomic context defined by late Keynesian regulatory arrangements and strategies of crisis management. While building on transnational intellectual networks (variously derived from Austrian economics, Ordoliberalism, Manchesterism and Chicago School economics), the institutional landscapes with which they collided had been shaped by opposed, state-interventionist and redistributive regulatory agendas – including, most prominently, Keynesianism and national-developmentalism. Conjuncturally specific "sites" for such neoliberalizing regulatory experiments included Pinochet's postnationalization Chile, post-IMF bailout Britain, Reagan's deindustrializing USA, and various crisis-stricken cities and regions across the older capitalist world attempting to attract "footloose" transnational capital investment through various forms of regulatory arbitrage.

During the 1980s, a new frontier of neoliberalization was opened, as a repertoire of neoliberal policy templates began to circulate transnationally and to acquire the status of all-purpose, "silver bullet" solutions to diverse regulatory problems and crisis tendencies (Figure 10.1, row 2). While this occurred in part through a "colonization" of extant, neo-Keynesian policy transfer networks (for instance, within the OECD, the World Bank and the IMF), it also involved the construction of new inter-jurisdictional circuits for the promotion, legitimation and delivery of neoliberal policy templates, mediated through an increasingly influential cadre of experts and "technopols," such as the infamous Chicago Boys. Through a series of trial-and-error maneuvers, manipulations, negotiations and struggles, many of the core neoliberalizing regulatory experiments of the 1970s – such as privatization, financialization, liberalization, workfare and urban entrepreneurialism – subsequently acquired "prototypical" status and became key reference points for subsequent projects of neoliberalization. Neoliberalizing forms of regulatory restructuring were thus now mobilized in diverse policy arenas by national, regional and local institutions not only in North America and western Europe, but also within an uneven, globally dispersed patchwork of postdevelopmental states and post-Communist zones, from Latin America, South Asia and sub-Saharan Africa to Eastern Europe and Asia. In order to facilitate the circulation, imposition and legitimation of market-based reform strategies, new political and extra-jurisdictional relays were constructed. Such fast policy networks were thickened by the late 1980s following the Latin American debt crisis and, subsequently, the collapse of the Soviet bloc.

In this way, the previous formation of disarticulated neoliberalization was transformed into a more tightly networked, transnationally orchestrated formation of mutually recursive, inter-referential policy reform strategies. Under these circumstances, neoliberalization projects no longer appeared as relatively isolated instances of market-disciplinary regulatory experimentation lodged within a hostile political-economic environment. Instead, patterns of reciprocal influence, coordination and exchange were established among neoliberalizing reform programs across otherwise diverse jurisdictional contexts and scales. Increasingly, such programs were recursively interconnected in order to accelerate, deepen and intensify their transnational circulation and implementation.

This deepening formation of neoliberalization was further consolidated during the 1990s, as market-disciplinary reform agendas were institutionalized on a world scale through an array of worldwide, multilateral, multilevel and supranational juridico-institutional reforms and rearrangements. This tendency is depicted in the lowest, fully shaded row of Figure 10.1, which outlines the deepening neoliberalization tendencies within each of the three main dimensions of regulatory restructuring, now including that of rule-regimes and parameterization processes. Prior to this period, postwar regulatory institutions such as the IMF, the World Bank, the GATT and, until the early 1970s, the Bretton Woods agreement, had established a broadly Keynesian framework for worldwide production and trade, a rule-regime that has been variously described as "embedded liberalism" or "progressive constitutionalism."[38] While these arrangements were destabilized during the 1970s and 1980s, it was not until the 1990s that a genuinely post-Keynesian, neoliberalized global rule-regime was consolidated. Through the construction, or market-disciplinary redesign, of global and supranational institutional arrangements, from the

OECD, the World Bank and the IMF to the WTO, the post-Maastricht EU and NAFTA, among others, neoliberalization processes now came to impact and restructure the very geoinstitutional frameworks governing national and subnational forms of regulatory experimentation. This tendentially neoliberalized geoinstitutional configuration is frequently referred to as the "Washington Consensus," but its regulatory elements and political-economic geographies cannot be reduced to a purely US-based hegemonic project. Rather, the new constitutionalism associated with the ascendant neoliberalized global rule-regime has also hinged upon conditionality agreements imposed by the WTO; supranational regulatory bodies and regional free-trade zones such as the EU, NAFTA, CAFTA, APEC and ASEAN; multinational organizations such as the G8 and the OECD; as well as quasi-independent global economic bodies such as the Bank for International Settlements.[39] The consolidation of such neoliberalized global and supranational rule-regimes, which are designed to impose market-disciplinary parameters upon national and subnational institutions and political formations, is arguably one of the most far-reaching consequences of the last four decades of neoliberalizing political-economic reform.

The dynamically mutating geographies of neoliberalization outlined above require critical researchers to track systematically the uneven development and transnational circulation of neoliberalized policy templates, and their variegated, path-dependent and contextually specific impacts, across diverse places, territories and scales. However, while this uneven development of neoliberalization processes has clearly been essential to the global landscape of post-1970s regulatory restructuring, it represents only one layering within a multidimensional process of institutional and spatial creative destruction. For, as the bottom row of Figure 10.1 indicates, neoliberalization processes have also transformed the very geoinstitutional frameworks within which regulatory uneven development unfolds, causing otherwise contextually specific forms of regulatory experimentation and interjurisdictional policy transfer to be canalized along tendentially market-disciplinary pathways. This rule-regime has certainly not diminished or dissolved the endemic path dependency and contextual specificity of neoliberalizing reform projects. But it *has* qualitatively transformed what might be termed the "context of context," that is, the political, institutional and juridical terrain within which locally, regionally and nationally specific pathways of regulatory restructuring are forged. No moving map of neoliberalization can be complete, we would argue, without attention to such macrospatial frameworks and politico-institutional parameters, for they have crucial implications for contextually situated processes of regulatory experimentation, whether market-disciplinary or market-restraining.

Scenarios of counter-neoliberalization

The medium- and long-term trajectories of contemporary patterns of regulatory restructuring are inherently unpredictable; they remain to be fought out through the conjuncturally embedded struggles provoked by the contradictions of earlier rounds of neoliberalization. Nonetheless, the preceding considerations suggest an approach for confronting such questions – one that attends simultaneously to global regulatory shocks and their place-, territory- and scale-specific ramifications, while avoiding dualistic transition models and associated declarations of neoliberalism's demise. Here we sketch several possible scenarios for future trajectories of regulatory restructuring. These are summarized in Figure 10.2 on the next page.

As should be immediately evident, Figure 10.2 is organized in direct parallel to Figure 10.1, except that the positioning of the shaded cells depicting the three dimensions of neoliberalization has now been inverted. The upper row presents each of the three dimensions of neoliberalization; the far left column lists four distinct scenarios for future pathways of regulatory restructuring. As indicated by the shaded pattern in the figure, each of the four scenarios entails a different degree and pattern of neoliberalization, defined in each case with reference to some combination among the three dimensions listed in the top row.

The scenario of *zombie neoliberalization* is depicted in the first row. In this scenario, despite its disruptive, destructive consequences, the global economic crisis of 2008–2009 does not significantly undermine the neoliberalization tendencies of the last four decades.[40] The neoliberalized rule-regime that had been consolidated during the 1990s and early 2000s may be recalibrated or reconstituted to restrain certain forms of financial speculation, but its basic orientation towards imposing market-disciplinary parameters on supranational, national, regional and local economies remains dominant. Orthodox neoliberal ideology is now increasingly called into question, but the political machinery of state-imposed market discipline remains essentially intact; social and economic policy agendas continue to be subordinated to the priority of maintaining investor confidence and a good business

	Dimensions of regulatory restructuring		
	Context-specific forms of regulatory experimentation	Systems of interjurisdictional policy transfer	Rule regimes and parameterization processes
Scenario 1: zombie neo-liberalization	Orthodox neoliberal ideology is severely undermined, but there is a continued neoliberalization of each of the three dimensions of regulatory restructuring, often through technocratic means Crisis tendencies and failures of market-driven regulatory arrangements contribute to a further entrenchment of neoliberalization projects as putative "solutions" to persistent regulatory dilemmas across scales, territories and contexts		
Scenario 2: disarticulated counter-liberalization	Tendential mobilization of market-constraining, redistributive and/or "push-back" regulatory experiments across dispersed, disarticulated contexts at local, regional and national scales	Continued neoliberalization of transnational policy transfer systems and rule-regimes Counter-liberalization projects remain relatively fragmented, disconnected and poorly coordinated – they have not significantly infiltrated multilateral, supranational or global institutional arenas Macrospatial rule-regimes continue to be dominated by market logics, despite persistent critiques from extra-institutional locations and "from below" (e.g., the global justice movement)	
Scenario 3: orchestrated counter-liberalization	Intensified orchestration, mutual recursion and tendential coevolution of market-constraining, redistributive regulatory experiments across increasingly interlinked contexts Thickening, intensification and extension of networks of policy transfer based upon (progressive or regressive) alternatives to market rule		Continued neoliberalization of rule-regimes: counter-liberalization projects may now begin to infiltrate macrospatial rule-making institutions (e.g., the World Bank, the European Union) but do not succeed in reorienting their basic market-driven orientations
Scenario 4: deep socialization	Continued intensification of (progressive or reactionary forms of) market-constraining, redistributive, re-embedding and socializing regulatory experimentation Continued elaboration and transnational consolidation of market-constraining, redistributive and socializing forms of cross-jurisdictional policy transfer Destabilization/dismantling of neoliberalized rule-regimes; construction of alternative, market-constraining, redistributive and socializing frameworks for macrospatial regulatory organization		

Figure 10.2. Counterneoliberalization: future pathways and scenarios

Note: Shaded cells denote the spheres of regulatory restructuring in which neoliberalization would be most pronounced.

climate; and policy agendas such as free trade, privatization, flexible labor markets, and urban territorial competitiveness continue to be taken for granted. In this scenario, as Patrick Bond argues, the most likely outcome of the current geoeconomic crisis is a "relegitimised neoliberalism and imperialism."[41] Consequently, there is a further entrenchment of market-disciplinary regulatory arrangements, a further lubrication and acceleration of neoliberalized systems of inter-jurisdictional policy transfer, and a further entrenchment of neoliberalized forms of regulatory experimentation across contexts.

In a second scenario, *disarticulated counter-neoliberalization,* a neoliberalized rule-regime and associated systems of neoliberal policy transfer persist, but meanwhile the global economic crisis offers new strategic opportunities, albeit within relatively dispersed politico-institutional arenas, for social forces and political alliances concerned to promote market-restraining or market-transcending regulatory strategies. Even prior to the most recent global financial crisis, there had been plenty of organized opposition to neoliberal policies by workers' movements, peasant movements, urban movements, various strands of the anti-globalization movement and, in some cases, by official social democratic, communist and populist political parties.[42] In the wake of the current economic crisis, there may be new strategic openings for such social movements and political organizations to pursue these market-restraining agendas, while in the process disseminating more broadly generative critiques of neoliberalized capitalism. In this scenario, however, such counter-neoliberalizing projects remain relatively disarticulated – that is, they are largely confined to localized, regionalized or, in some cases, nationalized parameters while still being embedded within geoinstitutional contexts that are dominated by market-disciplinary regulatory arrangements and policy-transfer networks. Clearly, the contextually specific regulatory experiments associated with disarticulated forms of counter-neoliberalization are a strategically essential frontier for exploring alternatives to a neoliberalized geoeconomic order. But, unless they are interconnected across places, territories and scales, and linked to institutional recalibrations, such initiatives confront systemic constraints that may undermine their medium- to long-term reproducibility, circumscribing their capacity for interspatial generalization.

Under a third scenario, *orchestrated counter-neoliberalization,* market-restraining forms of regulatory experimentation no longer occur in isolation, as relatively self-enclosed "outposts" of dissent, but are now recursively interconnected across places, territories and scales. Under these conditions, there are sustained efforts to create antisystemic networks of knowledge sharing, policy transfer and institution building among the diverse sites and scales of counter-neoliberal mobilization. This scenario may assume a relatively statist form – for instance, a coalition of neo-Keynesian, social democratic or ecosocialist national, regional or local governments, perhaps within or among key global regions. It may also assume a movement-based form – for instance, that of the World Social Forum, with its project of creating an alternative network of progressive policy transfer, linking activists and policy makers from diverse institutions, sectors and contexts across the world system.[43] Whether state-driven or movement-led, such networks gain significance and become increasingly well-coordinated in this scenario, possibly leading to the development of new, solidaristic and ecologically progressive visions for global economic regulation and interspatial relations. As we have argued, the creation of transnational networks for knowledge and policy transfer was essential to the consolidation, reproduction and evolution of neoliberalization processes during the last four decades, and such networks will surely be equally essential to any project(s) that aspire to destabilize or supersede market-disciplinary georegulatory arrangements. In the scenario of orchestrated counter-neoliberalization, however, the newly established, increasingly coordinated counter-neoliberalizing policy transfer networks still lack the capacity to infiltrate the echelons of global political-economic power, such as multilateral agencies, supranational trading blocs and powerful national governments. Consequently, even though the neoliberalized global rule-regime may be tendentially destabilized, it survives intact.

Can an alternative global rule-regime be forged? Under a fourth scenario, *deep socialization,* the neoliberalized global rule-regime is subjected to greater public scrutiny and popular critique. Subsequently, the inherited institutional frameworks of neoliberalization are infiltrated at all spatial scales by social forces and political alliances oriented towards alternative, market-restraining agendas. These might include capital and exchange controls; debt forgiveness; progressive tax regimes; nonprofit-based, cooperatively run, deglobalized credit schemes; intensified global redistribution; public works investments; and the decommodification and deglobalization of basic social needs such as shelter, water, transportation, health care and utilities. Out of the ashes of the neoliberalized global rule-regime emerges an alternative, social democratic, solidaristic and/or ecosocialist model of global regulation. The substantive political content of such a rule-regime is – indeed, has long been –

a matter of intense debate within the global Left.[44] But one of its core elements would be a radical democratization of decision-making and allocation capacities at all spatial scales – a prospect that stands in stark contrast to the principles of market discipline and corporate rule on which neoliberalization has been based.[45]

It should also be emphasized that not all alternatives to a neoliberalized rule-regime entail this progressive, solidaristic and radically democratic normative vision. As Michael Brie indicates, any number of regressive, even barbaric, scenarios are possible, including various forms of neoconservative, neototalitarian and neofundamentalist reaction, hyperpolarization, neoimperialism, remilitarization and ecological degradation.[46] Basic questions can also be posed regarding the geographical configuration of any future global rule-regime. Will it be increasingly China-centric, as Giovanni Arrighi predicts?[47] Will it be grounded on a multipolar world order, as Samir Amin hopes?[48] Will it entail an archipelago of progressively oriented interurban or intermetropolitan networks, coupled with new forms of worldwide sociospatial exclusion, as Allen J. Scott anticipates?[49] Or will it entail some other, yet-to-be envisioned formation of uneven spatial development and territorial organization? These questions cannot be resolved here; they are intended simply to provoke reflection and debate on the possible medium- to long-term consequences of both actual and possible counter-neoliberalization projects within each of the three dimensions of regulatory restructuring.

Conclusion: On the dialectics of regulatory transformation

This line of analysis is, admittedly, speculative, and much work remains to be done on a more concrete level to operationalize some of the methodological orientations presented here, at once with reference to the last four decades of neoliberalization processes and with reference to the contemporary conjuncture of crisis formation, particularly in relation to the transformation of urban landscapes. In our conceptualization, neoliberalization is not an all-encompassing global totality, but an unevenly developed *pattern* of restructuring that has been produced through a succession of path-dependent collisions between emergent, market-disciplinary regulatory projects and inherited institutional landscapes across places, territories and scales. Consequently, in order to consider the contemporary possibilities for transcending the influence of neoliberalization processes, whether within or among cities, it is necessary to distinguish various dimensions of their spatiotemporal articulation, including regulatory experimentation, inter-jurisdictional systems of policy transfer and global rule-regimes.

Counter-neoliberalizing regulatory experiments remain strategically crucial, especially in the urban context, but in the absence of orchestrated networks of counter-neoliberalizing policy transfer, they are likely to remain confined within particular places, scales and territories. Just as importantly, the construction of counter-neoliberalizing systems of policy transfer, whether among social movements, cities, regions or states, represents a major step forward for progressive activists and policy makers. But, in the absence of a plausible vision for an alternative global rule-regime, such networks are likely to remain interstitial, mere irritants to the global machinery of neoliberalization, rather than transformative threats to its hegemonic influence.

Our intention here, however, is not to prioritize any among these three levels of political engagement – all are strategically essential and have significant structural ramifications. Clearly, in the absence of viable, context-specific regulatory experiments, our imagination for what a global alternative to neoliberalization might look like will be seriously constrained. But just as importantly, if progressive urban analysts and activists focus their efforts predominantly upon locally and regionally specific "alternative economies," and bracket the broader systems of policy transfer and the geoinstitutional frameworks that impose regulatory rules upon such contexts, they will also be seriously limiting their ability to imagine – and to realize – a world in which processes of capital accumulation do not determine the basic conditions of human existence. From our point of view, therefore, "big picture" interpretive frameworks remain as essential as ever, not only for analyzing the sources, expressions and consequences of the contemporary global financial crisis, but also as structural and strategic reference points for mobilizing counter-hegemonic alternatives to currently dominant political-economic practices.[10] Local experiments do matter, and should be taken seriously, but so too should the broader institutional rule-regimes and interlocality policy relays that enframe context-specific pathways of regulatory reorganization. Hence the stress we have placed here on the inter- and extra-local dialectics of regulatory transformation.

Our analysis thus points towards two general conclusions for studies of urban regulatory landscapes and, more generally, for the study of supra-urban regulatory transformations. First, we can anticipate that trajectories of post-2008 regulatory restructuring will be powerfully shaped by the place-, territory- and scale-specific politico-institutional forms in which earlier rounds of neoliberalization were articulated. Second, our discussion suggests that, in the absence of counter-neoliberalizing strategies to fracture, destabilize, reconfigure and ultimately supersede the market-disciplinary rule-regimes that have prevailed globally since the late 1980s, the parameters for alternative forms of national, regional and local regulatory experimentation will continue to be sharply circumscribed.

Notes

1 Elmar Altvater, "Postneoliberalism or Postcapitalism," *Development Dialogue* 51 (Jan 2009): 73–88; Joseph Stiglitz, "The End of Neo-liberalism?," *Project Syndicate,* July 7, 2008, http://www.project-syndicate.org/commentary/the-end-of-neo-liberalism; Immanuel Wallerstein, "The Demise of Neoliberal Globalization," *MRZine,* January 2, 2008, http://mrzine.monthlyreview.org/2008/wallerstein010208.html.

2 Jamie Peck, Nik Theodore and Neil Brenner, "Postneoliberalism and its Malcontents," *Antipode* 41, no. 1 (2009): 94–116.

3 Neil Brenner, Jamie Peck and Nik Theodore, "Variegated Neoliberalization: Geographies, Modalities, Pathways," *Global Networks* 10, no. 2 (2010): 182–222.

4 But see John Clarke, "Living with/in and without Neo-liberalism," *Focaal* 51, no. 1 (2008): 135–47; Alfredo Saad-Filho and Deborah Johnston, eds., *Neoliberalism: A Critical Reader* (London, Pluto Press, 2005); Jamie Peck, "Geography and Public Policy: Constructions of Neoliberalism," *Progress in Human Geography* 28, no. 3 (2004): 392–405; as well as Brenner, Peck and Theodore, "Variegated Neoliberalization."

5 See Chapter 3 in the present volume, as well as Jamie Peck and Adam Tickell, "Neoliberalizing Space," *Antipode* 34, no. 3 (2002): 380–404.

6 James Mittelman, *The Globalization Syndrome* (Princeton, NJ: Princeton University Press, 2000), 4.

7 Ibid.

8 Karl Polanyi, *The Great Transformation* (Boston: Beacon Press, 1944), 140–41.

9 Jamie Peck, "Remaking Laissez-faire," *Progress in Human Geography* 32, no. 1 (2008): 3–43.

10 Philip McMichael, *Development and Social Change* (London: Sage, 1996).

11 Beverly Silver and Giovanni Arrighi, "Polanyi's 'Double Movement': The Belle Époques of British and U.S. Hegemony Compared," *Politics & Society* 31, no. 2 (2003): 325–55.

12 On the need for a "moving map" of neoliberalism, see David Harvey, *A Brief History of Neoliberalism* (Oxford: Oxford University Press, 2005), 88.

13 Bob Jessop, "Liberalism, Neoliberalism and Urban Governance," *Antipode* 34, no. 3 (2002): 452–72; Wolfgang Streeck and Kathleen Thelen, "Introduction: Institutional Change in Advanced Capitalist Economies," in *Beyond Continuity: Institutional Change in Advanced Political Economies,* ed. Wolfgang Streeck and Kathleen Thelen (Oxford: Oxford University Press, 2005), 1–39.

14 See Brenner, Peck and Theodore, "Variegated Neoliberalization."

15 Naomi Klein, *The Shock Doctrine* (New York: Metropolitan Books, 2007); Thomas Friedman, *The World Is Flat* (New York: Farrar, Straus and Giroux, 2005).

16   Harvey, *A Brief History of Neoliberalism;* Silver and Arrighi, "Polanyi's 'Double Movement'"; McMichael, *Development and Social Change;* and Stephen Gill, *Power and Resistance in the New World Order* (London: Palgrave, 2003).

17   Harvey, *A Brief History of Neoliberalism,* 87.

18   Ibid.

19   Brenner, Peck and Theodore, "Variegated Neoliberalization."

20   Ibid. See also Jamie Peck and Nik Theodore, "Variegated Capitalism," *Progress in Human Geography* 31, no. 6 (2007): 731–72; and Neil Brenner, *New State Spaces: Urban Governance and the Rescaling of Statehood* (Oxford: Oxford University Press, 2004).

21   Beth Simmons, Frank Dobbin and Geoffrey Garrett, "Introduction: The Diffusion of Liberalization," in *The Global Diffusion of Markets and Democracy,* ed. Beth Simmons, Frank Dobbin and Geoffrey Garrett (New York: Cambridge University Press, 2008), 1–63.

22   For a sustained critique see Jamie Peck, "Geographies of Policy: From Transfer-Diffusion to Mobility-Mutation," *Progress in Human Geography* 35, no. 6 (2011): 773–97; as well as Jamie Peck and Nik Theodore, *Fast Policy: Experimental Statecraft at the Thresholds of Neoliberalism* (Minneapolis: University of Minnesota Press, 2015).

23   Peck, "Geographies of Policy," 790.

24   The empirical analyses presented by Simmons, Dobbin and Garrett are, in fact, far more institutionally complex and geographically nuanced than their own use of the "diffusion" metaphor would imply. Interestingly, in their more concrete discussions of each of the four mechanisms of diffusion, the authors gesture towards an alternative conceptualization of neoliberalization that emphasizes multilevel, multicentric regulatory reorganization, institutional heterogeneity, policy contestation and path dependency. As such, their account actually breaks substantially with the mainstream diffusionist literature around which they frame their narrative (see Simmons, Dobbin and Garrett, "Introduction: The Diffusion of Liberalization").

25   This set of distinctions may well be applicable to other formations of regulatory restructuring – for instance, to "embedded liberalism" or "progressive constitutionalism" under postwar Fordist-Keynesian capitalism; or to late nineteenth-century classical liberalism. See John Ruggie, "International Regimes, Transactions, and Changes," *International Organization* 36, no. 2 (1982): 379–415; Gill, *Power and Resistance in the New World Order;* McMichael, *Development and Social Change;* and Silver and Arrighi, "Polanyi's 'Double Movement.'" For present purposes, however, these distinctions are mobilized to decipher the dynamics of regulatory restructuring associated with transnational neoliberalization.

26   See Chapter 3 in the present volume, as well as Peck and Tickell, "Neoliberalizing Space."

27   Peck, "Geographies of Policy"; Peck and Theodore, *Fast Policy.*

28   William Tabb, *The Long Default* (New York: Monthly Review Press, 1982).

29   Jamie Peck, *Workfare States* (New York: Guilford, 2001).

30   Johanna Bockman and Gil Eyal, "Eastern Europe as a Laboratory for Economic Knowledge: The Transnational Roots of Neoliberalism," *American Journal of Sociology* 108, no. 2 (2002): 310–52; Yves Dezelay and Bryant Garth, *The Internationalization of Palace Wars* (Chicago: University of Chicago Press, 2002); Jamie Peck and Nik Theodore, "Exporting Workfare/Imposting Welfare-to-Work," *Political Geography* 20, no. 4 (2001): 427–60; Jamie Peck and Nik Theodore, "Recombinant Workfare, across the Americas," *Geoforum* 42, no. 2 (2010): 195–208; Peck and Theodore, *Fast Policy.*

31   Gill, *Power and Resistance.*

32   Amongst the most pertinent questions to be pursued in the empirical investigation of rule-regimes are: (a) What is their scope: how broadly or narrowly do they extend across geographical space?; (b) What is their shape: do they encompass space comprehensively or unevenly? (c) What is their level

of intensity: how tightly or loosely do they circumscribe intrasystemic regulatory dynamics? (d) What is their level of internal variability: what types of politico-institutional differences are possible within them? and (e) What is their degree of malleability: to what extent can they be redefined through political negotiations or struggles?

33 See, for example, Otto Holman, "Asymmetrical Regulation and Multilevel Governance in the European Union," *Review of International Political Economy* 11, no. 4 (2004): 714–35; Adam Harmes, "Neoliberalism and Multilevel Governance," *Review of International Political Economy* 13, no. 5 (2006): 725–49; Richard Peet, *Unholy Trinity: The IMF, World Bank and WTO* (London: Zed, 2003).

34 Harmes, "Neoliberalism and Multilevel Governance," 732.

35 This representation is not intended to deny the presence of market-restraining regulatory projects within the shaded zones of the figure or, for that matter, to suggest that neoliberalization processes did not figure at all within the white quadrants. The goal, rather, is to demarcate analytically the general trajectory of market-disciplinary regulatory restructuring.

36 In a related article, we have analyzed these transformative processes as a shift from the uneven development of neoliberalization to the neoliberalization of uneven regulatory development. See Brenner, Peck and Theodore, "Variegated Neoliberalization."

37 Peck, "Remaking Laissez-faire."

38 Ruggie, "International Regimes"; Gill, *Power and Resistance.*

39 Gill, *Power and Resistance.*

40 Jamie Peck, "Zombie Neoliberalism and the Ambidextrous State," *Theoretical Criminology* 14, no. 1 (2010): 104–10.

41 Patrick Bond, "Realistic Postneoliberalism," *Development Dialogue* 51 (January 2009): 193.

42 Louise Amoore, ed., *The Global Resistance Reader* (New York: Routledge, 2005); Helga Leitner, Eric Sheppard and Jamie Peck, eds., *Contesting Neoliberalism: Urban Frontiers* (New York: Guilford, 2007).

43 Peter Marcuse, "Are Social Forums the Future of Social Movements?," *International Journal of Urban and Regional Research* 29, no. 2 (2005): 417–24.

44 See, for example, André Gorz, *Critique of Economic Reason* (New York: Verso, 1988); John Holloway, *Change the World Without Taking Power* (London: Pluto Press, 2002); Samir Amin, *The World We Wish to See* (New York: Monthly Review Press, 2009).

45 David Harvey, "The Right to the City," *New Left Review*, 53 (September/October 2008): 23–40; Mark Purcell, *Recapturing Democracy* (New York: Routledge, 2008).

46 Michael Brie, "Ways out of the Crisis of Neoliberalism," *Development Dialogue* 51 (January 2009): 15–32.

47 Giovanni Arrighi, *Adam Smith in Beijing* (New York: Verso, 2007).

48 Amin, *The World We Wish to See.*

49 Allen Scott, *Regions and the World Economy* (New York: Oxford University Press, 1998).

50 For an earlier version of this argument, see Jamie Peck and Adam Tickell, "Searching for a New Institutional Fix: The *after-*Fordist Crisis and Global-Local Disorder," in *Post-Fordism: A Reader,* ed. Ash Amin (Oxford: Blackwell, 1994), 280–315.

New Urban Geographies

11 Planetary Urbanization

with Christian Schmid

During the last several decades, the field of urban studies has been animated by an extraordinary outpouring of new ideas regarding the role of cities, urbanism and urbanization processes in ongoing global transformations.[1] Yet, despite these advances, the field continues to be grounded upon a mapping of human settlement space that was more plausible in the late nineteenth and early twentieth centuries than it is today.

The early twentieth century was a period in which large-scale industrial city-regions and suburbanizing zones were being rapidly consolidated around the world in close conjunction with major demographic, socioeconomic and environmental shifts in the erstwhile "countryside." Consequently, across diverse national contexts and linguistic traditions, the field of twentieth-century urban studies defined its theoretical categories and research object through a series of explicit or implied geographical contrasts. Even as debates raged regarding how best to define the specificity of urban life, the latter was universally demarcated in opposition to a purportedly "non-urban" zone, generally classified as "rural." As paradigms for theory and research evolved, labels changed for each term of this supposed urban-rural continuum, and so too did scholars' understandings of how best to conceptualize its basic elements and the nature of their articulation. For instance, the Anglo-American concept of the "suburb" and the French concept of *la banlieue* were introduced and popularized to demarcate further sociospatial differentiations that were occurring inside a rapidly urbanizing field.[2] Nonetheless, the bulk of twentieth-century urban studies rested on the assumption that cities – or, later, "conurbations," "city-regions," "urban regions," "metropolitan regions," "megacities," and "global city-regions" – represented a particular *type* of territory that was qualitatively specific, and thus different from the putatively non-urban spaces that lay beyond their boundaries.

The demarcations separating urban, suburban and rural zones were recognized to shift historically, but the spaces themselves were assumed to remain discreet, distinct, and universal. While paradigmatic disagreements have raged regarding the precise nature of the city and the urban, the entire field has long presupposed the existence of a relatively stable, putatively non-urban realm as a "constitutive outside" for its epistemological and empirical operations. In short, across divergent theoretical and political perspectives, from the Chicago School's interventions in the 1920s and the rise of the neo-Marxist "new urban sociology" and radical geography in the 1970s, to the debates on world cities and global cities in the 1980s and 1990s, the major traditions of twentieth-century urban studies embraced shared, largely uninterrogated geographical assumptions that were rooted in the late nineteenth- and early twentieth-century geohistorical conditions in which this field of study was first established.

During the last thirty years, however, the form of urbanization has been radically reconfigured, a process that has seriously called into question the inherited metageographical assumptions that have long underpinned urban theory and research. Aside from the dramatic spatial and demographic expansion of major megacity regions, which has been widely discussed,[3] recent decades have also witnessed several equally far-reaching implosions and explosions of the urban at all spatial scales. These include:

– *The creation of new scales of urbanization.* Extensively urbanized interdependencies are being consolidated within extremely large, rapidly expanding, polynucleated metropolitan regions around the world to create sprawling urban galaxies that stretch beyond any single metropolitan region and often traverse multiple national boundaries. Such mega-scaled urban constellations have been conceptualized in diverse ways, and the representation of their contours and boundaries remains a focus of considerable research and debate.[4] Their most prominent exemplars include, among others, the classic Gottmannian megalopolis of "BosWash" (Boston–Washington DC) and the "blue banana" encompassing the major urbanized regions in western Europe, but also emergent formations such as "San-San" (San Francisco–San Diego) in California, the Pearl River Delta in south China, the Lagos littoral conurbation in West Africa, as well as several incipient mega-urban regions in Latin America and South Asia.
– *The blurring and rearticulation of urban territories.* Urbanization processes are being regionalized and reterritorialized. Increasingly, former central functions, such as shopping facilities, corporate headquarters, multimodal logistics hubs, research institutions, cultural venues, as well as spectacular architectural forms, dense settlement patterns and other major infrastructural arrangements, are being dispersed

outwards from historic central city cores, into erstwhile suburbanized spaces, among expansive catchments of small- and medium-sized towns, and along major transportation corridors such as superhighways and rail lines.[5]

— *The disintegration of the hinterland.* Around the world, the hinterlands of major cities, metropolitan regions and urban-industrial corridors are being reconfigured as they are operationalized, infrastructuralized and enclosed – whether as back office and warehousing locations, global sweatshops, agro-industrial land-use systems, data storage facilities, energy generation grids, resource extraction zones, fuel depots, waste disposal areas, recreational areas or corridors of connectivity – to facilitate the metabolism of industrial urbanization and its associated planetary urban networks.[6]

— *The end of the wilderness.* In every region of the globe, erstwhile "wilderness" spaces are being transformed and often degraded through the cumulative socioecological consequences of unfettered worldwide urbanization, or are otherwise being converted into bio-enclaves offering "ecosystem services" to offset destructive environmental impacts generated elsewhere. In this way, the world's oceans, alpine regions, the equatorial rainforests, major deserts, the arctic and polar zones, and even the earth's atmosphere itself, are increasingly being interconnected with the rhythms of planetary urbanization at every geographical scale, from the local to the global.[7]

In our view, these geohistorical developments pose a fundamental challenge to the entire field of urban studies as we have inherited it from the twentieth century: its basic epistemological assumptions, categories of analysis, and sites of investigation require a foundational reconceptualization in order to remain relevant to the massive transformations of worldwide sociospatial and environmental organization we are witnessing today. Under contemporary conditions, therefore, the urban can no longer be understood with reference to a particular "type" of settlement space, whether defined as a city, a city-region, a metropolis, a metropolitan region, a megalopolis, an edge city, or otherwise. Consequently, despite its continued pervasiveness in scholarly and political discourse, the category of the "city" has today become thoroughly problematic as an analytical tool. Correspondingly, it is no longer plausible to rely upon the inherited urban/rural (or urban/non-urban) distinction to characterize the variegated differences that obtain between densely agglomerated zones and the less densely settled zones of a region, a territory, a continent or the globe. Today, the urban represents an increasingly worldwide condition in which all political-economic relations, infrastructural geographies and socioenvironmental landscapes are enmeshed.

This situation of *planetary urbanization* means, paradoxically, that even spaces that lie well beyond the traditional city cores and suburban peripheries – from territories of agro-industrial production, zones of industrialized resource extraction and energy generation, "drosscapes" and waste dumps, transoceanic shipping lanes, transcontinental highway and railway networks, and worldwide communications infrastructures to alpine and coastal tourist enclaves, "nature" parks and erstwhile "wilderness" spaces such as the world's oceans, deserts, jungles, mountain ranges, tundra and atmosphere – have become integral parts of a worldwide urban fabric. While the process of agglomeration remains essential to the production of this new worldwide topography,[8] political-economic spaces can no longer be treated as if they were composed of discrete, distinct, bounded and universal types of settlement. In short, in an epoch in which inherited notions of the rural and the countryside appear increasingly to be ideological projections derived from a largely superseded, preindustrial geohistorical formation, our image of the urban must likewise be fundamentally reinvented.

Already four decades ago, Henri Lefebvre put forward the radical hypothesis of the complete urbanization of society, a transformation that required, he argued, a radical epistemological shift from the analysis of urban form to the investigation of *processes* of urbanization.[9] However, a systematic application of this fundamental thesis has yet to be undertaken. Perhaps, in the early twenty-first century, the moment is now ripe for such an undertaking? In our view, the epistemological foundations of urban studies must today be fundamentally transformed.[10] The epistemological shift towards the analysis of planetary urbanization requires new strategies of concrete research and comparative analysis that transcend long-entrenched, city-centric assumptions regarding the appropriate object and parameters for urban research. In close conjunction with such new research strategies, the investigation of planetary urbanization will require major theoretical and conceptual innovations. We need, first of all, new theoretical categories through which to decipher emergent transformations of sociospatial organization, infrastructural configurations, political regulation, social mobilization and everyday life across places, scales, territories and landscapes. To this end, a new conceptual lexicon must be created for identifying the wide variety of urbanization processes that are currently reshaping the planet, and their intense contestation through diverse political strategies and social forces. Lastly, we require adventurous, experimental and boundary-exploding methodological strategies to facilitate the empirical investigation and visualization of these processes. Whether or not a distinct field of "urban" studies can persist amidst such theoretical, conceptual and methodological innovations is a question that remains to be explored in the years and decades ahead.

Notes

1   For critical overviews and assessments, see Saskia Sassen, "New Frontiers Facing Urban Sociology at the Millennium," *British Journal of Sociology* 51, no. 1 (2000): 143–59; Ananya Roy, "The 21st Century Metropolis: New Geographies of Theory," *Regional Studies* 43, no. 6 (2009): 819–30; and Edward Soja, *Postmetropolis: Critical Studies of Cities and Regions* (Cambridge, MA: Blackwell, 2000).

2   Robert Fishman, *Bourgeois Utopias* (New York: Basic Books, 1989); Ann Forsyth, "Defining Suburbs," *Journal of Planning Literature* 27, no. 3 (2012): 270–81.

3   For general overviews, see Tony Champion and Graeme Hugo, eds., *New Forms of Urbanization* (London: Ashgate, 2005); Allen J. Scott, ed., *Global City-Regions* (London: Oxford, 2001); and Ricky Burdett and Deyan Sudjic, eds., *The Endless City* (London: Phaidon, 2006).

4   See, for example, the initial explorations in Peter Hall and Kathryn Pain, eds., *The Polycentric Metropolis* (London: Earthscan, 2006); Arthur Nelson and Robert E. Lang, *Megapolitan America: A New Vision for Understanding America's Metropolitan Geography* (Chicago: APA Planners Press, 2011); and Richard Florida, Tim Gulden and Charlotta Mellander, "The Rise of the Mega-Region," *Cambridge Journal of Regions, Economy and Society* 1, no. 3 (2008): 459–76.

5   Edward Soja, "Regional Urbanization and the End of the Metropolis Era," in *The New Blackwell Companion to the City,* ed. Gary Bridge and Sophie Watson (Oxford: Blackwell, 2011), 679–89; Thomas Sieverts, *Cities without Cities: An Interpretation of the Zwischenstadt* (London: Routledge, 2003); Joel Garreau, *Edge City* (New York: Anchor, 1992).

6   See Chapter 13, in the present volume, as well as Nikos Katsikis, *From Hinterland to Hinterglobe: Urbanization as Geographical Organization,* (Doctor of Design Thesis, Harvard University Graduate School of Design, 2016); Roger Diener, Jacques Herzog, Marcel Meili, Pierre de Meuron and Christian Schmid, *Switzerland: An Urban Portrait,* 4 vols. (Basel: Birkhäuser, 2006); and Alan Berger, *Drosscapes* (Princeton, NJ: Princeton Architectural Press, 2007).

7   See William Boyd, W. Scott Prudham and Rachel Shurman, "Industrial Dynamics and the Problem of Nature," *Society and Natural Resources* 14 (2001): 555–70; Neil Smith, "Nature as Accumulation Strategy," *Socialist Register* 43 (2007): 1–21; Bill McKibben, *The End of Nature* (New York: Random House, 2006). This proposition is also further developed in an exhibition of the Urban Theory Lab, *Operational Landscapes* (Melbourne: Melbourne School of Design, 2015). For further details see: http://urbantheorylab.net/news/operational-landscapes-exhibition-in-melbourne; as well as Louise Dorignon, "And the Urban Exploded," *Society and Space*, online commentaries, accessed on January 20, 2016, http://societyandspace.com/material/commentaries/dorignon/.

8   Soja, *Postmetropolis*. See also, more recently, Allen J. Scott and Michael Storper, "The Nature of Cities: The Scope and Limits of Urban Theory," *International Journal of Urban and Regional Research* 39, no. 1 (2015): 1–15.

9   Henri Lefebvre, *The Urban Revolution*, trans. Robert Bononno (Minneapolis: University of Minnesota Press, 2003). See also Łukasz Stanek, Christian Schmid and Ákos Moravánszky, eds., *Urban Revolution Now: Henri Lefebvre in Social Research and Architecture* (London: Ashgate, 2014).

10 Neil Brenner and Christian Schmid, "Towards a New Epistemology of the Urban," *CITY* 19, no. 2–3 (2015): 151–82. See also Neil Brenner, ed., *Implosions/Explosions: Towards a Study of Planetary Urbanization* (Berlin: Jovis, 2014).

12 Urban Revolution?

The urban question has long been a flashpoint for intense debate among researchers concerned with the nature of cities and urbanization processes. Despite profound differences of methodology, analytical focus and political orientation, the major twentieth-century approaches to this question have taken an entity commonly labeled as *the city* (or some lexical variation thereof) as their primary unit of analysis and site of investigation.

This epistemological focus was canonized in the 1925 mission statement of urban sociology by Chicago School founders Ernest Burgess and Robert Park, laconically but confidently titled *The City*.[1] It subsequently evolved into a self-evident presupposition – so obvious that it did not require explanation – across diverse traditions of urban research. Indeed, despite their significant differences from Chicago School urban sociology, the major strands of mid- to late twentieth-century urban studies have likewise focused their analytical gaze primarily, if not exclusively, on "city-like" (nodal, relatively large, densely populated and self-enclosed) socio-spatial units. Whatever their specific methodological and political agendas, all major approaches to the urban question have either (a) documented the replication of city-like settlement types across larger territories; or (b) used a modifying term – mercantile, industrial, Fordist-Keynesian, post-Keynesian, post-Fordist, global, mega, neoliberal, ordinary, postcolonial and so forth – to demarcate its research terrain as a subset of a putatively more general sociospatial form, "the" city.

Of course, there have been many terms on offer for labeling the city-like unit in question – metropolis, conurbation, city-region, metropolitan area, megalopolis, megapolitan zone, and so forth – and these appropriately reflect the changing boundaries, morphologies and scales of human settlement patterns. And meanwhile, across and within the major traditions of urban theory and research, debates have long raged regarding the origins, dynamics and consequences of city-building, and more generally, regarding the functions of cities in relation to broader political-economic, sociocultural and demographic transformations. But underneath the tumult of disagreement and the relentless series of paradigm shifts, a basic consensus has persisted: the urban *problematique* is thought to be embodied, at core, in *cities* – conceived as settlement types characterized by certain indicative features (such as large populations, density and social diversity) that make them qualitatively distinct from a *non-city* social world (suburban, rural, countryside, wilderness) that is putatively located "beyond" or "outside" them.

In my current research endeavors, and in collaborations with Christian Schmid and others, we are developing a radically different way of conceptualizing the imprint and operationality of urban processes on the planetary landscape. Our aim is to supersede established understandings of the urban as a bounded settlement type or nodal condition in favor of multiscalar, territorially differentiated, morphologically variegated and rigorously processual conceptualizations. Several radical epistemological and methodological consequences flow from such a reorientation. Not least among these is the methodological requirement to supersede the urban/ non-urban divide that has long anchored the entire field of urban theory, research and practice.[2]

Implosions and explosions

Why should the urban/non-urban distinction be transcended, and why now? Clearly, settlement space has long been differentiated by place names, and it seems intuitive to demarcate the terrain of the urban, both historically and today, with reference to the world's great cities – London, New York, Shenzhen, Mumbai, Lagos and so forth. Even amidst the intense volatility associated with accelerated geoeconomic restructuring, such places clearly do still exist, and in fact, their size and strategic economic importance appear to be growing, not diminishing. But what, exactly, are these places, aside from names on a map that have been institutionalized by governments and branded as investment locations by growth coalitions? What distinguishes them qualitatively from other places within and beyond, say, the South East of England and western Europe; the US Northeast and North America; the Pearl River Delta and East Asia; Maharashtra and South Asia; or southern Nigeria and West Africa? Do they contain some special quality that makes them unique – their size, perhaps, or their population density? Their infrastructural outlays? Their strategic centrality in global flows of capital and labor? Or, on the other hand, have the sociospatial relations of urbanism that were once apparently contained within these units now exploded haphazardly beyond them, via the ever thickening commodity chains, infrastructural circuits, migration streams and circulatory-logistical networks that today crisscross the planet?

But, if this is the case, can any city, whatever its size, still be said to have coherent boundaries? Have the everyday social relations, interfirm networks, labor markets, built environments, infrastructural corridors and socioenvironmental footprints associated with such densified clusters now been extended, thickened, superimposed and interwoven to forge what Jean Gottmann once vividly described as an "irregularly colloidal mixture of rural and suburban landscapes" on national, international, continental and even global scales?[3] And, to the degree that all this is indeed occurring, shouldn't the inherited understanding of the urban as a distinctive settlement type be abandoned, or at least be radically reconceptualized?

This was the position advanced by Henri Lefebvre over four decades ago, when he opened his classic text *The Urban Revolution* with the provocative hypothesis that "society has been completely urbanized."[4] Although Lefebvre viewed complete urbanization as a virtual object – an emergent condition rather than an actualized reality – he suggested that the broad outlines of a complete formation of urbanization were already coming into relief during the 1960s in western Europe. They were evidenced, he argued, in the fragmentation and destruction of traditional European cities; in the formation of a large-scale territorial megalopolis stretching from England, Paris and the Ruhr region to Scandinavia; in the extension of logistical, commercial and tourist infrastructures deep into previously remote areas; in the construction of major industrial estates and large-scale housing ensembles in formerly peripheral locations in France, Spain and Italy; in the destruction of quasi-autonomous agrarian communities in formerly rural zones; and in wide-ranging processes of environmental degradation across the continent.[5] When actualized on a planetary scale, Lefebvre suggested, such tendencies would entail a relentless, if fragmentary, interweaving of an urban fabric – a "net of uneven mesh" – across the entire world, including terrestrial surfaces, watersheds and subterranean strata, the oceans and the atmosphere, all of which would be ever more directly operationalized to support the voracious pursuit of capitalist industrial growth.[6] Consequently, rather than conceiving the urban as a distinctive type of settlement space, to be contrasted to suburban, peri-urban, rural, wilderness or other putatively non-urban zones, Lefebvre argued that capitalist urbanization was better understood as an intricately layered web of "varying density, thickness and activity" that was now being stretched across the entire surface of the planet.[7]

In several striking formulations, Lefebvre characterized the planetary generalization of capitalist urbanization as a process of "implosion-explosion," a phrase he introduced to illuminate the mutually recursive links between capitalist forms of agglomeration and broader transformations of territory, landscape and environment. In a provocative, widely discussed diagram presented in the opening chapter of *The Urban Revolution*, Lefebvre used the notion of implosion-explosion to describe the broad constellation of historical-geographical transformations that would, he believed, herald the onset of complete urbanization on a world scale – specifically, "urban concentration, rural exodus, extension of the urban fabric, complete subordination of the agrarian to the urban."

When this "critical point" is reached, Lefebvre suggested, the condition of complete urbanization will no longer be hypothetical – a mere "virtual object" whose tendencies are selectively manifested in particular territories, whether in Europe or elsewhere. It would, rather, have become a basic parameter for planetary social and environmental relations, imposing new constraints upon the use, appropriation and transformation of the worldwide built and unbuilt environment, unleashing potentially catastrophic inequalities, conflicts and dangers, but also harboring new opportunities for the democratic appropriation, occupation and self-management of space at all scales. In the late 1980s, in one of his final texts, Lefebvre suggested that the critical point of complete urbanization – the "urban revolution" of his

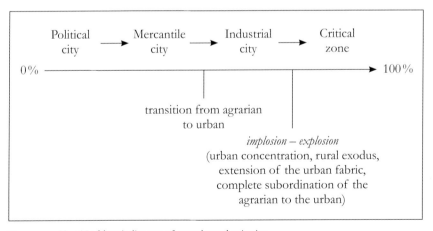

Figure 12.1: Henri Lefebvre's diagram of complete urbanization

earlier book's famous title – had actually been crossed, and thus that a "planetariza-tion of the urban" was now being realized in practice.[8]

Lefebvre's hypothesis has often been misinterpreted or caricatured as a vision of planet-wide densification, akin to the dystopian science fiction fantasies of writers such as H. G. Wells, J. G. Ballard or Isaac Asimov, in which the earth is envisioned as a continuous hardscape, a seamless skein of built-up, metallic or concrete infrastructure. More recently, however, Lefebvre's notion of a worldwide urban revolution has been productively reappropriated by critical urban theorists concerned to decipher some of the emergent patterns and pathways of uneven spatial develop-ment associated with early twenty-first-century urbanization processes.[9] For example, building upon several ideas from Lefebvre, radical urban theorist and critic Andy Merrifield has interpreted planetary urbanization as a simultaneous instrumental-ization and transformation of the erstwhile countryside within an unevenly inte-grated, thickly urbanized mesh of worldwide capitalist accumulation strategies:

> The urbanization of the world is a kind of exteriorization of the inside as well as interiorization of the outside: the urban *unfolds* into the countryside just as the countryside *folds* back into the city […] Yet the fault-lines between these two worlds aren't defined by any simple urban-rural divide, nor by anything North-South; instead, centers and peripheries are *immanent* within the accumulation of capital itself […] Therein centrality creates its own periphery, crisis-ridden on both flanks. The two worlds – center and periphery – exist side-by-side everywhere, cordoned off from one another, everywhere […] Absorbed and obliterated by vaster units, rural places have become an integral part of post-industrial production and financial speculation, swallowed up by an "urban fabric" continually extending its borders, ceaselessly corroding the residue of agrarian life, gobbling up every-thing and everywhere in order to increase surplus value and accumu-late capital.[10]

Within the unevenly woven skein of this planetary-urban condition, the colossal industrial operations, infrastructures and political ecologies of capitalist urbanization are no longer tightly concentrated within dense agglomerations or polycentric metropolitan regions, where they could be counterposed to the putatively "exterior" realm of rural existence – the vast, uninterrogated black box of the "non-city." Instead, the capitalist form of urbanization increasingly crosscuts, engulfs and supersedes the erstwhile urban/rural divide, stretching across and around the earth's entire surface, as well as into both subterranean and atmospheric zones. The resultant operational landscapes are composed of interwoven, planetary-scale socio-technical infrastructures for the key industrial, logistical and metabolic operations that support and sustain urban life – including resource extraction; fuel and energy generation; agro-industrial production and biomass appropriation; transportation and communications; as well as water supply, waste disposal and environmental management.[11] Thus understood, planetary urbanization unevenly intensifies inter-dependence, differentiation and polarization across and among places, territories and scales rather than generalizing "the" city as a universal spatial form or, for that matter, establishing the "borderless world" envisioned by an earlier generation of globalization boosterists.

Clearly, emergent formations of planetary urbanization are blurring, even exploding, long-entrenched spatial borders and ideological dualisms – not only between city and countryside, urban and rural, core and periphery, metropole and colony, society and nature, human and nonhuman, but also between the urban, regional, national and global scales themselves – thereby creating new configurations of a thickly yet unevenly urbanized landscape whose contours are extremely difficult, if not impossible, to theorize, much less to map, on the basis of inherited urban epistemologies. Such developments pose huge challenges for urbanists, planners and designers concerned to decipher, understand and shape emergent patterns and pathways of urbanization. Insofar as the basic conceptual grammar and meta-geographical framework of urban theory are inherited from a period of capitalist territorial organization that has now been largely superseded, it is essential to experiment with alternative "cognitive maps" that can more effectively grasp the rapidly changing geographies of our planetary-urban existence.[12]

Urbanization and its operational landscapes

In proposing and exploring this emergent agenda, our claim is decidedly not, as some urbanists have occasionally asserted, that cities (or, more precisely, zones of agglomeration) are dissolving into a placeless society of global flows, haphazard population dispersal, amorphous infrastructural plasma or borderless connectivity.[13] Nor are we suggesting that population density, interfirm clustering, agglomeration effects or infrastructural concentration – to name just a few of the conditions that are commonly associated with the phenomenon of cityness under modern capitalism – are no longer operationally significant features in contemporary economy and society. On the contrary, the approach proposed here remains fundamentally concerned with agglomeration processes, their changing role in regimes of economic development, and their variegated expressions in diverse morphological, infrastructural, institutional, demographic and spatial configurations – from large-scale urban regions, polycentric metropolitan territories and linear urban corridors to inter-urban networks and worldwide urban hierarchies. But in considering this constellation of issues, our work insists that "cities are just a form of urbanization," and thus that they must be understood as dynamically evolving sites, arenas and outcomes of broader processes of sociospatial and socioecological transformation.[14] In David Harvey's succinct formulation, "the 'thing' we call a 'city' is the outcome of a 'process' that we call 'urbanization'."[15]

But how, precisely, to theorize this *process* of urbanization and its variegated geographies? In fact, this task poses considerable challenges because, even though the concept of urbanization may initially appear to connote dynamic, processual qualities, it has actually long been thoroughly mired in the epistemological assumptions of methodological cityism, in which the city is treated as a self-evident, territorially enclosed and universally replicable sociospatial form. Along with other meta-concepts such as industrialization, modernization, democratization and rationalization, the concept of urbanization has a long history in the modern social and historical sciences, and has generally been used to invoke one of the putatively all-pervasive megaprocesses of modern capitalist social formations. Yet, in most accounts, urbanization refers, *tout court,* to the process of *city* growth: it is circumscribed, by definition, to refer only to the growth of large, and perhaps dense or diverse, settlements, generally in conjunction with some of the other macrotrends of capitalist modernity.

Although its origins may be traced to various strands of nineteenth- and early twentieth-century social theory, this city-centric conceptualization was paradigmatically embodied in American sociologist Kingsley Davis's classic, mid-twentieth-century definition of urbanization as the expansion of the city-based population relative to the total national population. Rather than defining cities in social, morphological or functional terms, Davis famously used arbitrary numerical population thresholds – generally 20,000 or 100,000 – to demarcate their specificity as settlement types.[16] Davis concisely summarized this strictly empirical understanding in the formula: $U = P_c / P_t$ (U = urbanization; P_c = population of cities; and P_t = total national population); and he subsequently devoted several decades of careful empirical research to its international application, eventually producing the first comprehensive worldwide survey of city population sizes.[17]

Davis's mid-century definition is today firmly institutionalized in the data collection systems that are still used by the United Nations (UN) and other international organizations, and it is also still rigidly entrenched within major strands of contemporary social science, urban planning, social policy and public health.[18] Indeed, it is precisely this empiricist, city-centric conceptualization of urbanization that underpins the hugely influential contemporary assertion that more than 50 percent of the world's population has now been relocated from the "countryside" to the "city." Aside from its empirical blind spots, which are considerable given the nonstandardized, nationally specific definitions of settlement types that are intermixed within the UN's global data tables, our work suggests that such a proposition is a quite misleading basis for understanding the contemporary urban revolution. It presupposes an ahistorical, universalizing and population-centric concept of the city that does not adequately grasp the extraordinary scale and diversity of agglomeration processes that are currently unfolding across the major world regions.[19] Just as importantly, the notion of a 50 percent urban threshold fails to illuminate the wide-ranging operations and impacts of urbanization processes that are unfolding far beyond the large centers of agglomeration, including in zones of resource extraction, agro-industrial production, forestry and rangelands, logistics and communications infrastructure, tourism, waste disposal and ecosystem services, which often traverse peripheral, remote and putatively "rural" or "wilderness" locations. While such operational landscapes may not contain the population densities, settlement properties, social fabric and infrastructural equipment that are commonly associated with large population centers, they have long played strategically essential roles in supporting the latter, whether by supplying raw materials, energy, water, food or labor, or through logistics, communications, ecological or waste processing functions.

Today, such landscapes are being comprehensively creatively destroyed through an unprecedented surge of mega-infrastructural investments, land enclosures and large-scale territorial planning strategies, often transnationally coordinated as speculative responses to global commodity price fluctuations, that are designed to support the accelerated growth of agglomerations around the world.[20] Their developmental rhythms and political ecologies are thus being linked more directly to those of the major urban centers via worldwide spatial divisions of labor and financial circuits; and their continuing commodification, enclosure and socioecological degradation are contributing directly to the forms of mass dispossession and displacement that are too often uncritically catalogued or even celebrated in contemporary mainstream urban policy discourse under the rubric of "rural-to-urban" demographic change.[21] Consequently, if we do indeed currently live in an "urban age," this condition must be explored not only with reference to the formation of global cities, metropolitan regions, megacity regions and worldwide interurban networks, but also in relation to the ongoing, if profoundly uneven, speculative and conflictual, operationalization of the entire planet, including terrestrial, subterranean, fluvial, oceanic and atmospheric space, to serve an accelerating, intensifying process of industrial urban development. Insofar as the dominant model of capitalist urbanization continues to be based upon the generalized extraction, production and consumption of fossil fuels, typically from zones located well beyond the major city centers, it is also directly implicated in a form of global ecological plunder that is permanently altering the earth's climate while infiltrating the earth's soils, oceans, rivers and atmosphere with unprecedented levels of pollution and toxic waste.

Rethinking the urban revolution

From this point of view, then, morphologically singular or population-centric approaches to the urban are totalizing, one-sided lenses into the emergent, uneven and variegated dynamics of planetary urbanization. This process cannot be understood adequately either with reference to intensified population growth within the world's largest cities, or simply as a replication of city-like settlement types across the earth's surface. Nor, on the other hand, can traditional notions of the hinterland or the rural adequately capture the processes of sociospatial, financial and ecological transformation through which formerly marginalized or remote spaces are being enclosed, operationalized, infrastructuralized and redesigned to support the continued agglomeration of socioeconomic activities within the world's megacity regions.[22] Instead, a new understanding of urbanization is needed that explores the mutually recursive relations between agglomeration processes and their operational landscapes, including the forms of land-use intensification, infrastructural expansion, sociometabolic transformation, logistical coordination, financial speculation and territorial redesign that accompany the latter at all spatial scales. In this understanding, the development, intensification and worldwide expansion of capitalism produces a vast, intensely variegated terrain of urbanized conditions that include yet progressively extend beyond the zones of agglomeration that have long monopolized the attention of urban researchers. As this erstwhile non-urban realm is increasingly subsumed within and operationalized by an uneven yet world-encompassing process of capitalist urbanization, the nature of the urban must itself be fundamentally reimagined and remapped, both in theory and in practice.

In collaboration with Christian Schmid, my own recent efforts to confront this challenge have hinged upon the core conceptual distinction between concentrated and extended urbanization.[23] *Concentrated urbanization* refers to the perpetual formation and restructuring of relatively dense agglomerations (cities, city-regions, megalopolises, megacity regions and the like). The geographies of concentrated urbanization broadly approximate those of cities, urban regions and metropolitan areas, as traditionally understood and visualized by urban researchers with reference to successive historical formations of urban territorial organization. These geographies are illustrated schematically in Figure 12.2, a map sequence by Constantinos Doxiadis from the 1960s, which depicts the expanding territorial extent of the London agglomeration during the last two centuries. As the figure shows, from a metropolitan perspective, apparent decentralization tendencies often entail a territorial consolidation of the agglomeration process on progressively larger scales across the landscape. Analogous, if place-specific, dynamics of concentrated urbanization have been imprinted on the landscapes of urbanization since the nineteenth century around the world. The vast literatures on urban form in the modern epoch have been essentially focused upon the variegated morphologies of concentrated urbanization across historical periods and geographical contexts.[24]

By contrast, *extended urbanization* denotes the production and perpetual reorganization of broader operational landscapes – including infrastructures for resource extraction, logistics and communication, energy and food production, water provision and management, waste disposal and environmental planning – that at once support and result from the dynamics of urban agglomeration.[25] Although it has

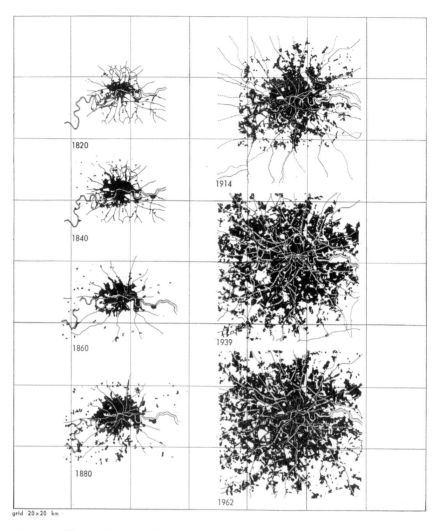

grid 20 x 20 km

Figure 12.2: The expanding scale of concentrated urbanization: London, 1820–1962, by Constantinos Doxiadis

largely been ignored or "black-boxed" by urban theorists under the rubric of the rural, the countryside and the hinterland – the proverbial supply regions and waste dumps for cities – this dynamically mutating realm of drosscapes, *terrains vagues,* in-between cities (*Zwischenstädte*), metapolis territories, horizontal urbanization, holey planes, *desakota* regions, quiet zones, fallow lands, liminal landscapes and un-building (*Abbau*) has long been integral to the urban process under capitalism.[26] During the last few decades, such landscapes of extended urbanization have become increasingly strategic in economic, geopolitical and ecological terms.[27] Quite strikingly, such landscapes have also recently acquired an unprecedented significance for designers concerned to address diverse social, architectural, infrastructural and material conditions that lie far beyond the confines of traditionally defined cities.[28] For present purposes, a visualization of worldwide transportation infrastructures (road, rail and marine transport) by Nikos Katsikis offers one among many possible representational strategies for interpreting such variegated connections and their systemic importance to the dynamics of planetary urbanization (Figure 12.3).

We believe that the distinction between concentrated and extended urbanization can provide a fruitful analytical basis for reconceptualizing the rapidly mutating geographies of the urban under contemporary conditions. It can also offer a perspective from which to explore Lefebvre's classic hypothesis of an urban revolution, both historically and in the contemporary period. From the point of view of concentrated urbanization, the urban revolution involves the spatial expansion and increasing strategic centrality of major metropolitan regions, as postulated by global city theorists and other, more recent commentators on the role of cities in economic life.[29] However, consideration of the *problematique* of extended urbanization introduces a more spatially variegated, territorially differentiated and multiscalar conceptualization of the Lefebvrian notion of an urban revolution, one that we consider essential for interpreting, investigating and visualizing emergent forms of planetary urbanization.

From this perspective, the contemporary urban revolution also entails the consolidation of a new relationship between urban agglomerations and their operational landscapes across vast zones of the world economy. The latter no longer serve simply as resource supply zones, "lagging" regions, staging grounds or waste dumps for city growth – the realms of "un-building" (*Abbau*) and planetary ecological degradation which Lewis Mumford observed with considerable alarm in the early

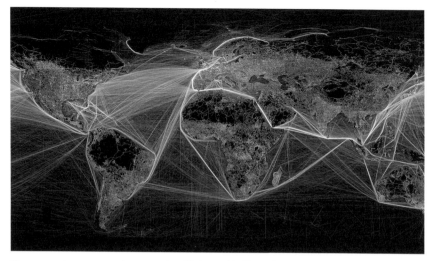

Figure 12.3: An emergent planetary urban fabric: worldwide road, rail and marine transport networks, by Nikos Katsikis

1960s.[30] Instead, the operational landscapes of extended urbanization are today themselves being more systematically enclosed, industrialized, infrastructuralized, financialized, interconnected and managed to serve specific functional purposes within the broader spatial divisions of labor and volatile geopolitical ecologies of a rapidly evolving planetary-urban system. This ongoing transformation of historically inherited hinterlands into heavily capitalized, financialized, transnationalized, geopolitically strategic and ecologically monitored operational landscapes represents one of the distinctive tendencies of the planetary urban revolution that is currently unfolding.[31]

Envisioning the planetary-urban

Despite its epistemologically and cartographically explosive message, the iconography used in the cover design of Lefebvre's *The Urban Revolution* – both in its original 1970 version and in its 2003 English translation – is strikingly conventional (Figure 12.4).

henri lefebvre
la révolution urbaine

◆ idées/gallimard

Henri Lefebvre

The Urban Revolution

Foreword by Neil Smith
Translated by Robert Bononno

Figure 12.4: Cover iconography, Henri Lefebvre's *The Urban Revolution* (1970 and 2003)

In the original French version, a classic image of urban density is adopted – a collage of large, iconic buildings pierced by an elevated subway train. In the more recent English translation, a similar, if more readily recognizable, iconography is chosen: one of Haussmann's great Parisian boulevards, forming a knife-like cut through the fabric of a dense urban landscape that stretches endlessly into the horizon.

Especially in light of my emphasis on the multifaceted, variegated and volatile character of emergent landscapes of planetary urbanization, it would clearly be ill-advised to attempt to represent them through any single, putatively iconic image, genre or cartographic method. Nonetheless, insofar as inherited approaches to the urban rest upon visual ideologies – for instance, of verticality, density and spatial boundedness – that naturalize "the" city as a unit of social life, the elaboration of critically reflexive counter-visualizations may provide an important basis for unsettling and ultimately superseding the latter, and thus for developing alternative interpretations of emergent patterns and pathways of urbanization. Among the many counter-visualization strategies that could be pursued in relation to such an endeavor, recent photographic work on colossal landscapes of industrialized resource extraction – for instance, by Edward Burtynsky, Garth Lenz and David Maisel – offers a particularly powerful set of interventions.[32]

In many of the most widely circulated images of such landscapes, the specter of worldwide ecological destruction is depicted with such richly aestheticized abstraction that some commentators have described this genre using phrases such as the "toxic sublime" or the "apocalyptic sublime."[33] In one notable series of aerial photographs of the Canadian Tar Sands by Garth Lenz (Figure 12.5), we are taken far from the large, dense, vertical landscapes of cityness, into a zone in which the earth's surface has been layered with a viscous sludge, traversed by muddy roads twisting around ponds filled with huge accumulations of toxic waste. Such images thus offer a dramatic, disturbing and unsettling visualization of the socially and ecologically disastrous operational landscapes of extended urbanization – Lefebvre might have described them as a form of "terricide" – that are being forged at a truly colossal scale to support and reproduce urban life under early twenty-first-century capitalism.[34]

Can Lenz's foreboding images of the Tar Sands offer a critical perspective through which to decipher our planetary-urban condition? If Haussmann's geometrical boulevards offered an iconic symbol for an earlier, city-centric formation of urban expansion, in which city dwellers were evicted from the center to create a built environment for urbanizing capital, perhaps Lenz's aerial photographs of industrialized terricide may provide an equally evocative metaphor for the worldwide form of *neo*-Haussmannization that has been unleashed under planetary urbanization.[35] The evictions, enclosures and dispossessions continue, but now on the scale of the entire planet, well beyond the inherited built environments of earlier rounds of urban development, leading to unprecedented social devastation, toxic contamination and environmental destruction. As Andy Merrifield explains:

> Baron Haussmann tore into central Paris, into its old neighborhoods and poor populations, dispatching the latter to the periphery while speculating on the center; the built urban form became simultaneously a property machine and a means to divide and rule; today,

Figure 12.5: Industrialized landscapes of resource extraction: Tar Sands, by Garth Lenz

neo-Haussmannization, in a similar process that integrates financial, corporate and state interests, tears into the globe, sequesters land through forcible slum clearance and eminent domain, valorizing it while banishing former residents to the global hinterlands of post-industrial malaise.[36]

It seems as urgent as ever, under these conditions, to develop new theories, analyses and cartographies that situate such operational landscapes – their land-use systems and infrastructural configurations; their labor regimes and property relations; their forms of governance; their ecological impacts; and their rapidly changing social fabrics – quite centrally within our understanding of the contemporary global urban condition. The epistemological perspectives proposed in our work on planetary urbanization are advanced in the hope that a new understanding of the urban may prove useful to ongoing struggles – *against* neo-Haussmannization, territorial enclosure, market fundamentalism and global ecological plunder; and *for* a different model of urbanization, an *alter*-urbanization, oriented towards the collective reappropriation and democratic management of "planetary space as the work of the human species."[37]

Notes

1   Robert Park and Ernest Burgess, eds., *The City* (Chicago: University of Chicago Press, 1967 [1925]).

2   For a detailed elaboration, see Neil Brenner and Christian Schmid, "Towards a New Epistemology of the Urban," *CITY* 19, no. 2–3 (2015): 151–82, as well as Neil Brenner, ed., *Implosions/Explosions: Towards a Study of Planetary Urbanization* (Berlin: Jovis, 2014).

3   Jean Gottmann, *Megalopolis* (New York: The Twentieth Century Fund, 1961), 5.

4   Henri Lefebvre, *The Urban Revolution,* trans. Robert Bononno (Minneapolis: University of Minnesota Press, 2003), 1.

5   See Henri Lefebvre, "The Right to the City," in *Writings on Cities,* ed. and trans. Eleonore Kofman and Elizabeth Lebas (Cambridge, MA: Blackwell, 1996), 69–72; Lefebvre, *Urban Revolution,* 1–23; Henri Lefebvre, "Reflections on the Politics of Space" and "The Worldwide Experience," in *State, Space, World: Selected Writings,* ed. Neil Brenner and Stuart Elden (Minneapolis: University of Minnesota Press, 2009), 190, 278.

6   Lefebvre, "Right to the City," 71; Lefebvre, *Urban Revolution,* 1–23.

7   Lefebvre, *Urban Revolution,* 4.

8   Henri Lefebvre, "Dissolving City, Planetary Metamorphosis," in Brenner, *Implosions/Explosions,* 566–71. The original essay was published in *Le Monde diplomatique* in May 1989 under the title, "Quand la ville se perd dans une métamorphose planétaire."

9   See, for example, Brenner, *Implosions/Explosions;* Łukasz Stanek, Christian Schmid and Ákos Moravánszky, eds., *Urban Revolution Now: Henri Lefebvre in Social Research and Architecture* (London: Ashgate, 2014); David Madden, "City Becoming World: Nancy and Lefebvre on Global Urbanization," *Environment and Planning D: Society and Space* 30, no. 5 (2012): 772–87; and David Harvey, "Lefebvre's Vision," in *Rebel Cities: From the Right to the City to the Urban Revolution* (London: Verso, 2013), ix–xviii.

10 Andy Merrifield, "The Right to the City and Beyond: Notes on a Lefebvrian Conceptualization," in Brenner, 523–32.

11 On the metabolic dimensions of urbanization processes, see Erik Swyngedouw, "Metabolic Urbanization: The Making of Cyborg Cities," in *In the Nature of Cities: Urban Political Ecology and the Politics of Urban Metabolism,* ed. Nik Heynen, Maria Kaika and Erik Swyngedouw (New York: Routledge, 2006), 21–40; and Daniel Ibañez and Nikos Katsikis, eds., *New Geographies 6: Grounding Metabolism* (Graduate School of Design, Harvard University, 2014). On the centrality of primary commodity production to world capitalist development, see Jason W. Moore, *Capitalism in the Web of Life* (New York: Verso, 2015); and Stephen G. Bunker and Paul S. Ciccantell, *Globalization and the Race for Resources* (Baltimore: Johns Hopkins University Press, 2005).

12 See Brenner and Schmid, "Towards a New Epistemology of the Urban"; as well as Jennifer Robinson, "New Geographies of Theorizing the Urban: Putting Comparison to World for Global Urban Studies," in *The Routledge Handbook on Cities of the Global South,* ed. Susan Parnell and Sophie Oldfield (New York: Routledge, 2014), 57–70; and Ananya Roy, "Worlding the South: Towards a Post-Colonial Urban Theory," in Parnell and Oldfield, *The Routledge Handbook on Cities of the Global South,* 9–20.

The concept of cognitive mapping is developed, via a reading of Kevin Lynch, in Frederic Jameson, "Cognitive Mapping," in *Marxism and the Interpretation of Culture,* ed. Lawrence Grossberg and Cary Nelson (Chicago: University of Illinois Press, 1992), 347–57.

13   The locus classicus of such arguments is Melvin Webber, "The Post-City Age," *Daedalus* 94, no. 4 (1968): 1091–110. For a critical review of more recent versions, see Stephen Graham, "The End of Geography of the Explosion of Place: Conceptualizing Space, Place and Information Technology," *Progress in Human Geography* 22, no. 2 (1998): 165–85.

14   Matthew Gandy, "Where Does the City End?," in Brenner, *Implosions/Explosions,* 86.

15   David Harvey, "Cities or Urbanization?," in Brenner, *Implosions/Explosions,* 61.

16   Kingsley Davis, "The Origins and Growth of Urbanization in the World," *American Journal of Sociology,* 60, no. 5 (1955): 429–37.

17   Kingsley Davis, *World Urbanization: 1950–1970, Volume II: Analysis of Trends, Relationships and Development,* Population Series no. 9 (Berkeley: Institute of International Studies, University of California, 1972); Kingsley Davis, *World Urbanization: 1950–1970, Volume I: Basic Data for Cities, Countries, and Regions,* Population Monograph Series no. 4 (Berkeley: Institute of International Studies, University of California, 1969).

18   See Neil Brenner and Christian Schmid, "The 'Urban Age' in Question," *International Journal of Urban and Regional Research,* 38, no. 3 (2015): 731–55.

19   See Christian Schmid, "Specificity and Urbanization: A Theoretical Outlook," in *The Inevitable Specificity of Cities,* ed. ETH Studio Basel (Zurich: Lars Müller Publishers, 2014), 282–97; Ananya Roy, "The 21st Century Metropolis: New Geographies of Theory," *Regional Studies* 43, no. 6 (2009): 819–30; and Robinson, "New Geographies of Theorizing the Urban."

20   See Martín Arboleda, "Financialization, Totality and Planetary Urbanization in the Chilean Andes," *Geoforum* 67 (2015): 4–13; Martín Arboleda, "In the Nature of the Non-City: Expanded Infrastructural Networks and the Political Ecology of Planetary Urbanisation," *Antipode* 48, no. 2 (2016): 233–51; and Mazen Labban, "Deterritorializing Extraction: Bioaccumulation and the Planetary Mine," *Annals of the Association of American Geographers* 104, no. 3 (2014): 560–76.

21   See Max Ajl, "The Hypertrophic City versus the Planet of Fields," in Brenner, *Implosions/Explosions,* 533–50; Timothy W. Luke, "Global Cities versus 'global cities': Rethinking Contemporary Urbanism as Public Ecology," *Studies in Political Economy* 70 (Spring 2003): 11–33; and Luke, "Developing Planetarian Accountancy: Fabricating Nature as Stock, Service and System for Green Governmentality," *Nature, Knowledge and Negation* 26 (2009), 129–59.

22   See Chapter 13 in the present volume.

23   For further elaborations, see Brenner and Schmid, "Towards a New Epistemology of the Urban"; Brenner and Schmid, "The 'Urban Age' in Question"; and the contributions to Brenner, *Implosions/Explosions.*

24   See, for example, Edward Soja's classic synthesis in *Postmetropolis: Critical Studies of Cities and Regions* (Malden, MA.: Blackwell, 2000). For a comprehensive historical overview, see Paul Bairoch, *Cities and Economic Development: From the Dawn of History to the Present,* trans. Christopher Braider (Chicago: University of Chicago Press, 1988).

25   The concept of extended urbanization was first introduced by Roberto-Luis Monte-Mór in his studies of the production of industrialized urban spaces and networks in the Brazilian Amazon. The term has subsequently also recently been used by Edward Soja in his studies of regional urbanization; another variation was developed by Terry McGee in his pioneering research on *desakota* regions in Southeast Asia. The key texts on extended urbanization by these and several other authors are included in Brenner, *Implosions/Explosions.* While we have been strongly inspired by these interventions,

we are using the notion of extended urbanization in the specific terms defined here. This usage is most consistent with that of Monte-Mór, but embeds his earlier conceptualization within our own developing epistemological and conceptual framework.

26　Several of these terms are discussed and elaborated in Alan Berger, *Drosscape: Wasting Land in Urban America* (Princeton, NJ: Princeton Architectural Press, 2006); Patrick Barron and Manuela Mariani, eds., *Terrain Vague: Interstices and the Edge of the Pale* (New York: Routledge, 2013); Thomas Sieverts, *Cities without Cities: an Interpretation of the Zwischenstadt* (London: Routledge, 2003); François Ascher, *Métapolis ou l'avenir des villes* (Paris: Editions Odile Jacob, 1995); Lars Lerup, *After the City* (Cambridge, MA: MIT Press, 2001); Norton Ginsburg, Bruce Koppel and T. G. McGee, eds., *The Extended Metropolis: Settlement Transition in Asia* (Honolulu: University of Hawaii Press, 1991); and Roger Diener, Jacques Herzog, Marcel Meili, Pierre de Meuron and Christian Schmid, *Switzerland: An Urban Portrait,* 4 vols., ed., ETH Studio Basel (Basel: Birkhäuser, 2006). On the metabolic and ecological preconditions for capitalist industrial development, see also Moore, *Capitalism in the Web of Life;* and Bunker and Ciccantell, *Globalization and the Race for Resources.*

27　See Arboleda, "In the Nature of the Non-City"; Labban, "Deterritorializing Extraction"; Luke, "Global Cities vs. 'global cities'"; and Chapter 13 in the present volume.

28　The growing concern of designers with the operational territories of urbanization is paradigmatically illustrated in, among other examples, the work of OMA on future scenarios for energy infrastructures in the North Sea (http://www.oma.com/projects/2008/zeekracht/), the projects of Lateral Office in the Arctic (http://lateraloffice.com/NEXT-NORTH-2011), Keller Easterling's writings on the geopolitics of subtraction (https://www.domusweb.it/en/architecture/2012/12/05/the-geopolitics-of-subtraction.html) and the various interventions of Neeraj Bhatia, Felipe Correa, Ana María Durán Calisto and others on oil and resource extraction urbanisms (see, for example, http://www.petropia.org/publications/articles/). See also Charles Waldheim and Alan Berger, "Logistics Landscape," *Landscape Journal* 27 (2008): 2–8; as well as Neeraj Bhatia, "The Cheap Frontier: Operationalizing New Natures in the Central Valley," *Scenario Journal* 5, Fall (2015): http://scenariojournal.com/article/the-cheap-frontier/.

29　See, for example, Michael Storper, *The Regional World* (New York: Guilford, 1996); Allen J. Scott ed., *Global City-Regions* (New York: Oxford University Press, 2001), Peter J. Taylor, *World City Network: A Global Urban Analysis* (New York: Routledge, 2005); Edward Glaeser, *Triumph of the City* (New York: Trantor, 2011). For a strong critique, see Brendan Gleeson, "The Urban Age: Paradox and Prospect," *Urban Studies* 49, no. 5 (2012): 931–43.

30　Lewis Mumford, "Mechanization and Abbau," in *The City in History* (New York: Harcourt, Brace, 1961), 450–52.

31　This transformation requires further collaborative research among urbanists, landscape architects and scholars of industrial extraction, agriculture, logistics, forestry and political ecology. For recent useful inroads towards such a dialogue, see Arboleda, "Financialization, Totality and Planetary Urbanization"; Labban, "Deterritorializing Extraction"; Luke, "Global Cities vs. 'global cities'"; and Luke, "Developing Planetarian Accountancy."

32　For a useful overview of such work, with specific reference to the photography of Burtynsky, see Merle Patchett and Andriko Lozowy, "Reframing the Canadian Oil Sands," *Imaginations: Journal of Cross-Cultural Image Studies* 3, no. 2 (2012); 140–69. A powerful presentation of David Maisel's work, along with critical commentary, can be found in his remarkable book *Black Maps: American Landscape and the Apocalyptic Sublime* (Göttingen: Steidl, 2013). A good overview of Lenz's work can be found in Becky Harlan, "Garth Lenz's Abstract Energyscapes," *National Geographic Online,* August 29, 2014: http://proof.nationalgeographic.com/2014/08/29/garth-lenzs-abstract-energyscapes/.

33 For discussion, see Patchett and Lozowy, "Reframing the Canadian Oil Sands."

34 On Lefebvre's notion of terricide, see Stuart Elden, "Terricide: Lefebvre, Geopolitics and the Killing of the Earth," Department of Politics, University of Warwick, unpublished manuscript, 2013.

35 On "neo-Haussmannization," see Merrifield, "The Right to the City and Beyond."

36 Ibid., 526.

37 Henri Lefebvre, "The Worldwide and the Planetary," in *State, Space, World: Selected Essays,* ed. Neil Brenner and Stuart Elden (Minneapolis: University of Minnesota Press, 2009), 206.

13 The Hinterland, Urbanized?

The lecture (it might also be a scholarly article, a research report, a policy brief, a design proposal, a strategic plan, or a grant application) opens with a familiar reminder of an apparently unassailable fact, delivered from a trusted source: in 2007 (or was it 2003?), United Nations (UN) statisticians had determined that more than 50 percent of the world's population was now living within cities. Anticipated by urban demographers since the 1950s, a momentous demographic threshold had been crossed: for the first time in history, humanity had become an urban species. Having thus framed the urban *problematique* as a world-historical, rural-to-urban demographic shift, and securely anchored it through the obligatory citation to a UN-Habitat or UN Population Division data table, more specific claims are then advanced – for instance, about the need to promote competitiveness, innovation, creativity, smart technology, good governance, sustainable infrastructure or ecological resilience within cities; about the urgency of addressing a range of urban "problems" in the spheres of economic development, public participation, housing, transportation, security, public health, environmental management and so forth; or about cities' potential to incubate solutions to proliferating planetary crises, whether geoeconomic, geopolitical or environmental.

Although its lineages can be traced to efforts to decipher the accelerated industrialization of capital, proletarianization of labor and infrastructuralization of landscape in the "paleotechnic cities" (Lewis Mumford) of nineteenth-century Euro-America, the notion of an urbanizing world has today become a seemingly ubiquitous interpretive frame. Much like the catch-all buzzword of "globalization" in the 1990s, the trope of a majority-urban world – an "urban age" – now serves as an epistemological foundation on which a huge array of conditions, dilemmas, conflicts and crises around the world are being analyzed, and in relation to which diverse public, private and nongovernmental modes of spatial intervention are being mobilized.[1]

Because the starting point of the lecture is so familiar, you ignore the author's framing gesture. Your thoughts drift as you wait for the real argument to begin – about the role of cities in current global transformations, about the ongoing restructuring of cities, and about strategic responses to the latter. The presentation soon turns to these questions, and a debate ensues – about cities. These, everyone appears to agree, represent the most elementary spatial units of the contemporary urban age. To what else could the concept of the urban possibly refer?

The urbanization *problematique*

All forms of knowledge and action presuppose interpretive frameworks that permit us to conceptualize and evaluate the social world, to render intelligible our place in the web of life, and to decipher the flow of change in which we are caught up and to which we contribute. Certain elements of these frameworks are reflexively grasped: we are consciously aware of their role in structuring value, experience and action; and we may, at times, subject them to critical examination, adjustment or even reinvention, especially during periods of accelerated restructuring, divisive social conflict and political turmoil. However, some aspects of these frameworks generally remain hidden from view; they intimately structure our everyday assumptions, interpretations and practices, but without themselves being accessible for reflexive interrogation. Only in retrospect, when they are being destabilized or superseded, can we more fully grasp the pervasive role of such naturalized *dispostifs* of understanding in the construction of our modes of social life.

To what degree do contemporary forms of global urban knowledge, embodied in the relentless repetition of the claim that we live in a majority-urban world, represent such a *dispostif* of unreflexively presupposed interpretive assumptions – a form, in short, of "spatial ideology" (Henri Lefebvre)?[2] Clearly, as Ross Exo Adams has recently argued, the notion of urbanization has long been used in strikingly atheoretical ways, as if it were a purely descriptive, empirical basis for referencing a natural, quasi-ontological tendency of human spatial organization, one that has existed for millennia, but which is said to have been accelerating dramatically during the last 150 years:

> Much like the weather, urbanization is something that exists "out there," a condition far too "complex" to present itself as an object to be examined in its own right and thus something which can only be mapped, monitored, compared and catalogued […] It thus becomes a term used to organize an ever-expanding set of "emerging" problems

whose analysis is limited to the particular elements that compose whatever happens to be emerging and the technologies used to register them, leaving the very milieu itself to, once again, remain a neutral background of human existence. At once transhistorical and bound to the immediate present, almost all depictions of the urban treat it as a capacity inherent to the human condition with which we organize ourselves in space.[3]

Despite the forceful warnings of Chicago School urban sociologists such as Louis Wirth against such analytically insubstantial conceptions already in the 1930s, this empiricist, naturalistic and quasi-environmental understanding of urbanization persisted in various forms throughout the twentieth century. In more recent decades, rather than being discredited, naturalistic models of urbanization have acquired a powerful new lease on life in the science of "big data," which tends to regard urban density as a condition that is basically akin to that of a closed biological system – subject to scientific "laws," predictable, and thus, technically programmable.[4]

Contemporary UN declarations of a majority-urban world, and most major strands of mainstream global urban policy, planning and design discourse, likewise grasp the phenomenon of urbanization via some version of this naturalistic, ahistorical and empiricist *dispositif*.[5] Here, urbanization is assumed to entail the simultaneous growth and spatial diffusion of cities, conceived as generic, universally replicable types of human settlement. Thus understood, the contemporary urban age represents an aggregation of various interconnected demographic and socioeconomic trends that have cumulatively increased the populations of large, dense urban centers. In this way, the urban age metanarrative has come to serve as a framework not only of interpretation, but of *justification*, for a huge, multiscalar assortment of spatial interventions designed to promote and perpetuate what geographer Terry McGee classically labelled "city dominance."[6] Around the world, the shared goal of such urbanization strategies is building the "hypertrophic city" (Max Ajl) – whether by densifying and extending extant megacity areas; by creating new urban settlement zones *ex nihilo* in pockets of the erstwhile countryside or along major transportation corridors; or by orchestrating rural-to-urban migration flows through a noxious cocktail of structural adjustment programs, land grabbing, agro-industrial consolidation, ecological plunder, and other forms of accumulation by dispossession that degrade inherited modes of social reproduction outside the large population centers.[7]

The vision of urbanization as *city* growth is, however, anything but self-evident. On a basic empirical level, the limitations of the UN's census-based data on urbanization are well-known and have long been widely discussed among critical demographers.[8] The simple but still apparently intractable problem, to which sociologist Kingsley Davis already devoted extensive critical attention in the 1950s, is that each national census bureau uses its own criteria for measuring urban conditions, leading to serious, persistent and seemingly absurd inconsistencies in comparative international data on urbanization.[9] In the current decade, for example, among those countries that demarcate urban settlement types based on a population size threshold (101 out of 232 UN member states), the criterion ranges from 200 to 50,000; no less than 23 countries opt for a threshold of 2,000, but 21 others specify the cutoff at 5,000.[10] A host of comparability problems immediately follow, since "urban" localities in one national jurisdiction may have little in common with those that are classified with the same label elsewhere. The use of various combinations of additional criteria in the other 131 member states – administrative, density-based, infrastructural and socioeconomic – adds several further layers of confusion to an already exceedingly heterogeneous international data set. Should certain administrative areas automatically be classified as urban? What population density criterion, if any, is appropriate? Should levels of non-agricultural employment figure into the definition of urban areas (as they do in India, albeit only for male residents)? In short, even this brief glimpse into the UN's data tables reveals that the notion of a majority-urban world is hardly a self-evident fact. It is, rather, a statistical *artifact* constructed through a rather crude aggregation of national census data derived from chronically inconsistent, systematically incompatible definitions of the phenomenon being measured.

Interiorizing the constitutive outside

Here arises a deeper theoretical problem with contemporary urban age discourse, and with the naturalized *dispositif* of urbanization from which it is derived. Even if the specificity of "city" growth relative to other forms of demographic, socioeconomic and spatial restructuring could somehow be coherently delineated (for instance, through consistently applied, geospatially enhanced indicators for agglomeration),[11] the question still remains: how to delineate the process of urbanization in *conceptual* terms? Despite its pervasive representation as a neutral, generic and objective background parameter within which spatial relations are situated, the process of urbanization must itself be subjected to careful theoretical scrutiny and critical interrogation.[12] Doing so reveals at least two major epistemological fissures – logically unresolvable yet perpetually recurrent analytical problems – within the hegemonic *dispositif* of urban knowledge.

First, in the mainstream interpretive framework, urbanization is said to entail the universal diffusion of "cities" as the elementary units of human settlement. As is widely recognized, however, these supposedly universal units have assumed diverse morphological forms; they have been organized at a range of spatial scales; they have been mediated through a broad array of institutional, political, social, military and environmental forces; and they have been differentially articulated to their surrounding territories, landscapes and ecologies, as well as to other, more distant population centers. Given the *de facto* heterogeneity of agglomeration patterns, can a universal notion of "the" city still be maintained? And, if we do reject the hegemonic equation of cityness with singularity, must we not also abandon the vision of urbanization as a universal process of spatial diffusion? Instead, heterogeneity, differentiation and variegation would have to be recognized, not simply as unstructured empirical complexity, but as intrinsic, systemically produced properties of the urbanization process itself.[13]

Second, in the hegemonic *dispositif*, urbanization is defined as the growth of "cities," which are in turn conceived as spatially bounded settlement units. This conceptual equation (urbanization = city growth), coupled with the equally pervasive assumption of spatial boundedness, logically requires differentiating the city-like units in question from a putatively non-urban realm located outside them. However, the demarcation of a coherent urban/non-urban divide at any spatial scale has proven thoroughly problematic, particularly since the accelerated worldwide industrialization of capital in the nineteenth century. Indeed, within the mainstream urban *dispositif,* the delineation of a non-urban "constitutive outside" is at once *necessary* – since it is only on this basis that cities' distinctiveness as such can be demarcated; and *impossible* – since (a) there are no standardized criteria for differentiating urban from non-urban settlement "types"; and (b) the apparent boundaries between urban settlements and their putatively non-urban exterior have constantly been exploded, imploded and rewoven at all spatial scales.

Despite the persistent naturalization of static, ahistorical settlement typologies (urban, suburban, rural, wilderness) in mainstream geographical discourse, the relentless territorial extension of large centers of agglomeration into their surrounding fringes and peripheries was widely recognized by twentieth-century urban planners and designers, from Ebenezer Howard, Otto Wagner and Benton MacKaye to Jean Gottmann, Constantinos Doxiadis, Ian McHarg and John Friedmann. Indeed, although it tends to be marginalized in canonical historical narratives, the relentless process of urban territorial extension was arguably one of the formative concerns in relation to which the modern discipline of urban planning was consolidated. The field, in other words, has long contained a reflexively territorial orientation, rather than being focused simply upon conditions within bounded settlement units.[14]

Just as importantly, as Lewis Mumford grimly recognized, the developmental pathways of capitalist agglomerations have always been intimately intertwined with dramatic, large-scale and long-term transformations of non-city spaces, often located at a considerable distance from the major centers of capital, labor and commerce. Mumford described this relation as an interplay between "up-building" and "un-building" (*Abbau*) – on the one side, colossal vertical, horizontal and subterranean industrial-infrastructural clustering; and on the other, the intensifying degradation of surrounding landscapes, ecosystems, watersheds, rivers, seas and oceans through their intensifying role in supplying cities with fuel, materials, water and food, and in absorbing their waste products.[15] From the original dispossession of erstwhile rural populations through territorial enclosure to the intensification of land use, the construction of large-scale infrastructural investments and the progressive industrialization of hinterland economies to support extraction, cultivation, production and circulation, the "growth of the city" (Ernest Burgess) has been directly facilitated through colossal, if unevenly developed, industrial and environmental upheavals across the planet. In precisely this sense, the rural, the countryside and the hinterland have never been reducible to a mere backstage "ghost acreage" that supports the putatively frontstage operations of large population centers.[16] Whatever their demographic composition, from the dense town networks of the Ganges Plain or Java to the barren wastelands of Siberia or the Gobi desert steppe, the spaces of the non-city have been continuously operationalized in support of city-building processes throughout the global history of capitalist uneven development.[17] Such spaces are, therefore, as strategically central to the processes of creative destruction that underpin the "urbanization of capital" (David Harvey) as are the large, dense urban centers that have long monopolized the attention of urbanists.[18]

Faced with the relentless interplay between the up-building and un-building of spatial arrangements, along with the perpetual explosion of urban conditions, relations and effects across the variegated territorial landscapes and ecologies of global capitalism, can a settlement-based conception of urbanization be maintained? Can the urban "phenomenon," as Henri Lefebvre famously queried, still be anchored exclusively within, and confined to, the city?[19] In fact, once the rigid analytical constraints imposed by such pointillist, methodologically territorialist assumptions are relaxed, the static, ahistorical dualisms of mainstream urban theory (city/countryside, urban/rural, interior/exterior, society/nature) can be swiftly superseded. New analytical horizons thereby open: the geographies of urbanization can be productively reconceptualized in ways that illuminate not only the variegated patterns and pathways of agglomeration, but the continuous production and transformation of an unevenly woven urban fabric across the many terrains of industrial activity (agriculture, extraction, forestry, tourism and logistics) that are today still being misclassified on the basis of inherited notions of the countryside, the rural, the hinterland and the wilderness.[20]

Given the totalizations, blind spots and blind fields associated with the inherited *dispositif* of urban knowledge, perhaps an urban theory *without an outside* may be well-positioned to wrest open some productive new perspectives for both research and action on emergent landscapes of planetary urbanization?

Designing other urbanizations

The theoretical maneuvers proposed here are intended not simply to permit the recognition of concrete, empirical complexity within, among and beyond urban centers, but as an epistemic basis for reconceptualizing the essential properties of the process under investigation, and thereby, to open up new horizons for understanding and influencing contemporary urbanization. As Christian Schmid and I have argued at length elsewhere, the epistemic fissures within contemporary urban discourse and practice can be transcended only through a radical break from the inherited urban *dispositif*, and from the one-sided vision of the urban condition which it anchors.[21] In any field of thought and action, new *dispositifs* of interpretation can only emerge when historical conditions destabilize inherited, doxic frameworks, and engender an intensive search for an alternative basis for understanding and transforming the world. As evidenced in the recent escalation of epistemological debates among critically oriented urbanists, the field of urban theory presently appears to be in the throes of such a search, despite sometimes dismissive backlash from advocates of established scholarly traditions.[22]

Against this background, the recent revival of interest in the rural, the countryside and the hinterland among many architects, landscape theorists and designers represents a highly salient, if still rather indeterminate, development. Will such engagements simply entail a change of venue for the operations of design – a strategic shift "back to the land" by architects in search of interesting new sites for their creative energies? Alternatively, might an architecturally grounded exploration of the world's non-city spaces help animate the project of developing new analyses, visualizations and designs of our emergent planetary urban fabric? Two concluding propositions may offer some orientation for such an endeavor:

– Inherited spatial vocabularies for describing non-city spaces – rural, countryside, hinterland, wilderness – are locked into an externalist framework that attempts to distinguish them, analytically and spatially, from the city. Such vocabularies and associated visualizations must today be transcended, not least in the design disciplines. Today, we need new ways of interpreting and mapping the planet's variegated territories, landscapes and ecologies of urbanization that are not opposed binaristically to the city, and that do not devalorize their operational significance – whether to capitalist industrial growth, to human life or to non-human ecologies – based upon a fetish of demographic criteria. The non-city is no longer exterior to the urban; it has become a strategically essential terrain of capitalist urbanization.

– The capitalist form of urbanization continues to produce contextually specific patterns of agglomeration, but it also relentlessly transforms non-city spaces into zones of high-intensity, large-scale industrial infrastructure – *operational landscapes*. In contrast to historically inherited hinterlands, in which various "free gifts" of nature embedded in the earth (food, materials, energy, labor, water) are appropriated to produce primary commodities, operational landscapes involve the industrial redesign of agricultural, extractive and logistical activities to engineer the most optimal social, institutional, infrastructural, biological and ecological conditions for (generally export-oriented) for capital accumulation in one or more sectors. Whereas hinterlands merely "host" primary commodity production within an inherited terrain, operational landscapes are consolidated through the active production of colossal urban-industrial spatial configurations that have been reflexively designed to accelerate and intensify the accumulation of capital on the world market.

The implications of these ideas for architectural and design interventions into the world's variegated non-city spaces remain to be elaborated. At minimum, they raise doubts about any approach that aspires to create fortified retreats or privatized enclaves (whether for ecosystem services, luxury consumption, private enjoyment or specialized industrial export activity) in the erstwhile countryside. Instead, they underscore the challenge of establishing politically negotiated, democratically coordinated, environmentally sane and socially meaningful modes of connectivity between the various places, regions, territories and ecologies upon which humans collectively depend for our common planetary life. As they mobilize their capacities to shape this emergent terrain of intervention, designers confront an important ethical choice – to help produce maximally profitable operational landscapes for capital accumulation, or alternatively, to explore new ways of appropriating and reorganizing the non-city geographies of urbanization for collective uses and for the common good.

The perspective outlined here is oriented towards a counter-ideological project, one to which designers working in and on non-city terrains are particularly well positioned to contribute. How can we visualize, and thereby politicize, the encompassing, but generally invisible, webs of connection that link our urban way of life to the "silent violence" of accumulation by dispossession and environmental destruction in the world's hinterlands and operational landscapes? Insofar as designers bring distinctive forms of spatial intelligence and visualization capacities to the sites in which they are engaged, they have an invaluable role to play in constructing new cognitive maps of the planet's unevenly woven urban fabric. Such maps may, in turn, provide much-needed orientation for all who aspire to redesign that fabric in more socially progressive, politically inclusive, egalitarian and ecological ways.

Insofar as these arguments challenge the dogma of the hypertrophic city – the widely prevalent assumption that ever larger cities represent humanity's inevitable future – they also open up a horizon for imagining a different form of urbanization, an *alter-urbanization*. Many urbanizations are, in fact, possible. Rather than being preordained through technological laws or economic necessity, urbanization projects are collective political choices, a medium and product of power, imagination, struggle and experimentation. Can we imagine, for example, a form of urbanization in which multiple settlement patterns and differentiated infrastructural arrangements – including metropolitan regions, intercity networks, small- and medium-sized towns and "quiet zones" – are cultivated within a holistic framework of territorial development, balanced resource management and ecological stewardship?[23] And can we envision a form of urbanization in which households and communities that choose to remain rooted in less densely settled or remote zones will enjoy access to viable public infrastructures, sustainable livelihoods and some measure of political control over the basic conditions shaping their everyday lives? Perhaps the agency of design in the world's non-city spaces is precisely to facilitate the imagination and production of these and many other alter-urbanizations.

Notes

1   For a critical overview of the convoluted history and contemporary proliferation of the majority-urban world proposition, see Neil Brenner and Christian Schmid, "The 'Urban Age' in Question," *International Journal of Urban and Regional Research* 38, no. 3 (2014): 731–55.

2   On the production of spatial ideology, see Henri Lefebvre, "Reflections on the Politics of Space," in *State, Space, World,* ed. Neil Brenner and Stuart Elden (Minneapolis: University of Minnesota Press, 2009), 167–84.

3   Ross Exo Adams, "The Burden of the Present: On the Concept of Urbanisation," *Society and Space,* article extras online, accessed December 14, 2015, http://societyandspace.com/2014/02/11/ross-exo-adams-the-burden-of-the-present-on-the-concept-of-urbanisation/.

4   Brendan Gleeson, "What Role for Social Science in the 'Urban Age,'" *International Journal of Urban and Regional Research* 37, no. 5 (2013): 1839–1851.

5   Brenner and Schmid, "The 'Urban Age' in Question."

6   Terry McGee, *The Urbanization Process in the Third World* (London: Bell & Sons, 1971).

7   Max Ajl, "The Hypertrophic City Versus the Planet of Fields," in *Implosions/Explosions: Towards a Study of Planetary Urbanization,* ed. Neil Brenner (Berlin: Jovis, 2014), 533–50; Mike Davis, *Planet of Slums* (London: Verso, 2006).

8   Tony Champion and Graeme Hugo eds., *New Forms of Urbanization* (London: Ashgate, 2007).

9   Kingsley Davis, "The Origins and Growth of Urbanization in the World," *American Journal of Sociology* 60, no. 5 (1955): 429–37.

10   Chandan Deuskar, "What Does Urban Mean?," *Sustainable Cities* blog, accessed on December 15, 2015, The World Bank, http://blogs.worldbank.org/sustainablecities/what-does-urban-mean.

11   For productive attempts to develop more consistent definitional strategies, see Shlomo Angel, *Planet of Cities* (Cambridge, MA: Lincoln Institute of Land Policy, 2012); as well as Hirotsugu Uchida and Andrew Nelson, "Agglomeration Index: Towards a New Measure of Urban Concentration," Working Paper 29, United Nations University, 2010, accessed December 15, 2015, https://www.wider.unu.edu/publication/agglomeration-index.

12   Neil Brenner and Christian Schmid, "Towards a New Epistemology of the Urban," *CITY* 19, no. 2–3 (2015): 151–82; Neil Brenner, "Theses on Urbanization," *Public Culture* 25, no. 1 (2013): 86–114; and Adams, "The Burden of the Present."

13   Such an approach is forcefully advocated by, among others, Christian Schmid, "Specificity and Urbanization: A Theoretical Outlook," in *The Inevitable Specificity of Cities*, ed. ETH Studio Basel (Zurich: Lars Müller Publishers, 2014), 282–92; Jennifer Robinson, "Cities in a World of Cities: The Comparative Gesture," *International Journal of Urban and Regional Research* 51, no. 1 (2011): 1–23; and Ananya Roy, "The 21st Century Metropolis: New Geographies of Theory," *Regional Studies* 43, no. 6 (2009): 819–30. On the systemic production of institutional and spatial variegation, see Neil Brenner, Jamie Peck and Nik Theodore, "Variegated Neoliberalization: Geographies, Modalities, Pathways," *Global Networks* 10, no. 2 (2010): 182–222.

14   See, in particular, John Friedmann and Clyde Weaver, *Territory and Function: The Evolution of Regional Planning* (Berkeley: University of California Press, 1979). In contrast, Peter Hall's *Cities of Tomorrow* (Cambridge, MA: Blackwell, 2002) embodies a resolutely city-centric approach to urban planning history.

15   Lewis Mumford, "A Natural History of Urbanization," in *Man's Role in Changing the Face of the Earth*, ed. William L. Thomas (Chicago: University of Chicago Press, 1956), 382–98; and "Paleotechnic Paradise: Coketown," in *The City in History* (New York: Harcourt, Brace, 1961), 446–81. See also the various contributions to Brenner, *Implosions/Explosions*.

16   Jason Moore, *Capitalism and the Web of Life: Ecology and the Accumulation of Capital* (New York: Verso, 2016); Gavin Bridge, "Resource Triumphalism: Postindustrial Narratives of Primary Commodity Production," *Environment and Planning A* 33 (2001): 2149–73.

17   Martín Arboleda, "In the Nature of the Non-City: Expanded Infrastructural Networks and the Political Ecology of Planetary Urbanisation," *Antipode* 48, no. 2 (2016): 233–51; and Arboleda, "Spaces of Extraction, Metropolitan Explosions: Planetary Urbanization and the Commodity Boom in Latin America," *International Journal of Urban and Regional Research*, DOI:10.1111/1468-2427.12290; and Mazen Labban, "Deterritorializing Extraction: Bioaccumulation and the Planetary Mine," *Annals of the Association of American Geographers* 104, no. 3 (2014): 560–76.

18   David Harvey, *The Urbanization of Capital: Studies in the History and Theory of Capitalist Urbanization* (Baltimore: Johns Hopkins University Press, 1985).

19   Henri Lefebvre, *The Urban Revolution*, trans. Robert Bononno (Minneapolis: University of Minnesota Press, 2003 [1970]); Brenner and Schmid, "Towards a New Epistemology."

20   On the concept of an "urban fabric," see Lefebvre, *The Urban Revolution;* and the contributions to Brenner, *Implosions/Explosions.* On the need to reinvent the inherited concept of the hinterland, see Neil Brenner, *Extended Urbanization and the Hinterland Question: Towards a Real Subsumption of the Planet?,* unpublished manuscript, Urban Theory Lab, Harvard GSD, December 2015; and Nikos Katsikis, "The Composite Fabric of Urbanization: Agglomeration Landscapes and Operational Landscapes,"

in *From Hinterland to Hinterglobe: Urbanization as Geographical Organization,"*. (Doctor of Design Thesis, Harvard University Graduate School of Design, 2016).

21 Brenner and Schmid, "Towards a New Epistemology of the Urban."

22 Neil Brenner and Christian Schmid, "Combat, Critique and Caricature in the Study of Planetary Urbanization," Urban Theory Lab, Harvard GSD and Institute for the Contemporary City, ETH Zurich, accessed December 15, 2015, http://www.urbantheorylab.net/publications/towards-a-new-epistemology-of-the-urban/.

23 The concept of "quiet zones" is derived from the ETH Studio Basel's pioneering study of urbanization in Switzerland: see Roger Diener, Jacques Herzog, Marcel Meili, Pierre de Meuron and Christian Schmid / ETH Studio Basel, *Switzerland: An Urban Portrait* (Basel: Birkhäuser, 2006).

14 The Agency of Design in an Age of Urbanization
dialogue with Daniel Ibañez

Daniel Ibañez (DI): You describe yourself as a critical urban theorist. What do you mean by this? '

Neil Brenner (NB): For me, theory is, at core, a means to interrogate, elucidate and reinvent the concepts and interpretations we presuppose to understand and act in the world, including in relation to all aspects of the built and unbuilt environment. Insofar as we always presuppose certain basic assumptions about how social relations and spatial arrangements are organized, and about how, when and why they change and can be changed, we are always already in the realm of theory. In this sense, theory is not separate from the realm of practice and action, but is a necessary, underlying precondition of pretty much everything we think and do. There is no "outside" to theory. The question is how reflexive, self-aware and self-critical we might be about the assumptions we presuppose as we shape our social, spatial and environmental practices.

As an urban theorist, I am concerned to clarify the concepts, metanarratives and framing assumptions we use in everyday life, scholarly discourse and professional practice to understand and influence cities and urbanization processes. As a critical urban theorist, I am particularly concerned with ideologies of the urban – the ways in which dominant understandings of spatial organization and environmental relations operate to legitimate political projects of city-building and urbanization that may reinforce determinate patterns of inequality, exploitation, dispossession, exclusion, social suffering and ecological destruction. I am equally interested in developing concepts that might help orient and empower social and political movements, as well as policy makers and designers, that are working to create more just, democratic and ecologically viable forms of urbanization.

In this sense, I believe, critical urban theory is essential to the struggle for alternative urban futures, and for new forms of urbanization – "*alter*-urbanizations" that diverge from the dominant profit-driven, socially divisive and ecologically disastrous form under which we now live. Unless we critically interrogate dominant urban concepts, modes of interpretation and systems of evaluation, which normalize various kinds of social injustices and ecological irrationalities, it is difficult to envision what such alternative urban futures might look like, and how they might be actualized.

DI How do you understand the contribution of critical theory to the pedagogical cultures and practices of design?

NB For some designers and planners, there is a strong resistance to theory, often derived from an urgent concern to change the world in a radical way. They view theory as something that detains them from their mission; they want to get busy confronting the big issues that inspire their work. I certainly appreciate that passion; I can well understand their concern to delve into the intricacies of the urgent problems they want to solve, which are plenty complicated and obviously require a lot of technical knowledge. Why get bogged down with philosophical or methodological abstractions, when there are serious problems in the world to be addressed?

Engaging with this kind of action-based resistance to theory has been very instructive for me. It has forced me to clarify my own views on why theory matters, not only for interpretation, but for action. My argument is a simple one: theory is actually a key tool for any intervention into the built or unbuilt environments of the world, even if it may be a step removed from the realm of immediate technical operations. In this view, theory provides an essential means of evaluation, imagination, contextualization and orientation for design and planning action. It is a basis for understanding the contexts, methods, agents, constituencies, possibilities, constraints, the lines of conflict and struggle, the potential outcomes and hazards, as well as the normative dimensions of the entire operation. Without theory, those fundamental dimensions of design intervention are impossible to analyze systematically, and with appropriate historical awareness and ethical-political reflexivity. In this sense, we are always already in the realm of theory; the key question is how reflexive we can be about the interpretive assumptions we are always presupposing in the work of design. Any practice of design that is not theoretically reflexive will be ineffectual, even blind. Theory is, therefore, an essential tool within a critically oriented, normatively attuned, contextually embedded and inter-contextually informed approach to design intervention.

DI Do you see a way of employing these critical-theoretical orientations in the everyday work of design?

NB The general argument I make to my students in the design disciplines is that we need to think not just about the site that a client (be it a corporation, a government or a nonprofit organization) has requested us to shape; we need to think more broadly about how our work might address some of the large-scale problems of modern capitalist society – social and territorial inequality, exploitation, displacement, alienation, economic crisis, environmental degradation, and so forth. But in order to do that, we cannot simply think of the site in terms of the building or even the neighborhood; we need to connect these scales up to much broader geographies of worldwide capitalism. The design disciplines must, in my view, avoid a purely formal or technical orientation, and must push back against the prevalent convention of simply implementing a client's vision of the site and its possibilities. Instead, we need to develop a broader normative and political vision of how architecture, planning and design can be relevant to addressing some of the deep social and environmental crises of contemporary capitalism – even if, and perhaps especially if, that entails recurrent conflicts with clients who control the resources required for the proposed intervention.

So, what I am really trying to offer is not so much a strategy, but a method. It is a method for connecting the work of design, architecture and planning to engagements with broader political-economic, social and environmental contexts and transformations, both within and beyond the city. I certainly can't figure out what the answer is on an abstract level, but I plead with my students to work as hard as they can, under the institutional, practical and contextual conditions in which they find themselves, to make these connections, and then to follow them quite systematically, beyond the sites of their specific projects, back out to the big problems of modern capitalism. I constantly urge them: don't simply accept narrow formal remits or technical standards, be more political, be more socially engaged, be more humanitarian, be more radical in your work! Use the powerful spatial intelligence of architecture, landscape and planning to promote more democratic, environmentally sane, socially just, culturally meaningful transformations in cities, territories, landscapes. I find that so many of my students are, in fact, urgently seeking out ways to make these types of connections, and they welcome the injunction to view the design disciplines as a basis for envisioning radically alternative futures.

DI We often hear that 50 percent of the world population is living in cities. You have argued forcefully that this is a totally misleading proposition. Why?

NB This is a widely quoted idea that is derived from the United Nations' data on global population levels. The attempt to measure the world's urban population has a long history in the UN, but despite appearances, it is anything but scientific. In fact it has long been based upon highly problematic empirical techniques and deeply problematic theoretical assumptions.[2]

   In one sense, it is clearly true that the world is becoming urban; the populations of large settlements are obviously increasing. And it is also certainly true that urbanization processes are transforming everyday life around the world, not least within the largest population centers. But, in order to count the number of people living in cities, you first have to have a coherent basis for defining what a city is, and where its spatial boundaries lie. As it turns out, this is not a simple matter. Indeed, there is massive disagreement on this issue among the national census bureaus upon which the UN bases its data on global urban population levels. Additionally, there are questions of interpretation. What exactly is a city, and why does it matter, and to whom, to say that a 50 percent global urban population "threshold" has now been crossed?

   I would raise two questions for anyone who embraces the idea of the "urban age," defined in these conventional terms. First, is it really useful to subsume the diversity of urban conditions and urbanization processes around the world under the universal, rather totalizing label of "the" city? Don't we actually need more differentiated categories to understand the ongoing transformation of the world's built and unbuilt environments, within and around the centers of agglomeration?

   Second, what about the supposed "rural" or "non-urban" domain outside of the dense population centers? Are the planet's "hinterlands" really irrelevant now, due to depopulation, migration or ecological degradation? Our research suggests that, on the contrary, the non-city landscapes of the world remain quite fundamental, in operational terms, to providing various kinds of material and metabolic support for urban-industrial life. This includes not only traditional and newly industrialized hinterland spaces, where the bulk of primary commodity production (mining, farming, biomass extraction and so forth) occurs, but increasingly, some of the world's most apparently remote places, such as the Arctic, the Amazon, the world's deserts and mountain ranges and oceans. Whether as resource extraction zones, agricultural and logistics landscapes, tourist enclaves, waste dumps or providers of "ecosystem services," these relatively low-population zones have been progressively operationalized, during the course of capitalist development, to support the industrial urbanization of the entire planet. They have been radically, often quite destructively, transformed – unevenly enclosed, infrastructuralized, territorialized – through their role in this process.

By contrast, the notion of an "urban age" implies a simple, linear, worldwide transition from the rural to the urban. It defines urbanization in purely demographic terms, and emphasizes the redistribution of populations between two basically static spatial containers, urban and rural. Like grains of sand moving through the bulbs of an hourglass, social, spatial and environmental change is assumed to happen simply through a redistribution of elements between unchanging units, urban and rural. The units themselves are assumed to be ontologically fixed, insulated from transformative processes which they merely host, without being structurally affected by them. This way of understanding urbanization arguably confuses far more than it illuminates about both poles of the supposed urban/rural dualism, as well as about the processes that are said to traverse them.

DI You have argued that, aside from its conceptual blind spots, the urban age concept is also empirically indefensible. What are some of the problems?

NB Measuring the world's urban population is very confusing and is based upon a statistical disaster. Every national government defines the city and the urban according to its own census categories and indicators. In some countries, it is a population threshold – for instance, 5,000 or 20,000, or 50,000. Sometimes, the census bureaus combine indicators, such as population size, density or employment conditions, to determine the conditions for urban settlements. In other contexts, the city is simply an administrative category, determined by governmental decisions. Furthermore, if one large country, such as China, India or Brazil, changes its criteria for defining cities (which occasionally happens), then the entire world's putative urban population level will be altered. When you dump all these different definitions into the UN global data tables, the results are fully chaotic – quite an empirical mess for an international organization that wields such widespread authority over global public discourse about cities. Even on a basic empirical level, the notion of a 50 percent global urban population "threshold" is indefensible: it is derived from the use of inconsistent, incompatible measurement criteria among the UN's member states. As such, it is little more than a vague, speculative generalization, disguised as an authoritative fact.

The real thrust of my critique, however, is that these are not simply empirical questions, problems of measurement. There are broader theoretical and interpretive issues at stake: what is the city, what is the urban, and for what purposes are corporations, governments, international organizations and so many others concerned with such putative "thresholds" of global urban life?

DI Against urban age ideology, you have argued for a much broader understanding of urbanization that includes not only cities, but vast zones that contain relatively low population sizes or densities. In many of your recent publications, you suggest that zones such as these have now become part of the planetary urban fabric. How is this so?

NB Our work in the book *Implosions/Explosions,* and subsequently, in the Urban Theory Lab, suggests that vast zones of the planet – including the world's rainforests, deserts, alpine zones, oceans and many other areas that may seem quite "remote" – are now being exploited and operationalized in order to support the agglomerations, the big cities, and the urban mode of life which they are generalizing.[3] But, due to their apparent geographical remoteness and relatively small populations, such hinterlands are never included in the conventional cognitive map of the urban age, which is totally agglomeration-centric: it treats the vast non-city zones of the world simply as an empty void, as a massive blank space on the world map. Even in the hugely influential, and in some ways quite provocative, nighttime lights map of the world, the emptiness of the unlit zones of the planet rather dramatically overwhelm the entire visualization. For me, that apparent emptiness is a far more striking aspect of the map than the sprawling imprint of the lit-up areas, which is widely used as a proxy for urban settlements. It is in this sense, I would argue, that the urban age concept is thoroughly ideological, because it directs our attention to the big settlements alone, treating them as quasi-self-propelled motors or "pods" of growth, without illuminating the profound ways in which urban life hinges upon intensively relational transformations of territories, landscapes and ecologies elsewhere, precisely in the dark zones of the nighttime lights image.

It is, meanwhile, essential to ask: what are the forms of dispossession and displacement in the so-called "countryside" that are contributing to the massive "rural-to-urban" migrations that are being naturalized or even celebrated by so many contemporary urban thinkers? What is actually happening in the larger territorial hinterlands of Latin America, South Asia, China or Africa, that is triggering the massive displacement of populations to the world's megacities? That question has got to be posed as an urgent and fundamental political issue, not least within the field of urban studies. Otherwise, we are simply taking for granted that the so-called rural-to-urban transition is necessary, irreversible, ecological and good, and then drawing arbitrary analytical boundaries around the "city," a scale that is arguably several steps downstream from the macroinstitutional, political-economic and ecological forces that actually animate contemporary urbanization processes.

In other words, rather than simply assuming that there is a natural, irreversible move from the countryside to the city, we have to look at particular policies, regulatory arrangements, institutions, property relations, power hierarchies, political struggles and geopolitical ruptures (including wars) that are animating the choreography of mass migration within and across different zones of the world economy. Across contexts, these processes are evidently tied to strategies of territorial enclosure, the intensification of land use, and new large-scale infrastructural investments for agro-industrial, extractive and logistical functions, which are undermining sustainable livelihoods and degrading ecological conditions in the erstwhile rural zones, while also concentrating the infrastructures of social reproduction in the big population centers. There are, of course, widely divergent patterns and pathways of enclosure, privatization, land-grabbing, industrial consolidation, infrastructuralization, financialization and environmental degradation across the global South. We have to look at these variegations, and their mediations through regulatory frameworks and political struggles in different contexts, instead of accepting the dangerously prevalent fable of a natural, necessary, global trend for populations to "choose" to move from the countryside to the city. But this means opening up the territory of the non-city, the variegated hinterlands of capitalist industrialization, to much more systematic interrogation by urban theorists and designers alike.

DI Could more participatory modes of governance be harnessed to counteract these tendencies? To what degree could a well-informed, politically active citizenry be a basis for developing alternative forms of urbanization?

NB There is, certainly, plenty of resistance in different parts of the world to these strategies of territorial enclosure, infrastructuralization, industrial transformation and financialization. Corporations cannot simply impose their will without a political structure that enables them simultaneously to privatize and to externalize the social and ecological costs of their activities. Nor can they pursue their accumulation strategies without the dissemination of ideologies that justify, legitimate or naturalize their activities, whether as so-called "best practices," structural necessities or pragmatic compromises. To the degree that political systems are democratically controlled at any spatial scale, there is always a possibility to appropriate state power to protect populations from the processes of accumulation by dispossession that are now being intensified around the world.

But meanwhile, neoliberalism – with its orientation towards privatizing local assets; increasing corporate control over investment decisions that affect society as a whole; and externalizing the social and ecological costs of capital accumulation – is still the dominant regulatory strategy of our time. We have plenty of evidence that relying purely on market forces to organize social life and territorial development will result in massive social disruptions and regulatory failures, including intensifying inequality, infrastructural shortfall, political fragmentation, public health crises, environmental destruction, democratic deficits and so forth. The private, profit-oriented control over investment decisions that, in practice, impact an entire city, territory or landscape, or indeed the whole planet, has been a social and ecological disaster. The question, then, is how to appropriate democratic, politically coordinated control over the city, and indeed the territory and the environment, as a *commons,* a collective resource that is actively produced and shared by all, rather than perpetuating a regulatory regime which permits the future of all to be decided by those with the exclusive discretionary power to make investment decisions on a profit-maximizing basis.

In the notion of French author Henri Lefebvre, *autogestion* – self-management, or grassroots control – must lie at the heart of any democratic form of territorial organization.[4] But Lefebvre, who was highly critical of the French Communist party, and also quite skeptical about Yugoslav autogestionary experiments in the 1970s, pointed out an irresolvable contradiction with this aspiration. Autogestion can only be activated from below, by the actors themselves; attempts to stimulate it from above undermine the basic principle of the grassroots. At the same time, however, without a larger-scale framework of institutional support and legal protection, the transformative impulses behind autogestionary, radically democratic mobilizations are hugely vulnerable to attack or even destruction by those who are most threatened by their demands.

So the problem is: how can a social formation be constructed in which political institutions are constantly open to being appropriated and transformed through initiatives from the bottom up, but without ever closing off that accessibility to future projects that promote new forms of transformation from below? Lefebvre himself suggested that if a fully autogestionary or self-managed society were ever established, the state would constantly be appropriated and transformed from below. As such, he somewhat mischievously suggested, it would "wither away" in the sense once postulated by Lenin in a radically different context. It is, obviously, a rather complicated proposition, both in theory and in practice.

DI What is the particular kind of agency that designers have in shaping urbanization processes?

NB That's the most urgent, and also the most vexing, question for the design disciplines today. When you operate on a site that is predetermined by a client, how can you use that opportunity, if your goal is to make a broader, socially progressive, politically inclusionary and ecologically sensible impact both within and beyond the site? If you understand the site as being mediated through, and embedded within, larger-scale political-economic and environmental processes, how can you use your circumscribed intervention to influence those larger power structures and metabolic flows? How, for example, might designers use their specific capacities and modes of intervention to push back against the broader rule-regimes of neoliberal capitalism?

The High Line in New York has become a paradigmatic, if now all-too-familiar, example of these dilemmas. Analyzed in a bounded manner, cut off from its context, it appears to be a beautiful, even radical, appropriation of the inherited urban infrastructure to produce an experience of landscape and ecology that is new, exciting, inspiring and powerful. But, if you look at its actual effect on the social relations of the surrounding zone, it has arguably served to increase spatial injustice, to accelerate gentrification and displacement, and in this way, to promote the construction of a closed, exclusionary city dominated by ruling class elites and the demands of tourists.

A well-intentioned designer might respond, plausibly enough, that it is better to commission a progressive, forward-thinking, aesthetically powerful and ecologically sensitive design, even within the limited parameters of a site, than to implement one that is more conservative, less experimental, less attractive, but which meets other criteria of inclusion, participation and so forth. I understand that stance very well, but I do not think a designer who is genuinely committed to a more radically democratic, egalitarian and socially diverse vision of the urban condition could ever be satisfied with that answer. The problem is with the definition of the site itself: it is too narrowly circumscribed, and that in turn limits our imagination of what an intervention could potentially accomplish. From my point of view, we need to push against that circumscribed definition of the site of design, to include broader elements, processes and struggles that connect up to what Henri Lefebvre called the "right to the city" – a radically democratic appropriation of the urban as it now exists, *and* a collective appropriation of the power to produce the urban, the possible spaces of the future, in a broader, more inclusive and democratically managed way.[5]

How to achieve such a grassroots, radically inclusive and transformative model of urban spatial development in practice is, of course, a major puzzle. But just by putting it on the agenda, and keeping it there, we can begin to push against a neoliberal rule-regime that grants the right to the city only to the wealthy, to property owners, to investors and developers, to finance capital. Clearly, designers have capacities that are urgently needed by developers, and by capital more generally, and they are capable of doing quite a bit more than simply reacting to market imperatives, selling that capacity to the highest bidder. They can also use their skills to promote a vision of the urban as a commons, a space that is produced, shared and constantly transformed by all. Designers probably have a much stronger negotiating position than they may often realize, because their technical skills and imaginative capacities harness immense potential to contribute quite powerfully to broader social, political and ecological transformations. I believe that designers could be a lot more politically and ethically selective, making value judgments about the appropriate normative parameters for their commissions, rather than simply assuming "there is no alternative" but to conform to market demands by accepting the client's assumptions and requirements.

Designers operate in many different organizational and financial structures, ranging from small-scale, independent consultancies to very large-scale international corporations like Arup or AECOM that command a massive labor force, technical apparatus and infrastructure. We need to think a lot more about various possible institutional, financial and technoscientific arrangements that might facilitate progressive or radical design work, and their implications for the social, spatial and environmental fabric of contemporary urbanism. In a purely profit-oriented framework, design will simply serve as a tool of profit-maximization and speculative investment – and thus, lead to the further consolidation of cities of exploitation, dispossession, exclusion, injustice and waste. But other frameworks are possible, in which design can be a powerful agent of progressive social change, social and cultural experimentation, democratization, empowerment, environmental reform and so forth. Even under current circumstances, with the continued dominance of market-authoritarian ideologies around the world, there appears to be an emerging demand for designers to contribute to producing a more socially integrated, ecologically balanced and territorially coherent urban fabric. And obviously, there is an urgent need for such progressive or radical design interventions, at every imaginable spatial scale. There is, therefore, plenty of work to do for socially progressive and radical designers, not least in reimagining how their own capacities might be more effectively harnessed to produce visions and strategies for alternative urbanisms and new pathways of urban and territorial transformation.

DI What is the role of visualization and representation strategies in the critical and political work of designers? Isn't this spatial intelligence one of the capacities that designers are particularly well positioned to contribute to the struggle for more socially just, democratically managed and ecological built environments?

NB Now that we have such elaborate geospatial data sources and technical platforms, we can rather easily produce apparently quite sophisticated, information-rich visualizations of countless territorial and ecological conditions at a range of spatial scales, from the very fine-grained to the planetary. As a result, we may actually begin to believe the illusion that we have truly created a photographic replication of the world's complexity. To me, that assumption produces what we might think of as a new cartographic positivism: the hubristic belief that the map is a mimetic reflection of life.

DI Perhaps somewhat like the famous Borges parable, "On Exactitude in Science," in which the desire for mimesis eventually forces the cartographer to expand the map to the scale of the entire Empire it aspires to represent?

NB Yes, exactly. But the conceit of mainstream geospatial approaches is slightly different, suggesting that, simply through the layering of many forms of finely grained spatial data in the visualization machine, we can create a diagram that actually captures the complexity of the "empire" – precisely without, as in the Borges parable, having to build a map that is actually scaled to the size of the entire world. Pushing back against that hubristic desire, I would insist that there is not, and never can be, a single diagram of the urban. In the Urban Theory Lab, we are always wrestling with the question of whether you can still use that vast, increasingly powerful geospatial machinery in a critically reflexive way. In our work thus far, we have been pursuing an explicitly anti-mimetic approach to mapping, trying actively to resist the photographic illusion. Our aspiration is to create a culture of counter-visualization as we approach the *problematique* of urbanization – in other words, to build maps that explicitly draw attention to their own artifice, to their own status as abstractions, constructions and interpretations, rather than presenting themselves as if they were actually capturing the full complexity of the urban process. Here, in other words, abstraction becomes a counter-ideological push-back – a classic Marxian move that now takes visual form.

At the same time, we insist that the machine itself, the contemporary apparatus of geospatial data visualization, with its satellite networks and its large-scale information processing systems, is based upon very specific metageographical constructions, determinate modes of interpretation that are directly connected to a range of institutions (states, corporations) that are actively trying to reshape the world's urban and territorial landscapes. In this sense, geospatial data hardly offer a neutral, passive lens for representing the "real."[6] We thus also need to direct our critical representational capacities back towards that machine, revealing the agency of the lens itself, even as we continue to harness the capacities of that lens (and, of course, many others) to try to represent the planetary "empire" of the urban under capitalism. Doing so would be the spatial embodiment of the kind of critical-theoretical reflexivity to which my textual work has long been committed. For us, then, the project of counter-visualization is absolutely essential to the collective work of envisioning, and ultimately producing, alternative forms of urbanization.

DI So, you are basically saying that mapping should be a political statement?

NB Architecture, landscape architecture and planning too – all of the design disciplines. They should be political statements, but not simply in the sense that state institutions define the political. They should be political statements in the radically autogestionary sense of mobilizing their imaginative visions, practical capacities, forms of spatial intelligence and modes of territorial intervention to help empower people to appropriate, share and transform the urban in and through their everyday lives.

Notes

1   Thanks are due to Professor Chris Roach, California College of Architecture (CCA), for permission to build upon elements from an earlier dialogue he conducted with Neil Brenner, published in *The AGENT,* California College of the Arts/CCA (March 2014). We also thank Adam Tanaka for editorial assistance.

2   See Neil Brenner and Christian Schmid, "The 'Urban Age' in Question," *International Journal of Urban and Regional Research* 38, no. 3 (2014): 731–55.

3   Neil Brenner, ed., *Implosions/Explosions: Towards a Study of Planetary Urbanization* (Berlin: Jovis, 2014). See also Neil Brenner and Christian Schmid, "Towards a New Epistemology of the Urban," *CITY* 19, no. 2–3 (2015): 151–82; and Neil Brenner "Theses on Urbanization," *Public Culture* 25, no. 1 (2013): 86–114.

4   Henri Lefebvre, *State Space World,* ed., Neil Brenner and Stuart Elden; trans. Gerald Moore, Neil Brenner and Stuart Elden (Minneapolis: University of Minnesota Press, 2009).

5   Henri Lefebvre, "The Right to the City," in *Writings on Cities,* ed. and trans. Eleonore Kofman and Elizabeth Lebas (Cambridge, MA: Blackwell, 1996): 63–184; David Harvey, "The Right to the City," *New Left Review,* 53 (September/October 2008): 23–40. For further elaborations, see Neil Brenner, *Place, Capitalism and the Right to the City,* Keynote Lecture, Creative Time Summit, New York City, November 2013: available at https://www.youtube.com/watch?v=V_dk7-8Hms8.

6   This argument is developed further in Neil Brenner and Nikos Katsikis, *Is the World Urban? Towards a Critique of Geospatial Ideology* (New York: Actar, forthcoming). See also, foundationally, Laura Kurgan, *Close Up at a Distance: Mapping, Technology, and Politics* (Cambridge, MA: Zone Books, 2013).

15 Assemblage, Actor-Networks and the Challenges of Critical Urban Theory

with David J. Madden and David Wachsmuth

The field of urban studies is today confronted with significant theoretical, conceptual, epistemological and methodological challenges. As was also the case in the late 1960s and early 1970s, when debates on the urban question destabilized inherited Chicago School ontologies, established paradigms of urban research now appear increasingly limited in their ability to illuminate contemporary urban transformations and struggles.[1] As in previous rounds of debate on the urban question, the source of the contemporary "urban impasse" is the restless periodicity and extraordinary slipperiness of the urban phenomenon itself.[2] Even more so than in the 1970s, urbanization today "astonishes us by its scale; its complexity surpasses the tools of our understanding and the instruments of practical capacity."[3] At the turn of the twenty-first century, Edward Soja aptly captured this state of affairs:

> It may indeed be both the best of times and the worst of times to be studying cities, for while there is so much that is new and challenging to respond to, there is much less agreement than ever before as to how best to make sense, practically and theoretically, of the new urban worlds being created.[4]

Some strands of urban studies, particularly those rooted in the professionalized routines of academic disciplines, remain mired in outdated research agendas that only partially grasp the contours, dynamics and consequences of emergent urban transformations. Fortunately, however, there is elsewhere considerable intellectual adventurousness on display, as urbanists across the social sciences and humanities, as well as in the cognate fields of planning, architecture and design, grapple creatively with the tasks of deciphering the rapidly transforming worldwide landscapes of urbanization.[5] Among the key agendas for such researchers is to investigate the evolving positionalities of cities – and urban landscapes more generally – within such large-scale, long-term trends as geoeconomic restructuring, market-driven regulatory change (including both privatization and liberalization), the worldwide informalization of labor, mass migration, environmental degradation, global warming, the creative destruction of large-scale territorial landscapes and the intensification of polarization, inequality, marginalization, dispossession and social conflict at all spatial scales.

In the face of these trends and transformations, there is an increasingly urgent need to rethink our most basic assumptions regarding the site, object and agenda of "urban" research. The "urban question" famously posed four decades ago by Lefebvre, Harvey and Castells remains as essential as ever, but it arguably needs to be *reposed,* in the most fundamental way, in light of early twenty-first-century conditions. Do we really know, today, where the "urban" begins and ends, or what its most essential features are, socially, spatially or otherwise? At minimum, the town/country divide that once appeared to offer a stable, self-evident, basis for delineating the specificity of city settlements, today appears increasingly as an ideological remnant of nineteenth-century industrial capitalism that obfuscates the patterns and pathways of contemporary urbanization processes.[6] More radically still, a case can be made that Lefebvre's postulate of an incipient process of "complete" or "planetary" urbanization is today being actualized in practice. Despite pervasive sociospatial unevenness and persistent territorial inequality, the entire fabric of planetary settlement space is now being both extensively and intensively urbanized.[7] In the face of this prospect, and especially given the unprecedented pace, scale and volatility of contemporary worldwide urbanization, it is essential to consider whether inherited concepts and methods for understanding and influencing urban life remain adequate. The oft-repeated mantra that a global "urban transition" has recently occurred due to the putative fact that over half of the world's population now lives within cities does not even begin to capture the analytical, representational and political complexities associated with grasping the contemporary global urban condition.

It is, we would argue, not a moment for intellectual modesty or a retreat from grand metanarratives, as advocated by some poststructuralists a few decades ago. On the contrary, from our point of view, there is today a need for ambitious, wide-reaching engagements – theoretical, concrete and practical – with the planetary dimensions of capitalist urbanization across places, territories and scales. It would be problematic, however, to suggest that any single theory, paradigm or metanarrative could, in itself, completely illuminate the processes in question.[8] Theoretical ambition need not be pursued through the construction of reductionist, simplifying or totalizing frameworks. The task, rather, is to create concepts, interpretations and methods that open up new questions and horizons – at once for thought, imagination and action. Accordingly, in contrast to some of the more closed models of urbanism that prevailed during the high points of Chicago School urban research in the 1930s through the 1960s and, in a different way, within the structuralist Marxisms of the 1970s, we believe that critical urban theory today must embrace and even celebrate a certain degree of eclecticism. Today more than ever, there is a need for a collaborative, open-minded spirit to prevail in urban studies, particularly among those scholars who are most committed to confronting the daunting challenges of reconceptualizing the parameters and purposes of this research field. When such scholars make divergent or opposed theoretical, conceptual and methodological choices, useful opportunities may emerge to clarify the stakes of such choices, and their possible implications.[9]

In that spirit, our goal here is to evaluate critically an influential new tendency in urban studies associated with actor-network theory (invariably referred to by its initials, ANT), an approach to social science developed by Bruno Latour, Michel Callon, John Law and their followers.[10] Although ANT has influenced several important strands of contemporary urban thinking, its most dedicated proponents in urban studies have presented the concept of "assemblage" as its analytical centerpiece and as the basis for a new ontology of the urban.[11] Accordingly, we refer to this newly emergent ANT-based strand of urban studies generically as "assemblage urbanism."[12]

Given our remarks above regarding the unstable situation of contemporary urban studies, we welcome the efforts of assemblage urbanists to transcend certain inherited, intellectually constraining assumptions regarding the urban question, and on this basis, to open up new analytical windows into the various forms in which that question is being posed and fought out today. However, as we detail below, our own orientations for such an endeavor diverge considerably from those that have been proposed by scholars advancing an ANT-based framework. While *empirical* and *methodological* applications of the assemblage concept have generated productive insights in various strands of urban studies by building on political economy, we suggest that the *ontological* application favored by several influential contemporary ANT urbanists contains significant drawbacks. In explicitly rejecting concepts of structure in favor of a "naïve objectivism," this approach deprives itself of key explanatory tools for understanding the sociospatial "context of contexts" in which urban spaces and locally embedded social forces are positioned.[13] Relatedly, such approaches do not adequately grasp the ways in which contemporary urbanization continues to be shaped and contested through the contradictory, hierarchical social relations and institutional forms of capitalism. Finally, the normative foundations of such approaches are based upon an ahistorical, decontextualized standpoint rather than an immanent, reflexive critique of actually existing social relations, power hierarchies and institutional arrangements. Taken together, these considerations suggest that assemblage-based approaches can most effectively contribute to critical urban theory when they are linked to theories, concepts, methods and research agendas derived from a reinvigorated, multiscalar geopolitical economy.

In outlining these arguments, our intention is not to patrol the boundaries of theoretical innovation or methodological experimentation in urban studies. Rather, we hope to contribute to a broader debate regarding the challenges of contemporary critical urban theory, and about which conceptual choices, analytical frameworks and methodological strategies will be most effective for confronting them. Because we do not believe there is any single correct solution to such challenges, our questions are intentionally open-ended – an invitation for further dialogue. The goal is thus to open up new horizons for thought, imagination and action in relation to emergent forms of urbanization.

Actor-networks, assemblages and the urban question

During the last decade, ANT has become an increasingly prominent stand of poststructuralist social theory and social science.[14] Known as the "sociology of associations" or "sociology of translation," ANT grew out of science studies, and sees all things, as its name implies, as networks of actors. Networks are understood to be working alliances of multifarious composition. Actors, or actants, are simply things that act – anything that resists or impacts other things. Actants in ANT, famously, are human as well as non-human, animate as well as inanimate, material as well as ideational, large and small, those things called "natural," "cultural," and "social." As Bruno Latour puts it in an early programmatic statement, ANT starts from the ideas of irreducibility and infinite combinability: "Nothing can be reduced to anything else, nothing can be deduced from anything else, everything may be allied to everything else."[15] Despite the singular term "theory" in its name, ANT actually contains several intertwined layers of argumentation. It is a method for framing field sites and research objects, and more generally, an argument for what social science should and should not be. Perhaps most generally, it entails both an ontology and an epistemology – an account of what exists, and a linked set of claims about how to generate valid knowledge regarding the latter.

Ostensibly opposed to essentialism of any sort, ANT sees the world as immanent, contingent, heterogeneous, and ontologically flat, disclosing no other levels, final explanations or hidden core. ANT is thoroughly constructivist, although it has a number of criticisms to make of the standard language of social construction.[16] Whereas mainstream social constructionism asserts the social character of what appears "natural," ANT calls into question the society/nature division itself, rejecting the analytical coherence of both the "social" and the "natural" as categories. The prime ANT injunction that flows from this position is "to follow the actors themselves."[17] This should be done, actor-network theorists argue, while staying true to the "principle of generalized symmetry," which holds that both human and nonhuman actors should be described using common concepts.[18]

It is impossible to point to a specific set of empirical findings or conclusions that are drawn from actor-network studies, although diverse aspects of human/non-human networks have been investigated. For example, studies in this tradition often seek to uncover the heterogeneity and multiplicity of ostensibly well-integrated networks. Actants often attempt to make themselves "obligatory passage points" that are necessary for the continued success of the network. When all is running correctly, networks often manage to "black-box" themselves, hiding their artificiality under the illusion of integrality. This black-boxing only becomes apparent when networks fall apart due to quasi-entropic decay, strategic missteps or intentional refusal on the part of one or another actant.

While ANT has influenced diverse urban thinkers during the last decade, its core arguments have been most systematically imported into urban studies via the concept of assemblage, which has recently been presented as the conceptual lynchpin and ontological foundation for a radically new approach to the urban question. Although the word "assemblage" is sometimes used in a descriptive sense, to describe the coming-together of heterogeneous elements within an institution, place, built structure or art form, its philosophical usage in English derives principally from the work of Gilles Deleuze and Félix Guattari.[19] Their concept of *agencement* was translated as "assemblage" by Brian Massumi in the English version of *A Thousand Plateaus* published in the late 1980s, and this convention was generally preserved through a "loose consensus" among subsequent translators and commentators.[20] But the concept of assemblage has subsequently been mobilized in multifarious ways, only some of which are explicitly Deleuzoguattarian.[21] Aside from the heterodox, broadly Deleuzoguattarian strand of architectural theory and criticism developed as of the late 1980s in the now-defunct journal *Assemblages,* the dominant inflection of assemblage thinking in contemporary urban studies is most tightly associated with the tradition of ANT, as summarized above.

On a descriptive level, an assemblage-theoretical approach to the urban question entails viewing the city as a bundle of networks. As Thomas Bender explains:

> The metropolis […] is made up of networks – human networks, infrastructural networks, architectural networks, security networks; the list could be almost infinite, and they are not confined by a circumferential boundary […] Networks agglomerate into assemblages, perhaps a neighborhood, or a crowd at a street festival, or a financial center like Wall Street in New York City. The metropolis, then, is an assemblage of assemblages.[22]

In itself, however, the emphasis on the networked character of contemporary urbanism is relatively uncontroversial, and resonates with any number of approaches to urban studies that have not been influenced by ANT.[23] However, beyond this general emphasis on urban networks, the major advocates for an ANT-based approach to urbanism have larger ambitions, proposing an extremely wide array of ontological, analytical and/or normative purposes to which the concept of assemblage may be applied, and attributing to it some rather impressive explanatory capabilities.

The influential recent work of urban geographer Colin McFarlane illustrates this tendency.[24] Rather than disavowing the idea's mercurial nature, McFarlane affirms it, noting that the term "assemblage" is "increasingly used in social science research, generally to connote indeterminacy, emergence, becoming, processuality, turbulence, and the sociomateriality of phenomena."[25] According to McFarlane, as a motif within urban studies, the notion of assemblage is primarily focused upon "sociomaterial transformation," "grammars of gathering, networking and composition," and "interactions between human and nonhuman components" that as "co-functioning" can be "stabilized" or "destabilized" through "mutual imbrication."[26] Assemblages are processual relationships that "cannot be reduced to individual properties alone."[27] Assemblage thinking highlights processes of composition and recognizes diverse forms of human and nonhuman agencies – while striving to avoid reification, reductionism and essentialism. In this sense, McFarlane contends, assemblage thinking has an "inherently empirical focus."[28] As urban theory, assemblage thought asks how urban "things" – including, quite appropriately, the urban itself – are assembled, and how they might be disassembled or reassembled.

McFarlane outlines three specific contributions that assemblage approach can make to the development of critical urban theory. First, he sees assemblage thought as an empirical tool for engaging in thick description of "urban inequalities as produced through relations of history and potential."[29] He suggests that by paying detailed, ethnographic attention to processes of assemblage, urbanists may better understand how actually existing urban situations are constituted and, on this basis, may be better equipped to imagine alternatives to those situations. Second, McFarlane notes, assemblage thought can help attune researchers to the problematic of materiality – that is, to the significance and purported agency of materials themselves, "whether [they] be glossy policy documents, housing and infrastructure materials, placards, banners and picket lines, new and old technologies, software codes, credit instruments, money, commodities, or of course the material conditions of urban poverty, dispossession and inequality."[30] By "distributing agency across social and material" entities, such that both human and non-human forms of agency may be considered coevally, "assemblage thinking diversifies the range of agents and causes of urban inequality, while potentially multiplying the spaces of critical intervention."[31] Third, McFarlane sees the assemblage idea as activating a more general critical "imaginary" and political sensibility containing a distinctive image of the desirable city-to-come.[32] While noting the risk of the idea's co-optation by various elitist or oppressive projects, McFarlane offers "cosmopolitanism" as a "normative political project of urban assemblage."[33]

For McFarlane then, the concept of assemblage is said to open up a variety of new urban questions – or, at least, new orientations towards inherited urban questions – as well as new sites of analysis, methodological tools, targets of critique and political visions. As an illustration of the potential of this discourse, McFarlane briefly discusses his own work on urban informality in Mumbai, where he observed "the crucial role that various materialities play in the constitution and experience of nequality, and in the possibilities of a more equal urbanism."[34] Here, marginalized city dwellers "recycle" the city by gathering "materials [...] from local construction debris, riverbeds, manufacturing waste, or patches of tree cover."[35] Unequal access to infrastructure and other resources is shaped by the state and various other powerful actors. For some activists, the material networks of the city can be used as objects of resistance and tools of protest, generating a subaltern form of urban cosmopolitanism or "one-worldism" that militates for a new urban commons.[36] McFarlane suggests that an assemblage-based urban imaginary can produce "new urban knowledges, collectives and ontologies" that invoke and pursue new rights to the city among the most marginalized city-dwellers.[37]

Insofar as they enable urban scholars to question outdated categories and epistemologies, to demarcate new objects and terrains of urban research, and to highlight the political stakes and consequences of previously taken-for-granted dimensions of urban life, the analyses advanced by proponents of assemblage urbanism open up some important new perspectives on the urban question. The question, however, is how much and what type(s) of intellectual and political work the concept of assemblage, and the mode of analysis associated with it, can plausibly be expected to accomplish. Despite their contributions, we believe that assemblage-theoretical approaches to the urban question remain too broadly framed, at times even indeterminate, to realize their proper analytical potential. And this very indeterminacy, we argue below, amounts to a retreat from precisely those analytic vantage points and political positions that enable urban theory to engage in the project of critique.

In our view, the power of assemblage-theoretical approaches to urban studies may be most productively explored when their ontological dimensions are eschewed entirely, and when, correspondingly, their conceptual, methodological, empirical and normative parameters are circumscribed rather precisely. Against interpretations of this concept as the basis for "transforming the very ground of urban studies" and as "an alternative ontology for the city," we argue here for a much narrower, primarily methodological application.[38] The concept of assemblage is most useful, we contend, when it is mobilized in the context of a broader repertoire of theories, categories, methods and research agendas that are not derived internally from ANT. In elaborating these concerns, we are particularly interested in addressing what we view as the highly ambiguous status of political economy, and the concept of capitalism itself, within assemblage-theoretical approaches to urban studies. This issue is inextricably intertwined with the still larger question of the goals, tools and techniques of critical urban theory.

The spectre of political economy

At the outset, it might appear that radical urban political economy and the new theoretical idioms associated with assemblage urbanism could coexist and even mutually transform each other's methodological orientations, descriptive categories and objects of analysis.[39] However, an often-unstated but nonetheless pervasive agenda of assemblage urbanism seems to be a redescription of urban processes, transformations and inequalities with almost no reference to the key concepts and concerns of radical urban political economy – for instance, capital accumulation, class, property relations, land rent, exploitation, commodification, state power, territorial alliances, growth coalitions, structured coherence, uneven spatial development, spatial divisions of labor and crisis formation, among others. Most frequently, this displacement is often simply enacted, accompanied by neither an explicit critique of political-economic concepts nor a clear argument for how assemblage-based approaches might better illuminate the dimensions of contemporary urbanization to which such concepts have generally been applied. Yet the social relations, institutions, structural constraints, spatiotemporal dynamics, conflicts, contradictions and crisis tendencies of capitalism do not vanish simply because we stop referring to them explicitly – especially under conditions in which their forms are undergoing deep metamorphoses, they arguably still require explicit theorization and analysis in any critical account of the contemporary global urban condition.

At the same time, however, among many of the major practitioners of assemblage-based approaches, there appears to be considerable confusion as to whether such categories should be mobilized to deepen, extend, transform or supersede the analysis of capitalist structurations of urbanization. Does the term "assemblage" describe a type of hitherto-neglected *research object* to be studied in a broadly political-economic framework – thus generating a political economy of urban assemblages? Is assemblage analysis meant to extend the *methodology* of urban political economy in new directions, thus opening up new interpretive perspectives on dimensions of capitalist urbanization that have been previously neglected or only partially grasped? Or does the assemblage approach offer a new *ontological* starting point that displaces or supersedes the intellectual project of urban political economy?

Following from these questions, Figure 15.1 identifies what we view as the three major articulations between assemblage thinking and political economy that have been developed in the recent urban studies literature. The rows in the table represent both the core logical positions in terms of which this articulation may be

Form of articulation	Relation to urban political economy	Exemplary research foci	Representative authors
1: Empirical *Political economy of urban assemblages*	Assemblage is understood as a specific type of research object that can be analyzed through a political-economic framework and/or contextualized in relation to historically and geographically specific political-economic trends.	Technological networks within and among cities (for instance, electrical grids); intercity networks; assemblages of territory, authority and rights	Saskia Sassen; Stephen Graham and Simon Marvin; Harris Ali and Roger Keil
2: Methodological *Assemblage as a methodological extension of urban political economy*	Assemblage (often in conjunction with the closely related concept of as "metabolism") is presented as a methodological orientation through which to investigate previously neglected dimensions of capitalist urbanization. The core concerns of critical urban political economy remain central, but are now extended into new realms of inquiry.	The production of socionatures; infrastructural disruption or collapse; flows of energy, value, substances, policies, microbes, people, ideas	Stephen Graham; Eugene McCann and Kevin Ward; Erik Swyngedouw; Maria Kaika; Matthew Gandy; Thomas Bender
3: Ontological *Assemblage as an "alternative ontology for the city"*	Assemblage analysis displaces the investigation of capitalist urban development and the core concerns of urban political economy (for instance, the commodification of urban space, inequality and power relations, state intervention, polarization, uneven spatial development).	Urban materialities and infrastructures, including buildings, highways, artifacts, informal settlements, communications systems, traffic flows, interurban networks	Bruno Latour and Emilie Hermant; Ignacio Farías; Colin McFarlane; Richard G. Smith; Alan Latham and Derek McCormack; Manuel Tironi

Figure 15.1: Articulations of assemblage analysis and urban political economy

Note: references in the fourth column refer to works cited in the text.

understood and the major analytical strategies that have been adopted in practice by researchers who have been influenced, in varying degrees, by ANT.

The first row demarcates the use of assemblage as a distinctive type of research object within urban political economy. Saskia Sassen for example, uses the assemblage concept to refer to a particular historical interrelation of territory, authority and rights, while Stephen Graham and Simon Marvin's *Splintering Urbanism* conceives of infrastructure networks as "sociotechnical *assemblies* or 'machinic complexes' rather than as individual causal agents with identifiable 'impacts' on cities and urban life."[40] A similar approach is developed by Harris Ali and Roger Keil in their studies of transnational infectious disease transfer between global cities.[41] These authors do not draw on assemblage thinking as an ontological foundation, but instead mobilize certain propositions from such approaches in order to reframe concrete urban analysis on an *ad hoc* basis. Consequently, authors working in this tradition tend to analyze the assemblages they have identified along more or less political-economic lines – in effect, they are engaged in a political economy of urban assemblages.

In the second row, assemblage thinking generates a predominantly methodological approach that builds upon urban political economy while extending and reformulating some of its core elements and concerns, in part through selective appropriations from ANT, to study various phenomena associated with, for example, infrastructure failure, policy transfer and urban socionatures.[42] This procedure parallels the ways in which the cognate field of urban political ecology has used the idea of "metabolism" to capture the interconnected yet fluid dynamics that characterize the production of urban socionatures.[43] As these authors note, the metabolism concept has a long heritage in political economy, as well as obvious affinities with some strands of contemporary assemblage analysis.[44] Urban political ecology explicitly connects these two positions, using the concept of metabolism and selected methodological tools from ANT to build upon and reformulate the treatment of socionatures within critical urban political economy. For these authors, the concept of metabolism serves simultaneously as a way to characterize objects of inquiry (particularly urban socionatural networks) and also as an explanatory and theoretical device. On the one hand, as Erik Swyngedouw observes, the metabolic circulation of matter causes it to become "'enrolled' in associational networks that produce qualitative changes and qualitatively new assemblages."[45] On the other, urbanization itself is retheorized as "a metabolic circulatory process that materializes as an implosion of socionatural relations, a process which is organized through socially articulated networks and conduits."[46] Such arguments amount to a substantial rethinking of urban theory, but it is one that retains the central concerns, concepts and analytical orientations of political economy within a methodologically expanded framework.[47]

Finally, in the third row, ANT subsumes the entire conceptual apparatus and explanatory agenda of urban studies. Authors working in this manner look to ANT as a way to reconceptualize the fundamental character of the urban social world. The urban landscape is now conceived as a huge collection of human and nonhuman actants within a flat ontology devoid of scalar or territorial differentiations. Ways of understanding the city based on concepts from political economy or spatial sociology are considered illegitimate; categories of sociospatial structuration such as scale and territory are understood primarily as data to be interpreted rather than as analytical, explanatory or interpretive tools. In this way, the *problematique* of assemblage formation comes to function as a radical ontological alternative to political economy: assemblage is no longer merely a conceptual motif, an empirical tool or a methodological orientation, but the ontological basis for an alternative mapping of the urban social universe. Representative examples of this position include Bruno Latour and Emilie Hermant's study of Paris, Ignacio Farías's programmatic statement on ANT and urban studies, Colin McFarlane's theoretical articles, and several contributions to Ignacio Farías and Thomas Bender's edited volume on assemblage urbanism.[48]

Distinguishing between these three broad ways of articulating assemblage thought and political economy should clarify that there is no single "assemblage urbanism," and therefore no coherence to arguing for or against the concept of assemblage in general terms. At the same time, as the preceding discussion indicates, we believe that some of its specific manifestations are more defensible than others. Specifically, we would argue that the merits of levels 1 and 2 – the empirical and methodological levels – have been convincingly demonstrated in the urban studies literature, and certainly warrant further elaboration in future theoretical and substantive research. Through selective appropriation of insights from ANT and other sources, these strands of assemblage thinking have productively extended the methodological toolkit, research focus and interpretive orientation of urban political economy. However, for reasons we now elaborate, we are skeptical regarding the possible contributions of analyses conducted on level 3 of the table – assemblage as an ontology – particularly with regard to their relevance to the project of *critical urban studies*.

An ontology of naïve objectivism

A notable strength of ANT is its attention to the multiple materialities of socionatural relations. Additionally, approaches derived from ANT have pioneered the analysis of how and when nonhuman actants, from buildings and building materials to infrastructural grids, forms of energy and even weather systems, may generate significant forms of "reactive power" or agency.[49] But, without recourse to political economy or to another theoretical framework attuned to the structuration of urban processes (whether by capital, states, territorial alliances or social movements), an ontologically inflected appropriation of assemblage analysis confronts serious difficulties as a basis for illuminating the contemporary global urban condition.

In particular, the descriptive focus associated with ontological variants of ANT and assemblage urbanism leaves unaddressed important explanatory questions regarding the broader (global, national and regional) structural contexts within which actants are situated and operate – including formations of capital accumulation and investment/disinvestment; historically entrenched, large-scale configurations of uneven spatial development, territorial polarization and geopolitical hegemony; multiscalar frameworks of state power, territorial alliance formation and urban governance; and the politico-institutional legacies of sociopolitical contestation around diverse forms of dispossession, deprivation and discontent. In explicitly rejecting concepts of structure as remnants of an outdated model of social science explanation, or in simply ignoring the questions raised by such concepts, ontological approaches to assemblage analysis deprive themselves of a key explanatory tool for understanding the sociospatial, political-economic and institutional contexts in which urban spaces and locally embedded social forces are positioned. Within such a framework, moreover, there is no immanent principle for distinguishing relevant and irrelevant actants, whether of a human or nonhuman nature. Indeed, as Bender suggests, such approaches risk engaging in an "indiscriminate absorption of elements into the actor-network" with the "effect of levelling the significance of all actors."[50] The result of this procedure is a metaphysics of association based on what

Andrew Sayer has elsewhere aptly termed a "naïve objectivism."[51] This mode of analysis presupposes that the "facts" – in this case, those of interconnection among human and nonhuman actants – speak for themselves, rather than requiring mediation through theoretical assumptions and interpretive schemata.

The intellectually problematic and politically neutralizing consequences of such positions are very much in evidence within recent applications of ANT to the investigation of contemporary urban development. Consider, for example, McFarlane's account of informal housing in Mumbai, which offers a broad description of housing arrangements in a marginalized neighborhood of that city.[52] The experience of poverty and inequality, he shows, is crucially mediated through the building materials and infrastructural elements that comprise the built environment. On this basis, McFarlane appropriately suggests that the materiality of informal housing in Mumbai deserves more analytical attention due to its important role in mediating the everyday experience of poverty. As he indicates, housing is "both *made* and *edited,* in contexts of deeply unequal resources and precarious lives."[53] But does the thick description of assemblages offered in his analysis suffice to illuminate the specific forms of inequality and deprivation under investigation? To what degree does an assemblage-theoretical analysis help explain the underlying contexts and causes of urban sociospatial polarization, marginalization and deprivation, whether in Mumbai or elsewhere?

While McFarlane's rendering of assemblage may shed valuable light on the dynamics of making and editing, and on the broad spectrum of socionatural processes involved in the latter, it is precisely the "contexts of deeply unequal resources and precarious lives" that are bracketed in his analysis.[54] This bracketing is problematic insofar as it leaves underspecified the question of what historical geographies of land ownership, dispossession, deprivation and struggle generated and entrenched the unequal distribution of resources and the precarious life-conditions in the areas under discussion. After all, many of the details McFarlane gives of informal housing materiality – found construction materials, vertical modular construction, accreted rather than planned built forms, and the like – would equally well describe sociomaterial conditions within other zones of informality and marginalization in megacities across Latin America, the Middle East and South Asia.[55] Yet the shantytowns and squatting settlements within each of these global regions are positioned differentially within any number of broader historical geographies of power – for instance, global divisions of labor and circuits of capital investment/

disinvestment; legacies of colonial and postcolonial statecraft; modes of geopolitical control, subordination and intervention by imperial powers and global institutions such as the World Bank and the International Monetary Fund; patterns of agro-industrial transformation and associated rural-urban migration; state strategies to shape urbanization through speculative real estate development, infrastructural production, housing policy and slum clearance; and forms of social movement mobilization at various spatial scales. In an analytical maneuver that is typical of this strand of assemblage analysis, contexts such as these are scarcely mentioned, much less theorized or systematically analyzed. However, without a sustained account of this *context of context*, the analysis remains radically incomplete.[56]

While the assemblage ontology focuses on the materials themselves, it is essential to consider the political-economic structures, institutions and power relations in which they are embedded. In McFarlane's account of informal housing in Mumbai, the building materials are understood to be highly polysemic and promiscuous. Graffiti paint, unadorned brick, dirt in backyard gardens, corrugated metal – each can be an expression of precarious impoverishment or of dominating, aestheticized prosperity, depending upon its context. In a telling illustration of his conception of sociomaterial assemblages, McFarlane asks, "what [is] the particular agency of Richard Florida's sleek PowerPoint presentations of the 'creative city' […] when set against existing local urban plans?"[57] But is the real issue here the sociomateriality of PowerPoint or the structural contexts, institutional locations and geo-ideological circuits in which this technique is deployed? It is quite possibly the case that policy entrepreneurs who are aligned with real estate developers will use sleek PowerPoint presentations while, say, working-class housing activists will not. But what matters about the PowerPoint presentations are the projects of ideological legitimation towards which they are mobilized; the words, phrases, and narratives they contain have a nonarbitrary relationship to historically and geographically situated, differentially empowered social movements, forces, alliances and institutions. Substitute a PowerPoint presentation focused on the purported benefits of the creative class or a state-subsidized office tower for one focused on residential displacement, political disempowerment or labor rights, and it is an assemblage with a very different form and function, even though it may appear identical in purely material terms.

An empirical focus on such assemblages could be helpful in unraveling certain aspects of such dynamics, but this would entail exploring their contested instrumentalities within the political-economic, institutional and geo-ideological force fields mentioned above. By contrast, an ontological conception of assemblage substitutes for such considerations a naïve objectivism that is difficult to reconcile with the basic questions about power, inequality, injustice, politicization, struggle and mobilization that lie at the heart of critical urban theory.[18]

Actuality, possibility and critique

The major theoretical proponents of ANT have been explicitly hostile to what they see as "critical sociology"; this generalization applies to significant strands of assemblage analysis as well.[19] Perhaps for this reason, those branches of critical urban studies that have incorporated assemblage thinking into their intellectual apparatus have tended to marry it to more explicitly political-economic approaches which supply a strong dose of critical energies. The authors whose work is positioned on the empirical and methodological levels of Figure 15.1 thus rely extensively upon urban political economy to ground the critical elements of their respective analyses. By contrast, advocates of ANT argue explicitly against critical social science – as in Latour's account of his own position as "harsh and [...] truly obnoxious" towards critical sociology, seeing in the "infatuation with emancipation politics" a renunciation of a properly scientific attitude.[60]

At the same time, other urbanists, including several authors discussed above, have sought explicitly to link assemblage analysis to critical urban theory. Thus Farías extols ANT's "radicality," while McFarlane argues that assemblage urbanism is concerned with the relationship between the actual and the possible, and specifically, with the question of how formations of the urban might "be assembled differently."[61] The issue, however, is not whether the actual and the possible are related, but *how*. Here, we believe, there is a fundamental distinction worth making between the dialectical approaches to critique that often motivate political-economic analyses and those derived internally from assemblage analysis. In McFarlane's account, which formulates a position that is typical of much assemblage thinking, potentiality is exteriority: any assemblage may, in principle, be decomposed and a new one formed by incorporating new sociomaterialities; these new elements, which lie outside the extant assemblage, supply the possibility for different arrangements of human and nonhuman relations. This possibility is ontologically presupposed rather than being understood as historically specific or immanent to the sociomaterial relations under investigation. Although McFarlane introduces fruitful normative categories such as the right to the city, the commons and cosmopolitanism, the assemblage approach appears to operate primarily by describing alternatives unreflexively, as abstract possibilities that might be pursued.[62] Unfortunately, however, this approach offers no clear basis on which to understand how, when and why particular critical alternatives may be pursued under specific historical-geographical conditions or, more generally, why some possibilities for reassemblage are actualized over and against others that are suppressed, marginalized or excluded.

Critical theory, by contrast, holds that capitalism and its associated forms contain the possible as an immanent, constitutive moment of the real – as contradiction and negation.[63] Specific historical structures produce determinate constraints on the possibility for social transformation, as well as determinate, if often hidden or suppressed, openings for the latter. Within such a framework, the impulse towards critique is not an external, normative orientation or a mental abstraction, but is embedded within, and enabled by, the same structures, contradictions and conflicts that constrain the realization of what might be possible. From this point of view, a key challenge for any critical theory is to explicate reflexively its own conditions of emergence – not simply as a matter of individual opposition or normative commitment, but in substantively historical terms, as an essential moment within the same contradictory, dynamically evolving social totality it is concerned to decipher and ultimately to transcend.[64]

When we compare this immanent, dialectical conception of negation with the externalist normative orientation of assemblage theory, we also find a major difference in political outlook. Despite its stated goal of expanding our understanding of agency into nonhuman realms, ontological forms of assemblage thinking are not well equipped to identify the specific human agents, social forces and institutional configurations that might promote emancipatory forms of social transformation. Instead, a passive-voice politics prevails in which assemblages and actor-networks are anonymously, almost mysteriously destabilized or dismantled. McFarlane argues, for example, that "urban assemblages are structured through various forms of power relation and resource and information control."[65] But if this is the case, it is essential to explore who (or what, as the case may be) is doing the structuring to whom. In a world animated by passive interactions among actants, the force field of struggle among diverse sociopolitical agents battling to appropriate and reappropriate urban space is relegated to the background.[66] While there are strands of assemblage theory that have successfully articulated powerful, even radical, visions of alternative futures, it seems impossible to pursue the latter without engaging with the fundamentally political dimensions of human agency.[67] In short, perhaps because of the inert way that they interpret the world, ontological variants of assemblage thought do not offer much guidance for how to change it.

Reassembling assemblage urbanism?

In a recent assessment of contemporary urban theory, Ananya Roy argues that "it is time to blast open [the] theoretical geographies" associated with late-twentieth-century urban studies and thus to produce new "geographies of theory" that can come to terms with the contemporary global urban moment in both North and South.[68] Our goal in this chapter has been to assess the degree to which various emergent strands of assemblage-theoretical urban studies can contribute to this wide-ranging intellectual and political task. While we are broadly sympathetic to the empirical research agendas and methodological orientations that have been opened up through such discussions, we have expressed a range of reservations regarding the more ontologically grounded applications of assemblage urbanism, which offer no more than a partial, if not misleading, basis for critical urban studies.

By way of conclusion, we want to reiterate the need for intellectual adventurousness and experimentation in this research field, and to underscore the ways in which, notwithstanding its blind spots, the debate on urban assemblages is productively contributing to such impulses. Despite the confident, and occasionally polemical declarations by the defenders of inherited frameworks, it is certainly not the case that critical urban theory, as it currently exists, has ready-made analytical tools for deciphering the rapidly transforming condition of worldwide urbanization.[69] And surely, the questions posed by assemblage urbanists – for instance, regarding human/nonhuman interfaces, networked interdependencies and the production of sociomaterial infrastructures – are essential ones. Such questions deserve serious, sustained exploration in future forays into the urban question.

Today, new forms of urbanization and world-making co-constitute each other in a volatile context of geoeconomic, geopolitical and environmental crisis, ongoing market-driven regulatory experimentation and intense sociopolitical contestation at all spatial scales. As the urban condition becomes worldwide, it does so not through the absolute territorial expansion of an inherited urban object, but rather through the emergence of qualitatively new, genuinely planetary forms of urbanization in which a densely if unevenly urbanized fabric of sociospatial and political-economic interconnectivity is at once stretched, thickened and continually redifferentiated across places, territories and scales, throughout the space of the entire globe. This becoming-worldwide (in Lefebvre's terms, *mondialisation*) of the urban is not simply a quantitative expansion of city populations or an outwards extension of inherited metropolitan jurisdictional boundaries, but has entailed a qualitative reconstitution of the urban itself in which a host of inherited spatial oppositions – for instance, city/suburb, urban/rural, core/periphery, built/unbuilt, North/South, human/nonhuman, society/nature – are being fundamentally rearticulated, if not superseded entirely.[70]

In light of these unprecedented trends and transformations, a key challenge for any critical approach to urban theory is to generate a new lexicon of spatial differentiation through which to grasp emergent forms of uneven geographical development in ways that capture their tendential, planet-wide systematicity as well as their equally pervasive volatility, precariousness and mutability. Could it be precisely here, faced with the extraordinary challenge of mapping a worldwide yet internally hierarchized and differentiated urban ensemble, that the conceptual and methodological gestures facilitated through assemblage approaches become most productive? Whereas the concept of "structured coherence" presented by David Harvey in the 1980s confronted this problem at the scale of an individual urban region, there is today a need to decipher the variegated articulations among the disparate spatial, political-institutional and ecological elements of the emergent planetary urban configuration.[71] This task is especially urgent given the continued circulation of ideological projections of world capitalism as a heterarchical, cosmopolitan, flexible, borderless and creative "world order" that mask an entrenched, repressive agenda of (reconstituted) market fundamentalism, accumulation by dispossession and deepening environmental catastrophe. Because assemblage thinking opens up the prospect for thinking space as a relationally overdetermined plenitude, it may offer useful insights for exploring and mapping these emergent geographies of dispossession, catastrophe and possibility. But, as we have suggested, such an exercise will be most effective when it is linked systematically to the intellectual tools and political orientations of critical geopolitical economy.[72]

Even though the urban process has taken on new forms in its planetary formation, we have suggested that it remains a fundamentally capitalist urban process. In our view, the capitalist dimension of urbanization – mediated, of course, through state institutions, regulatory strategies, political alliances, social struggles and systemic crisis tendencies at all spatial scales – figures crucially in producing and reproducing contemporary geographies of deprivation, dispossession and marginalization, both within and among metropolitan regions, throughout the world. Consequently, for urban theory to remain intellectually and politically relevant, it must continue to explore the prospects for the critique of capitalism that are immanent within contemporary sociospatial relations and ecological dynamics.

The approach to critical urban theory proposed here is not grounded upon a transhistorical metaphysics of labor, a structuralist or universalizing framing of the urban, a totalizing concept of capital, or a class-theoretical reductionism. Instead, through a spiral movement involving a dialectic of theoretical abstraction, methodological experimentation and concrete research, it reflexively subjects its own explanatory apparatus to continual reevaluation and reconstitution in light of the ongoing trends, contradictions and struggles associated with contemporary forms of sociospatial restructuring.[73] Against this background, a key challenge is to link the analytical and methodological orientations of assemblage urbanism to the tools of geopolitical economy in ways that contribute to a genuinely critical approach to ongoing planetary urban transformations – one that is attuned not only to local specificities and contingencies, but also to broader, intercontextual dynamics, trajectories, constraints and struggles.[74] In short, the task of understanding the present age of planetary urbanization can be confronted effectively neither through the inert categories of traditional urban theory nor via the conceptual quietude to which some strands of assemblage thought are unfortunately susceptible. Instead, we must continue to seek out the ingredients – intellectual and political – for a critical imagination that is oriented towards the possibility of a radically different type of worldwide space, and by implication, a different form of urbanization.[75] This, in turn, requires forging a critical urban theory that is capable of grasping our rapidly urbanizing planet "by the root."[76]

Notes

1 See, for instance, Manuel Castells, *The Urban Question: A Marxist Approach,* trans. Alan Sheridan (Cambridge, MA: MIT Press, 1979); David Harvey, *Social Justice and the City* (Baltimore: Johns Hopkins University Press, 1973); and Henri Lefebvre, *The Urban Revolution,* trans. Robert Bononno (Minneapolis: University of Minnesota Press, 2003).

2 Nigel Thrift, "An Urban Impasse?," *Theory, Culture & Society* 10, no. 2 (1993): 229–38.

3 Lefebvre, *Urban Revolution,* 45.

4 Edward W. Soja, *Postmetropolis: Critical Studies of Cities and Regions* (Cambridge, MA: Blackwell, 2000), xii.

5 Ananya Roy, "The 21st Century Metropolis: New Geographies of Theory," *Regional Studies* 43, no. 6 (2009): 819–30; Jennifer Robinson, "New Geographies of Theorizing the Urban: Putting Comparison to Work for Global Urban Studies," in *The Routledge Handbook on Cities of the Global South,* ed. Susan Parnell and Sophie Oldfield (New York: Routledge, 2014), 57–70; Saskia Sassen, "New Frontiers Facing Urban Sociology at the Millennium," *British Journal Sociology* 51, no. 1 (2000): 143–59; Peter Taylor, *World City Network: A Global Urban Analysis* (New York: Routledge, 2004) and Soja, *Postmetropolis.*

6 David Wachsmuth, "City as Ideology," *Environment and Planning D: Society and Space* 32, no. 1 (2014): 75–90.

7 See Chapter 13 in the present volume.

8 This claim applies not only to the contemporary conjuncture: urbanization has always been an "open system" insofar as its basic patterns and consequences cannot be derived from any single theoretical framework or causal mechanism. See Andrew Sayer, *Method in Social Science: A Realist Approach,* 2nd ed. (London: Routledge, 1992).

9 See, for example, Robinson, "New Geographies of Theorizing the Urban."

10 Bruno Latour, *Reassembling the Social: An Introduction to Actor-Network-Theory* (New York: Oxford University Press, 2005); Bruno Latour and Emilie Hermant, *Paris: Invisible City,* trans. Liz Carey-Libbrecht (2006), http://www.bruno-latour.fr/virtual/EN/index.html; John Law and John Hassard, eds., *Actor Network Theory and After* (Malden, MA: Blackwell, 1999). For a critical overview see Noel Castree, "False Antitheses? Marxism, Nature and Actor-Networks," *Antipode* 34, no. 1 (2002): 111–46.

11 See, for example, Ash Amin, "Rethinking the Urban Social," *CITY* 11, no. 1 (2007): 100–14; Ash Amin and Nigel Thrift, *Cities: Reimagining the Urban* (London: Polity, 2002); and Stephen Graham and Simon Marvin, *Splintering Urbanism* (New York: Routledge, 2001). For more explicitly assemblage-theoretical engagements with the urban question, see Colin McFarlane, "Assemblage and Critical Urbanism," *CITY* 15, no. 2 (2011): 204–24; Colin McFarlane, "The City as Assemblage: Dwelling and Urban Space," *Environment and Planning D: Society and Space* 29, no. 4 (2011): 649–71; Thomas Bender, "Reassembling the City: Networks and Urban Imaginaries," in *Urban Assemblages: How Actor-Network Theory Changes Urban Research,* ed. Ignacio Farías and Thomas Bender (New York: Routledge, 2010), 303–23; and Ignacio Farías, "Introduction: Decentring the Object of Urban Studies," in Farías and Bender, *Urban Assemblages,* 1–24.

12 We argue below, however, that it is both possible and desirable to mobilize the assemblage concept in a manner that does not entail an embrace of ANT and its associated ontologies.

13 On "naïve objectivism" see Sayer, *Method in Social Science.* On the need for an investigation of the "context of contexts" see Neil Brenner, Jamie Peck and Nik Theodore, "Variegated Neoliberalization: Geographies, Modalities, Pathways," *Global Networks* 10, no. 2 (2010): 182–222.

14 For a critical evaluation, see Castree, "False Antitheses?"

15 Bruno Latour, *The Pasteurization of France,* trans. Alan Sheridan and John Law (Cambridge, MA: Harvard University Press, 1993), 163.

16 Bruno Latour, "The Promise of Constructivism," in *Chasing Technoscience: Matrix for Materiality,* ed. Don Ihde and Evan Selinger (Bloomington, IN: Indiana University Press, 2003): 27–46.

17 Latour, *Reassembling the Social,* 12.

18 Michel Callon, "Some Elements of a Sociology of Translation: Domestication of the Scallops and the Fishermen of St. Brieuc Bay," in *Power, Action and Belief: A New Sociology of Knowledge?,* ed. John Law (London: Routledge, 1986), 196–223.

19 For descriptive uses of the concept see, for example, Saskia Sassen, *Territory, Authority, Rights: From Medieval to Global Assemblages* (Princeton, NJ: Princeton University Press, 2006); and David Madden, "Revisiting the End of Public Space: Assembling the Public in an Urban Park," *City & Community* 9, no. 2 (2010): 187–207. For its philosophical grounding, see Gilles Deleuze and Félix Guattari, *A Thousand Plateaus,* trans. Brian Massumi (Minneapolis: University of Minnesota Press, 1987) as well as Manuel DeLanda, *A New Philosophy of Society: Assemblage Theory and Social Complexity* (New York: Continuum, 2006).

20 John Phillips, "Agencement/Assemblage," *Theory, Culture & Society* 23, no. 2–3 (2006): 108.

21 See George Marcus and Erkan Saka, "Assemblage," *Theory, Culture & Society* 23, no. 2–3 (2006): 101–6; Stephen Collier, "Global Assemblages," *Theory, Culture & Society* 23, no. 2–3 (2006): 399–401.

22 Bender, "Reassembling the City," 316.

23 See, for example, William Cronon, *Nature's Metropolis: Chicago and the Great West* (New York: Norton, 1991); Manuel Castells, *The Rise of the Network Society* (Cambridge, MA: Blackwell, 1993); and Taylor, *World City Network.*

24 McFarlane, "Assemblage and Critical Urbanism"; McFarlane, "The City as Assemblage."

25 McFarlane, "Assemblage and Critical Urbanism," 8.

26 Ibid., quotes from 8, 10, 11.

27 Ibid., 11.

28 Ibid., 14.

29 Ibid., 12.

30 Ibid., 24.

31 Ibid., 31.

32 Ibid.

33 Ibid., 32.

34 Ibid., 25.

35 Ibid., 26.

36 Ibid., 33.

37 Ibid., 35.

38 Farías, "Introduction," 8, 13.

39 For discussion and elaboration, see Castree, "False Antitheses?" as well as Ignacio Farías, "Interview with Stephen Graham," in *Urban Assemblages: How Actor-Network Theory Changes Urban Research,* ed. Ignacio Farías and Thomas Bender (New York: Routledge, 2010), 197–203.

40 Sassen, *Territory, Authority, Rights;* Graham and Marvin, *Splintering Urbanism,* 31.

41 Harris S. Ali and Roger Keil, "Securitizing Network Flows: Infectious Disease and Airports," in *Disrupted Cities,* ed. Stephen Graham (New York: Routledge, 2010): 111–30.

42 See, for example, Stephen Graham, "When Infrastructures Fail," in Graham, *Disrupted Cities,* 1–26; Eugene McCann and Kevin Ward, eds., *Mobile Urbanism: Cities and Policymaking in the Global Age* (Minneapolis: University of Minnesota Press, 2010); and Erik Swyngedouw, "Metabolic Urbanization: The

Making of Cyborg Cities," in *In the Nature of Cities: Urban Political Ecology and the Politics of Urban Metabolism,* ed. Nik Heynen, Maria Kaika and Erik Swyngedouw (New York: Routledge, 2006), 21–40.

43 Swyngedouw, "Metabolic Urbanization"; Maria Kaika, *City of Flows: Modernity, Nature and the City* (New York: Routledge, 2005); and Matthew Gandy, "Rethinking Urban Metabolism: Water, Space and the Modern City," *CITY* 8, no. 3 (2004): 363–79.

44 John Bellamy Foster, *Marx's Ecology: Materialism and Nature* (New York: Monthly Review Press, 2000).

45 Swyngedouw, "Metabolic Urbanization," 26.

46 Ibid., 35.

47 For a parallel, equally cautious methodological orientation to urban assemblages, see Bender, "Reassembling the City."

48 See, for example, Latour and Hermant, *Paris: Invisible City;* Farías, "Introduction"; McFarlane, "Assemblage and Critical Urbanism" and McFarlane, "The City as Assemblage." See also Richard G. Smith, "Urban Studies without 'Scale': Localizing the Global through Singapore" and Alan Latham and Derek McCormack, "Globalizations Big and Small: Notes on Urban Studies," both in Farías and Bender, *Urban Assemblages,* 73–90 and 53–72. Another example is Manuel Tironi, "Gelleable Spaces, Eventful Geographies," in Heynen, Kaika and Swyngedouw, *In the Nature of Cities,* 27–52.

49 In his foundational statement, *Reassembling the Social,* Latour offers the standard reference point on these matters in the context of a rather sweeping critique of twentieth-century social science. See also the lucid statement by Jane Bennett in *Vibrant Matter: A Political Ecology of Things* (Durham, NC: Duke University Press, 2010); and Jane Bennett, "The Agency of Assemblages and the North American Blackout," *Public Culture* 17, no. 3 (2005): 445–65.

50 Bender, "Reassembling the City," 305.

51 Sayer, *Method in Social Science,* 45.

52 McFarlane, "Assemblage and Critical Urbanism."

53 Ibid., 26; italics in original.

54 Ibid.

55 Ananya Roy and Nezar AlSayyad, eds., *Urban Informality: Transnational Perspectives from the Middle East, Latin America and South Asia* (Lanham, MD: Lexington Books, 2004).

56 Brenner, Peck and Theodore, "Variegated Neoliberalization."

57 McFarlane, "Assemblage and Critical Urbanism," 30–31.

58 See Chapter 2 in the present volume, as well as, for example, Peter Marcuse, "From Critical Urban Theory to the Right to the City," *CITY* 13, no. 2–3 (2009): 185–97; Edward W. Soja, *Seeking Spatial Justice* (Minneapolis: University of Minnesota Press, 2010).

59 Bruno Latour, "Why Has Critique Run out of Steam? From Matters of Fact to Matters of Concern," *Critical Inquiry* 30, no. 2 (2004): 225–48; Latour, *Reassembling the Social.* For critical discussion, see David J. Madden, "Urban ANTs: A Review Essay," *Qualitative Sociology* 33, no. 4 (2010): 583–90.

60 Latour, *Reassembling the Social,* 12, 52. On ANT's contradictory merger of a neopositivist insistence on the separation of science from politics with its antipositivist recognition that the knowing subject interacts with the known object, see Madden, "Urban ANTs."

61 Farías, "Introduction," 3; McFarlane, "Assemblage and Critical Urbanism," 16.

62 McFarlane, "Assemblage and Critical Urbanism."

63 Herbert Marcuse, "A Note on Dialectic," in *The Essential Frankfurt School Reader,* ed. Andrew Arato and Eike Gebhardt (New York: Continuum, 1990), 444–51; Henri Lefebvre, *State, Space, World: Selected Writings,* ed. Neil Brenner and Stuart Elden (Minneapolis: University of Minnesota Press, 2009); and Bertell Ollman, *Dance of the Dialectic* (Chicago: University of Illinois Press, 2003). See also Chapter 2 in the present volume.

64   Moishe Postone, *Time, Labor and Social Domination: A Reinterpretation of Karl Marx's Critical Social Theory* (New York: Cambridge University Press, 1993).

65   McFarlane, "Assemblage and Critical Urbanism," 15.

66   On such struggles, see the contributions to Neil Brenner, Margit Mayer and Peter Marcuse, eds., *Cities for People, Not for Profit: Critical Urban Theory and the Right to the City* (New York: Routledge, 2011).

67   See, for example, Bennett, *Vibrant Matter.*

68   Roy, "The 21st Century Metropolis," 820. See also Robinson, "New Geographies of Theorizing the Urban."

69   See, for example, Allen J. Scott and Michael Storper, "The Nature of Cities: The Scope and Limits of Urban Theory," *International Journal of Urban and Regional Research* 39, no. 1 (2015): 1–15.

70   For Lefebvre's concept of *mondialisation,* see the texts included in *State, Space, World.*

71   On the concept of "structured coherence," see David Harvey, *The Urban Experience* (Baltimore: Johns Hopkins University Press, 1989); as well as Neil Brenner, "Between Fixity and Motion: Accumulation, Territorial Organization and the Historical Geography of Spatial Scales," *Environment and Planning D: Society and Space* 16, no. 5 (1998): 459–81. For a critical-anthropological reflection on the same set of issues, see Aihwa Ong and Stephen Collier eds., *Global Assemblages* (Cambridge, MA: Blackwell, 2004).

72   Bender, "Reassembling the City." See also, foundationally, Doreen Massey, *For Space* (London: Sage, 2005).

73   Sayer, *Method in Social Science.*

74   See Christian Schmid, "Specificity and Urbanization: A Theoretical Outlook," in *The Inevitable Specificity of Cities,* ed. ETH Studio Basel (Zurich: Lars Müller Publishers, 2014), 282–97; as well as Roy, "The 21st Century Metropolis"; Robinson, "New Geographies of Urban Theorizing."

75   Lefebvre, *State, Space, World.*

76   Karl Marx, *Early Writings,* ed. and trans. T. B. Bottomore (New York: McGraw-Hill 1963), 52.

16 Introducing the Urban Theory Lab

Contemporary urban research stands at a crossroads. As scholars struggle to decipher current forms of urbanization, they are forced to confront the limitations of inherited approaches to urban questions, and consequently, to face the difficult challenge of inventing new theories, concepts and methods that are better equipped to illuminate emergent spatial conditions, their contradictions and their implications at diverse sites and scales around the world. The result of these efforts is an intellectual field in disarray.

Perhaps more so than ever before since the consolidation of radical approaches to urban theory in the 1970s, there is today fundamental disagreement regarding the basic dimensions of what Manuel Castells famously referred to as "the urban question" – its constitutive elements, its empirical expressions and its political implications.[1] There are also deep questions of theorization, conceptualization, interpretation and method that remain chronically unresolved across many realms of urban knowledge and action.[2] Today, self-described urbanists appear to have only one thing in common – the desire to investigate, understand and reshape "urban" spaces, however the latter may be demarcated in analytic, political or strategic terms. Early twenty-first-century urbanists are likely to disagree on nearly everything else – the conceptualization of what they are trying to study or transform, the justification for why they are doing so, and the elaboration of how best to pursue this goal.

The Urban Theory Lab (UTL) has been established to grapple with this state of affairs. Through a combination of research and pedagogy, our aim is to mobilize the resources of theory to help advance the collective project of understanding and shaping the contemporary urbanization process.

A lab for theory? The starting point of the UTL is the strong contention that *theory matters*. While most labs are oriented towards empirical forms of experimentation, the UTL's agenda is to proceed experimentally with theories, concepts and methods. Of course, such an endeavor requires deep, wide-ranging engagement with concrete, contextually grounded research on all manner of urban phenomena – economic, regulatory, cultural, architectural, experiential, political. But the primary goal of this theoretico-experimental endeavor is, as French regulation theorist Michel Aglietta once proposed in a powerful critique of empiricist economics, "the development of concepts and not the 'verification' of a finished theory."[3]

Theoretical and conceptual frameworks shape perceptions of the urban landscape, interpretations of the built environment and practices of urban intervention. Such frameworks have a massively structuring impact on concrete urban investigations, because they condition "how we 'carve up' our object of study and what properties we take particular objects to have."[4] In this sense, questions of theory and concept formation lie at the heart of all forms of urban research and practice, even the most empirical, locally embedded and detail-oriented. They are not mere background conditions or framing devices, but constitute the very interpretive fabric through which urbanists weave together metanarratives, normative-political orientations, analyses of empirical data and strategies of intervention.

Perhaps, then, it is through the work of theory that we can begin to clarify the sites, scales, morphologies and trajectories of contemporary urbanization processes, as well as the social forces, institutional arrangements, political strategies, spatial ideologies and power relations through which the latter are produced. In the context of the UTL, this work is understood as an ongoing, reflexive, practico-analytic exercise in demarcating the what, the why and the how of historical and emergent formations of urbanization across places, territories and scales. If the aspiration towards a generalized clarification of such matters should prove elusive, a well-tempered but critical approach to urban theory may still seek to accomplish a more modest but essential task: that of illuminating the wide-ranging implications, whether methodological, empirical or political, of particular theoretical choices at various levels of abstraction – from concept, norm, representation, model and map to scheme, plan, strategy, intervention and projection.[5]

The UTL seeks to promote experimental theoretical forays into emergent urban conditions and urbanization processes around the world. Such high-risk, speculative endeavors may lead into blind alleyways or dead ends, signifying a misconceived conceptual orientation, methodological strategy or research pathway. But, with persistence, patience, reflexivity and a bit of good teamwork, these ventures may also foreshadow breakthroughs towards new epistemological, analytical or practical horizons, yielding potentially fruitful perspectives for thought, representation, imagination or action in relation to our rapidly changing planetary urban landscape. The UTL aims to create a collaborative intellectual and pedagogical space in which such theoretical experiments may be pursued – rigorously, ambitiously and collaboratively.

There is plenty of room for debate regarding the inheritance of twentieth-century urban theory and its potential applications to emergent twenty-first-century formations of planetary urbanization. But the work of the UTL is premised on the assumption that contemporary challenges in urban theory must be confronted in reflexive dialogue with earlier efforts to demarcate the contours of the urban question, always understood in the historical-geographical context(s) of their production and appropriation in urban research and practice. In each case, these traditions must be appropriated critically, in relation to the uncertainties, dilemmas and concerns of the present moment. This hermeneutic of intellectual appropriation permits older texts and traditions of urban studies – for instance, the concept of "un-building" (*Abbau*) developed by Lewis Mumford; the "radiant urbanism" of Louis Wirth; the regional fabric of urbanization envisioned by Ludwig Hilberseimer; or the approach to "planetary zoning" of Constantinos Doxiadis – to be rediscovered from new angles and for new purposes. It also opens up the exciting prospect of resituating hitherto subterranean, marginalized or counterhegemonic traditions of urban theory into the analytic heartlands of contemporary debates on urban questions.

The UTL is concerned with nearly all forms of urban knowledge, including urban ideologies and ideologies of urbanization – since it is, after all, via the realm of ideology that powerful institutions (states, corporations) and social forces narrate, justify and mobilize their own strategies of intervention into social relations and built environments at every imaginable spatial scale.[6] Crucially, the UTL's endeavor is conceived, fundamentally, as a form of *critical* urban theory. The metanarratives on urbanization elaborated in our work will not be understood as neutral, scientific depictions of historical or contemporary trends. Instead they will be positioned – reflexively embedded within our own global space/time context; and positional – reflexively attuned to the institutionalized geographies of power, injustice and struggle with which the landscapes of modern capitalist urbanization are enmeshed.[7] As pursued here, therefore, the goal of critical urban theory is not only to illuminate historical and contemporary forms of this politics of space, but to excavate its variegated historical geographies for possibilities, often suppressed through ideological totalization or institutional violence, that point towards alternative forms of shared urban/planetary social life and spatial organization.[8] This ineluctable horizon of possibility – the prospect of more radically democratic, socially just, culturally liberating and ecologically sane forms of urbanism at a planetary scale – serves simultaneously as an epistemological starting point and as a politico-normative orientation for the work undertaken in the UTL.

Just as urban questions defy inherited disciplinary boundaries, so too must the work of the UTL draw upon a broad array of intellectual tools, methods and materials to animate its explorations. This means that the fragmentation of urban conditions and sociospatial realities enforced through disciplinary divisions of labor must be rejected in favor of approaches that draw upon intellectual resources from across the social sciences, the humanities and the legal, planning and design disciplines, among other fields.[9] The UTL's work must avoid sectarian orthodoxies, seeking theoretical inspiration and methodological traction through eclectic combinations of work from heterodox approaches in each of these intellectual worlds. Regardless of how such theoretical appropriations are sutured together, they are not metaphysical commitments but strategic orientations: they become intelligible only in relation to specific research questions, objects/sites of inquiry, pathways of exploration and politico-normative concerns. Consequently, the UTL's search for theories, concepts and methods adequate to the manifold challenges of understanding twenty-first-century urbanization must necessarily be open-ended – it may yield unexpected results or produce surprising new horizons for further investigation and strategic intervention. Long-trusted approaches or assumptions may prove stale, misleading or obsolete; and ideas previously ignored, dismissed or viewed with suspicion may unexpectedly acquire powerful new applications as perspectives and agendas evolve. Such theoretical and epistemological gymnastics must be welcomed as routine research maneuvers rather than being viewed as analytical setbacks, detours or roadblocks.

One additional challenge lies at the heart of our work – namely, that of connecting urban theory to new visualizations of urbanization processes. We view the projects of urban theory and urban mapping/cartography as inextricably connected. Inherited urban theories necessarily entail specific mappings of the world, whether they are reflexively articulated or tacitly presupposed. Accordingly, our research seeks to excavate the cartographic assumptions and visualization strategies that underpin the major traditions of twentieth- and early twenty-first-century urban theory. On this basis, we aim to develop new ways of visualizing urbanization that supersede inherited metageographical binarisms (for instance, urban/rural, town/

country, city/non-city, society/nature, human/nonhuman) and thus offer new perspectives for understanding the variegated and deeply polarized geographies of our urbanizing planet. Unless urban theories can be translated into spatial representations that are appropriate to emergent conditions, inherited metageographical binarisms will continue to haunt our understanding of urban processes, and will seriously impede our capacity to shape them.

This endeavor is closely connected to a strong critique of contemporary mapping technologies. During the last several decades, new visualizations of diverse terrestrial conditions – from population distributions and densities, land use patterns and infrastructural arrangements to human environmental impacts – have been produced and widely disseminated. Unlike traditional representations of such conditions, which have usually been derived from census and topographic surveys, these new visualizations have been based upon the use of remote sensing technologies (in particular, satellites) and new techniques of geospatial analysis (such as geographic information systems [GIS]) to measure and map the phenomena under investigation. From the popular diffusion of nighttime lights images and the everyday use of global positioning systems (GPS) and Google Earth to the proliferation of satellite images derived from more specialized forms of spatial data on populations, settlements, infrastructures and landscapes, geospatial visualizations have become a commonplace reference point used to illustrate or justify diverse interpretations of the world's built and unbuilt landscapes at nearly every conceivable spatial scale.

While geospatial data and images can indeed be used productively to illuminate urbanization processes, their deployment to date has been severely hindered by the perpetuation of what might be termed the *photographic illusion*. This entails the treatment of geospatial visualizations as if they were mimetic, photographic representations of spatial conditions and distributions. In fact, such visualizations are never a direct "mirror of nature" (Richard Rorty), but are invariably mediated through metageographical assumptions that are embedded within spatial taxonomies, coding systems and techniques of data processing. The scaling, pixelation and color-coding of geospatial information are thus never purely technical operations, but necessarily rest upon theoretical presuppositions and interpretive procedures that are masked by the image's apparent "facticity."[10]

For this reason, a critique of geospatial ideology is a necessary precondition for any reflexive appropriation of remotely sensed data and images in investigations of contemporary urbanization processes. By revealing the pervasive yet often hidden metageographical assumptions that invariably underpin geospatial visualizations, our work subjects them to critical interrogation and, where appropriate, radical reinvention via the vibrant, experimental approaches to visual representation that are under development across the design disciplines and within emergent strands of radical cartography. In this way, the development of new theories of urbanization can be translated into new visualizations of ongoing spatial transformations across places, sites, territories and scales. Such visualizations may in turn inspire and animate the development of new theoretical perspectives (concepts, methods, analytical orientations, research strategies) through which to investigate, to render intelligible, and ultimately, to influence the shape and pathway of planetary urbanization. This dialectic of theory development and visual experimentation must remain a central, animating force in our work, continually opening up new horizons and possibilities for inquiry, imagination, explanation, provocation and action.

In the years ahead, we hope to explore a variety of questions and to pursue diverse forms of research, analysis and mapping starting from these general epistemological premises. While our present agendas focus on the broad *problematique* of planetary urbanization, we hope that the intellectual agendas, orientations and methods developed in this work may prove useful to urbanists grappling with a wide range of issues and problems. Our own projects and aspirations will necessarily continue to evolve in critical dialogue with others, and in relation to a rapidly evolving, deeply conflictual worldwide landscape of urbanization, urban restructuring and sociopolitical contestation.

Notes

1   Manuel Castells, *The Urban Question: A Marxist Approach,* trans. Alan Sheridan (Cambridge, MA: MIT Press, 1977).

2   Edward Soja, *Postmetropolis* (Oxford: Wiley-Blackwell, 2000); Ananya Roy, "The 21st Century Metropolis: New Geographies of Theory," *Regional Studies* 43, no. 6 (2009): 819–30.

3   Michel Aglietta, *A Theory of Capitalist Regulation,* trans. David Fernbach (New York: Verso, 1979), 66.

4   Andrew Sayer, "Defining the Urban," *GeoJournal* 9, no. 3 (1984): 281. See also Andrew Sayer, *Method in Social Science: A Realist Approach,* 2nd ed. (London: Routledge, 1992).

5   Examples of such an exercise include Andrew Sayer, "Postfordism in Question," *International Journal of Urban and Regional Research* 13, no. 3 (1989): 666–95; Jamie Peck, "Struggling with the Creative Class," *International Journal of Urban and Regional Research* 29, no. 4 (2005): 740–70; Brendan Gleeson,

The Urban Condition (London: Routledge, 2014); Neil Brenner and Christian Schmid, "The 'Urban Age' in Question," *International Journal of Urban and Regional Research* 38, no. 3 (2014): 731–55; and Chapter 15 in the present volume.

6   David Wachsmuth, "City as Ideology," *Environment and Planning D: Society and Space* 32, no. 1 (2014): 75–90; Kanishka Goonewardena, "The Urban Sensorium: Space, Ideology, and the Aestheticization of Politics," *Antipode* 37, no. 1 (2005): 46–71.

7   See David Harvey, *Rebel Cities* (London: Verso, 2012); Andy Merrifield, *Dialectical Urbanism* (New York: Monthly Review Press, 2006); Peter Marcuse and Ronald van Kempen, eds., *Of States and Cities: The Partitioning of Urban Space* (New York: Oxford University Press, 2002); Jenny Künkel and Margit Mayer, eds., *Neoliberal Urbanism and Its Contestations* (New York: Palgrave, 2012); and Loïc Wacquant, *Urban Outcasts: A Comparative Sociology of Advanced Marginality* (London: Polity, 2007).

8   The concept of a "politics of space" is derived from Henri Lefebvre, "Reflections on the Politics of Space," in *State, Space, World: Selected Writings,* ed. Neil Brenner and Stuart Elden (Minneapolis: University of Minnesota Press, 2009), 167–84. On the politics of critique in critical urban theory, see Chapters 2 and 9 in the present volume, as well as Peter Marcuse, "Whose Right(s) to What City?," in *Cities for People, Not for Profit: Critical Urban Theory and the Right to the City,* ed. Neil Brenner, Margit Mayer and Peter Marcuse (New York: Routledge, 2011), 24–41.

9   Henri Lefebvre, "Fragmentary Sciences and Urban Reality," in "The Right to the City," in *Writings on Cities,* ed. and trans. Eleonore Kofman and Elizabeth Lebas (Cambridge, MA: Blackwell, 1996), 94–96.

10   See Laura Kurgan, *Close up at a Distance: Mapping, Technology and Politics* (Cambridge, MA: Zone Books, 2013); and Neil Brenner and Nikos Katsikis, "Is the Mediterranean Urban?," in *Implosions/Explosions: Towards a Study of Planetary Urbanization,* ed. Neil Brenner (Berlin: Jovis, 2014), 428–59. For Rorty's philosophical critique of correspondence theories of truth, see his *Philosophy and the Mirror of Nature* (Princeton, NJ: Princeton University Press, 1979).

17 Coda: Critical Urban Theory, Reloaded?

dialogue with Martín Arboleda

Martín Arboleda (MA): I would like to begin by addressing your current work on planetary urbanization, some of which is summarized in the *New Urban Geographies* section of this book. In your collaborative project with Christian Schmid and in many of your recent writings, you suggest that an emergent process of extended urbanization is producing an urban fabric that, instead of only being concentrated in specific nodal points or metropolitan regions, is now also woven throughout vast stretches of the world, rendering obsolete the traditional distinction between city and country. Some version of this idea seems to have already been present in your early writings on the scalar dimensions of urban questions and on the rescaling of state space under neoliberal capitalism. Could you elaborate on the genealogy of the notion of planetary urbanization in your work? What theories or circumstances have shaped it into its current form?

Neil Brenner (NB): I turned to the issue of scale in my earlier work in an attempt to supersede a narrowly place-based understanding of the urban, in a scholarly and political context defined by debates on "globalization." This work emerged in the mid- to late-1990s, when global city theory was gaining momentum and generating interesting new perspectives on contemporary urbanism. Around the same time, Bob Jessop, Jamie Peck and other regulationist-inspired scholars were leading the way towards a reflexively spatialized approach to state theory in the context of newly emergent localisms, regionalisms and systems of multilevel governance. Building upon these discussions and the methodological innovations they were introducing, my own "scalar turn" involved an effort to explore the role of distinctively post-Keynesian, neoliberalized state spatial strategies in facilitating what was then understood as an accelerating globalization of urban space. Global city formation, the new localisms and the new regionalisms were, I argued, also tightly intertwined with rescaled forms of state intervention, in which major urban regions were emerging as strategic targets for institutional reorganization, policy innovation, infrastructure development, megaprojects and so forth. A scale-attuned approach proved very useful for researching such issues, because it enabled me to explore the strategic importance of urban governance in the remaking of national state space during that period, as well as the ways in which rescaled state institutions were contributing to an accelerating process of urban and territorial restructuring. In this multiscalar approach to urban governance, cities and local economies were not treated as discrete, bounded units, but were analytically embedded within dynamically changing, multitiered geoeconomic and geopolitical hierarchies.[1]

In the context of those discussions, and building upon the approach to scale that had previously been developed by radical geographers such as Neil Smith and Erik Swyngedouw, I was concerned to question the traditional geographical binarisms in terms of which the city and the urban had long been defined. Instead of contrasting the urban to suburban or rural territories, a scalar approach entails distinguishing the urban from non-urban scales, and thus embeds the urban within a broader, hierarchically structured, fluidly mutating landscape of uneven spatial development. In such a conception, the urban is not a horizontally articulated settlement type positioned on an areal surface (and correspondingly contrasted with other settlement types, whether suburban, rural or whatever), but is woven into a vertical hierarchy of scales. Here, the urban stands in contrast to the regional, the national, the supranational and the global, each of which is constituted and transformed relationally through sociospatial processes (for instance, capital accumulation, state regulation, migration, political mobilization) that are internally differentiated along scalar dimensions. This generalization applies whether we are considering questions of urban economic development or urban governance, or any other process that produces a distinctively urban scale of sociospatial organization. In each case, a scalar delineation of the urban requires us to contrast it to supraurban scales of strategy, activity and institutionalization, rather than to putatively "non-urban" settlement types or territories.

My current work on planetary urbanization builds upon the methodological foundations of that earlier scalar turn and the research which flowed from it. And it certainly continues my critique of the mainstream, place-based approaches to the urban question that have long dominated the field of urban studies. However, rather than privileging a purely scalar lens, this more recent work brings the territorial dimensions of urbanization back into focus much more systematically than I did in my earlier explorations. In effect, this work combines a reflexively multiscalar approach with a conceptualization of capitalist urbanization as a process of territorialization and reterritorialization which encompasses a range of different spatial conditions, landscapes and ecologies, at once within and beyond zones of metropolitan agglomeration. It continues my earlier attempt to destabilize the urban/non-urban binarism, but via a different methodological route.

In this conception, the urban no longer describes a discrete settlement type or land-use condition, but refers to the vast force field of variegated sociospatial and ecological transformations associated with capitalist industrialization, at once within large, dense cities as well as across the diverse types of industrialized hinterlands, or "operational landscapes," that have been constructed to support urban modes of existence. Building upon Lefebvre's earlier writings on generalized urbanization, the notion of the urban is accordingly extended to encompass most of the planet, and to include zones of industrial primary commodity production (agricultural, livestock and extractive landscapes, industrial forests and fisheries, and so forth), logistics and waste management infrastructures, as well as the oceans, underground or subterranean zones, and even the earth's atmosphere. Along with my collaborators, we have thus proposed an approach to "urban theory without an outside": insofar as much of the planet is now being operationalized through urbanization processes (albeit obviously in contextually specific patterns and intensities across places, regions and territories), it no longer appears productive to define the urban through a contrast to putatively "non-urban," exterior zones.

But this proposal opens up a range of new conceptual and methodological challenges that we have only just begun to explore: how to conceptualize the patterns of sociospatial differentiation and uneven spatial development that are crystallizing within this unevenly woven, variegated and constantly mutating fabric of planetary urbanization? As Christian Schmid and I have argued in some of our recent texts, we need new vocabularies, a new grammar of spatial differentiation, to investigate and to theorize the modes of connection and disconnection between zones of agglomeration and other kinds of places, territories and landscapes across the planet.[2]

Let me hasten to emphasize: we are not suggesting that agglomerations are unimportant; and nor are we claiming that the whole world has become a single mega-agglomeration, a seamless, metallic grid in which there are no population density gradients, akin to the Death Star in the *Star Wars* films or the planet of Trantor in Isaac Asimov's sci-fi classic *Foundation*. Rather, we are proposing to add a new dimension to urban theory, extended urbanization – the production of operational landscapes that support, and are in turn continually transformed by, the forms of concentrated urbanization on which urban researchers have long focused their analytical gaze. These increasingly industrialized, infrastructuralized and enclosed operational landscapes are only bluntly or partially illuminated through inherited concepts of the hinterland, the countryside or the rural, so we have quite a lot of work to do to develop a theory that relates them dialectically, and in historically specific ways, to the geographies of (concentrated) urbanization during the last 150 years or so.

I should also hasten to add that, in proceeding in this way, I am in no way attempting to abolish concepts of scale or territory, or for that matter those of place or network. Each of those concepts – scale, territory, place and network – remain central to critical sociospatial theory; indeed we might also need others, such as landscape and socionature, to capture the overdetermined multiplicity of sociospatial structuration under modern capitalism.[3] The point is simply that I would no longer define the urban primarily or exclusively in either scalar or territorial terms. The methodological directions in which I am working are still, therefore, very much at odds with the proposals for a "human geography without scale" and a "flat ontology" that were elaborated in what we might now view as the endgame of some of the scale debates that generated so much academic controversy in the early to mid-2000s.[4]

MA The notion of the operational landscape could definitely unsettle many commonsense assumptions regarding the boundaries of the urban. Is that why the cover of your 2014 edited volume on planetary urbanization, *Implosions/Explosions,* includes a photograph of an apparently non-urban setting, basically to assert that the boundaries of the urban are much more unstable than what has been historically considered?[5]

NB The cover of *Implosions/Explosions* is an aerial photograph of the Tar Sands in Northern Alberta by Garth Lenz, a photographer and environmental activist concerned to document the massive wave of large-scale ecological destruction that is currently under way in that part of Canada today. This is a huge area, approximately the size of Florida, that is effectively being enclosed, infrastructuralized, industrialized, financialized and plundered to supply fossil fuels to the big population centers of North America and beyond. It is now well documented that entire watersheds and ecosystems in and around the Tar Sands are being permanently destroyed, not to mention the devastating public health impact over many generations in the surrounding settlements, and especially among First Nations populations.[6] Much like the landscape photography of Edward Burtynsky and David Maisel, Garth Lenz's images thus function as a provocative metaphor for a global process of industrial socioenvironmental degradation and dispossession that is increasingly inseparable from the accelerated growth and expansion of metropolitan regions around the world. If we define the urban in terms of the broader set of relationships (social, politico-institutional and ecological) and infrastructures (systems of extraction, communication, transportation, energy production, water and food supply, and so forth) that support agglomerations, then operational landscapes such as this one have to be included quite centrally within the urban *problematique*.

This is, I believe, precisely what Lefebvre was urging us to do with his concept of the urban fabric. This fabric is today getting woven ever more densely and intensively around the entire planet; it cannot be reduced to the nodal points and metropolitan clusters on which urbanists have long focused their gaze. For me, there is simply no way to look at the Tar Sands of Northern Alberta without connecting the operationalization of that landscape to historical and contemporary processes of capitalist, fossil-fuel-based urbanization. We need to connect the dots – analytically, cartographically and politically – between these grim landscapes of industrial mega-extraction, ecocide and dispossession, and the everyday socioecological metabolism of metropolitan regions around the world.

And you are certainly right that I intend this cover image as a strong provocation. Rather than using an iconic image such as a skyscraper, a waterfront development project, a dense urban neighborhood or a satellite image of a megacity, we chose to foreground a different, but arguably equally essential, kind of colossal infrastructure that supports and materializes the urbanization process. The cover image of the Tar Sands is thus intended as a spatial metaphor for the broader argument we have been making about extended urbanization. But one could also have chosen other non-city sites and infrastructures to illustrate the variegated conditions associated with extended urbanization – for example, a New Panamax container ship, the Great Pacific garbage patch, an oil rig in the North Sea, a gas pipeline in the Sahara Desert, the orbital pathways of space junk, a highway cutting through the Amazon, a palm oil plantation on Sumatra, a mining enclave in northern Chile, western Australia, the Gobi desert or Siberia, a hydroelectric dam in the Himalayas or Andes, the transoceanic undersea cable network, or a Monsanto plant breeding lab in Maui.

MA Considering that the notion of operational landscape is intended to render visible the dense networks of socioecological mediations that feed contemporary urbanization processes, what relationship exists between your formulation of extended urbanization and the concept of metabolic urbanization as outlined by the Marxist school of Urban Political Ecology (UPE)?[7] Does your work build upon the UPE framework, or do you intend a reformulation of its agendas?

NB There are strong parallels here, in that both approaches react against certain binaristic understandings of the city and its putative "outsides." Additionally, both approaches aim to deconstruct reified visions of urban materiality in favor of process-based reconceptualizations that emphasize metabolism, circulation, socio-ecological creative destruction and so forth. In the case of UPE, the primary concern is to supersede the inherited society/nature divide (as well as that between the human and the non-human world) by analyzing cities and urban regions as complex socionatural assemblages in which metabolic flows and social relations coalesce to produce historically specific spatial configurations of power. I have found this approach highly productive for my own thinking about urban questions. For example, the Marxian concept of metabolism is absolutely fundamental for the project of reinventing critical urban theory. And many of the methodological insights and imperatives of UPE have figured quite centrally in our efforts to develop a theorization of planetary urbanization.

But there are also some ambiguities in the UPE project, or at least in its elaborations during the last decade or so. As Hillary Angelo and David Wachsmuth have argued, much of UPE research has actually focused on the traditional, bounded city: despite its radical, far-reaching methodological potential, its research object has often been delineated in a relatively traditional way, simply as an urban agglomeration in which metabolic transformations are said to be situated.[8] Angelo and Wachsmuth make a powerful argument that the Lefebvrian potentialities of UPE – to develop a socionatural and metabolic approach to urbanization, and not merely to the city – have yet to be fully explored. There is no doubt that some of the pioneering UPE researchers, such as Matthew Gandy, Maria Kaika and Erik Swyngedouw, have effectively exploded this tendency towards "methodological cityism" by exploring some of the large-scale mega-engineering projects and colossal infrastructural configurations that support, and indeed constitute, urban life under modern capitalism. Yet, it is also clear that we still have quite a lot of work to do to analyze and theorize the extended geographies and ecologies of urbanization upon which the construction and reproduction of large, densely packed metropolitan agglomerations necessarily depends. The tools of UPE are essential for that project, but they arguably need to be applied more systematically beyond the city's boundaries, to explore the large-scale, uneven and variegated geographies of planetary urbanization as a whole.

MA Although one could argue that the common history of city and country goes back thousands of years, your periodization of this dialectic seems to be circumscribed to the history of capitalism. Why do you apply your theory of urbanization in this way, rather than as a more general historical principle?

NB Insofar as human settlements have always hinged upon wider social, economic, infrastructural and ecological connections to their surrounding territories, as well as upon long-distance networks of trade, the distinction between concentrated and extended urbanization may initially appear as a transhistorical basis for exploring a wide range of city/non-city flows and power configurations associated with empire, extraction, trade and civilization, from the early emergence and growth of cities and interurban trade networks in premodern world systems, prior to the worldwide extension of capitalism. In this sense, the framework does initially appear to resonate with the kinds of arguments that, for example, both Lewis Mumford and Jane Jacobs explored regarding the relation of the city to its surrounding rural ecosystem during world history, or with classic work on cities and territories by urban economic historians such as Paul Bairoch.[9] But, in our work, we are most directly concerned with the historical specificity of the capitalist form of urbanization. We mobilize the distinction between concentrated and extended urbanization as an analytical device for that particular purpose, rather than as the basis for a world-historical, *longue durée* analysis of cities and their territories or environments.

Here, I think we are consistent Lefebvrians: we build strongly upon Lefebvre's suggestion that the capitalist form of urbanization is tightly interconnected with the increasing generalization of industrialization in the nineteenth century and subsequently. On the one hand, urbanization assumes a particular form within any social formation that is based on the generalized accumulation of capital, with associated processes of commodification of labor and land, and territorial enclosure.[10] But, most importantly for us, the capitalist form of urbanization undergoes a further qualitative transformation when capital accumulation is more widely industrialized, that is, when the labor process, capital circulation and the organization of metabolic flows (materials extraction, energy production, biomass appropriation, water and food supply, waste management and so forth) are intensively rationalized, through the systematic mobilization of science and technology embodied in assemblages of machinery, equipment and infrastructure, to intensify surplus value extraction.

Such dynamics of capitalist industrial transformation have massive implications for spatial organization, not only within large-scale industrial cities, but across the variegated landscapes of inherited hinterlands and even, in some cases, formerly "wasteland" or "wilderness" zones. Having previously been enclosed as capitalist private property, they are now also more extensively rationalized, infrastructuralized, planned and financialized to support the sociometabolic operations of capital accumulation: the institutionalized appropriation of nature's "free gifts" (food, energy, materials) is now more actively, directly and systematically intensified, accelerated and managed within specifically capitalist modes of territorial organization.[11] Through capitalist industrialization, hinterlands are thus transformed into "operational landscapes."[12] Above and beyond the initial moment of territorial enclosure, intrinsically capitalist forms of spatial organization are now consolidated to intensify profit-driven modes of agricultural cultivation, resource extraction, energy production, logistics, forestry and environmental management within rapidly evolving, worldwide spatial divisions of labor. In an important sense, the transformation of hinterlands into operational landscapes, which is expressed through an increasingly planetary explosion of extended urbanization, represents a tendency towards the real subsumption of territory under capital.[13]

Historically, following David Harvey's pioneering work, radical urban theory has focused mainly on the implications of capitalist industrialization for the rationalization and relentless transformation of cities' built environments – for instance, their subordination to the imperatives of profit-based production and circulation; and their recurrent subjection to processes of crisis-induced creative destruction, in which the forward motion of capitalist development renders them dysfunctional and even obsolete, leading to accelerated restructuring and new formations of spatial organization. Thus, our standard periodizations of urban development focus on city form, regional expansion and inter-city relations, from the mercantile, industrial, corporate-monopoly and Fordist-Keynesian formations of urban development up through our present, globalized or neoliberalized constellations. But, in our work, we are already finding that powerful processes of reterritorialization and creative destruction – of sociospatial infrastructures, socioenvironmental relations and institutional-regulatory systems – have simultaneously been rippling across the landscapes of extended urbanization as well, especially since the 1850s.

Though they are clearly connected to broader cycles of capitalist industrialization and crisis formation, we do not yet have a strong understanding of exactly how – by what mechanisms and in what temporal rhythms – such creative destruction processes in the operational landscapes of extended urbanization are articulated to those within and among metropolitan agglomerations. But it seems clear that we need to explore much more systematically the variegated connections – analytical, spatial and historical – between processes of concentrated and extended urbanization within the evolving, crisis-riven spatial divisions of labor of modern capitalism. Just as city-centric, nodal understandings of agglomeration have become increasingly problematic, so too are inherited externalist and place-based understandings of the hinterland, the rural and the wilderness now revealed as analytically and politically limiting. Rather than perpetuating such inherited conceptual dualisms, we need to reconnect these mutually constitutive, dialectically interlinked force fields of capitalist sociospatial and environmental transformation within a reinvigorated theory of uneven, variegated and planetary capitalist urbanization. Within this framework, then, the variegated geographies of the urban result from the co-evolution of agglomeration processes and the continuous construction/transformation of operational landscapes during successive worldwide regimes of capitalist industrialization.

At this stage of our work, having demarcated the problem in theoretical terms, a number of complex empirical-historical questions arise regarding the changing relations between metropolitan agglomerations and operational landscapes at various spatial scales since the 1850s. For example: What kinds of large-scale metabolic infrastructures – for materials, energy, food and water supply, and for waste management – have supported successive historical regimes of capitalist industrial urbanization in different zones of the world economy? How have the social, institutional, infrastructural and environmental geographies of inherited hinterlands been transformed as the production of primary commodities (food, fuel, fiber, materials) has become progressively industrialized? How have such geographies been creatively destroyed during periods of geoeconomic crisis or geopolitical volatility, or when specific primary commodity sectors undergo rapid industrial restructuring and/or financialization? How have such transformations facilitated, and been accelerated by, specific patterns and pathways of metropolitan development? To what degree are "urban effects" – such as land-use intensification, expanded infrastructural investment, enhanced connectivity and large environmental impacts – increasingly being generated within such operational landscapes, beyond the world's major metropolitan centers? How have the dialectics of concentrated and extended urbanization mediated, and been transformed by, large-scale labor migration patterns since the 1850s? How have they been mediated by, and contributed to, geopolitical strategies and conflicts within and among major states, empires and regulatory institutions – for instance, around issues related to control over resources, energy and food supplies?

Vast literatures exist on many of these topics, of course, but they are only rarely connected in analytical terms to the questions about capitalist urbanization that are emerging in our work. We are hopeful that exploring these and related questions will prove fruitful for the development of new approaches to urban theory, history and geography that can help illuminate emergent forms of planetary urbanization, as well as their historical antecedents since the generalized industrialization of capital in the nineteenth century.

MA In what ways do you think this approach could help inform planning practice and policy making?

NB I definitely think of what I am doing as a form of critical urban theory, and thus, as an attempt to unsettle the taken-for-granted assumptions within much of mainstream urban discourse – academic, governmental and corporate. In my view, a purely city-centric understanding of urbanization is both intellectually misleading and politically irresponsible because, whether intentionally or not, it erases or "black-boxes" the multifarious transformations of socioenvironmental relations that support the operations of metropolitan agglomerations. The notion that cities are self-propelled engines of economic growth is an ideological fable: it hides the large-scale infrastructural and ecological links that embed cities within vast landscapes of extraction, production, distribution and power.

Consider, for example, the problem of informal housing in megacities, which is today, appropriately enough, a major concern for urban scholars, policy makers and planners around the world. Our approach suggests that the very delineation of this focal point, the megacity, is already too narrow. Instead of starting with informal housing as it appears within big cities and on their peri-urban fringes, we need to ask: what are the broader conditions in property relations, labor markets, agricultural production, land-use systems and environmental arrangements that have contributed to the mass displacement of formerly rural populations into the big cities, where informal housing settlements are then constructed? All of those processes mostly form a "blind field" within mainstream urban age discourse, because it is focused unilaterally on the agglomeration – the internal built environment of the city. Its starting point – the naturalized assumption of cityness as the necessary spatial form of our shared global modernity – effectively erases the ongoing processes of enclosure, expulsion, ecological plunder and territorial reorganization that not only accompany, but actively mediate and animate, the construction and expansion of metropolitan regions.

What happens to our understanding of planning and policy intervention on the housing question in the world's megacities if we include these operational landscapes, and their geographies of violent dispossession and ecological destruction, within our assessment of emergent challenges and potential responses? To some extent, some inherited twentieth-century approaches to territorial and spatial planning – *l'aménagement du territoire* or *Raumordnung* – open up a productive optic through which to confront such issues, even though they have historically been largely centered on the imperatives of state control, internal colonization and economic management. Our perspective affirms that the city remains as strategic as ever as a point of intervention, but we argue that so too are many processes of socioterritorial and ecological transformation that are positioned "upstream" from the city and/or are configured at much broader spatial scales – regional, national, continental, planetary. Insofar as many putatively "urban" problems are rooted in broader political-economic, environmental and territorial transformations, our approach suggests that policy makers in the United Nations, international organizations and national governments could productively broaden their understanding of the site of intervention, such that they may begin to address root causes rather than merely downstream, local consequences. This is obviously a proposition that requires further concretization and contextualization in relation to specific issues. We hope to elaborate its implications in the future in several policy arenas.

MA Looking beyond concepts of density and population thresholds in contemporary accounts of urbanization is extremely urgent, both intellectually and politically. However, by problematizing the non-urban realm to such an extent, isn't there a danger that the notion of the urban is stretched too broadly, and starts to lose coherence?

NB That is an entirely reasonable question, one that frequently arises when we present these ideas. But it is also one that can be clarified quite simply.

First: our approach does not deny the existence or importance of densely agglomerated metropolitan regions; it simply suggests that we cannot understand them coherently if we subsume them under the singular, universal and generic label, "city." We need to analyze the diverse processes of urbanization that produce and transform such zones of agglomeration, rather than viewing them as examples of a general type or universal form. Agglomeration has many causes; it yields diverse consequences; it is materialized in differentiated patterns at various spatial scales; and it unfolds through variegated developmental pathways. In short, there is no singular form of "the" city.

Second, our stronger claim is that a reinvented, expanded concept of urbanization can also begin to illuminate sociospatial, infrastructural and environmental transformations in the operational landscapes, beyond the dense zones of population settlement, in direct relation to the agglomeration processes that have long monopolized the analytical gaze of urban researchers. Crucially, however, in suggesting that such zones are being urbanized, in the specific sense outlined above, we are not claiming that everything is the same, that the whole world is a single urban sheet, or that the invocation of urbanization could somehow explain all dimensions of life. Rather, we are simply suggesting (a) that the patterns and pathways of such operational landscapes can be productively understood in relation to changing conditions within the zones of agglomeration which they support; and (b) that our understanding of agglomeration processes will, in turn, be limited if we do not analytically connect them to the production of operational landscapes, that is, to the dynamics of extended urbanization.

In sum, then, our emphasis is on variegated, uneven and dialectical processes of urbanization rather than singular types or universal forms of "the" city. The claim is that urbanization is a process of intense sociospatial differentiation — to use Lefebvre's terminology once again, it is at once global (generalizing), fragmented and hierarchical.[14] The task is to illuminate the specific ways in which, since the large-scale industrialization of capital, such processes have produced and transformed sociospatial configurations at every spatial scale, across terrestrial, subterranean, oceanic and atmospheric spaces. Even though this theoretical reframing is still relatively speculative, I believe that it already offers more coherent, productive analytical tools for exploring processes of sociospatial differentiation under early twenty-first-century capitalism than the hegemonic epistemology of the urban that currently prevails, with its homogenizing use of the singular concept of "the" city and its totalizing universalization of the urban/rural dichotomy.

MA In various chapters of this book, you wrestle with two seemingly antagonistic ways to approach the urban question. On the one hand, you argue consistently that the urban is a theoretical construct, one that can be produced only through a process of conceptual abstraction. On the other, you also highlight the importance of focusing on the experiential plane, and on everyday life, in order to grasp the lived practices that produce specific urban effects, including many of the ideological ones you subject to critical scrutiny in the preceding chapters. How can critical urban studies deal with the recurrent tension between these two dimensions of the urban – as concrete abstraction and as lived experience?

NB A dialectical approach is always desirable, and it is certainly essential for relating the experiential and the structural dimensions of urbanization. Today, there appears to be a widening disjuncture between categories of practice – the everyday concepts that we have inherited to understand the spatial organization of the world – and the relentless search for more adequate categories of critical analysis that might help us decipher contemporary processes of sociospatial and environmental transformation. As David Wachsmuth has incisively argued, the naturalized category of cityness, and the closely associated urban/rural distinction, persist in everyday consciousness and political discourse, even though in theoretical terms they have become deeply problematic, even ideological, insofar as they distort our understanding of sociospatial relations.[15] This is a huge problem and paradox in our current work on planetary urbanization, one that Christian Schmid has also productively addressed using a Lefebvrian framework.[16]

The United Nations continues to base its global population data tables on a crude urban/rural distinction, which is an appallingly imprecise basis for understanding patterns of demographic and spatial change across regional and national contexts. The notion that less densely settled zones are "rural" is still widely presupposed around the world, across territories and cultures, within the social sciences and policy discourse. So, clearly, on the level of experience, of everyday cognitive maps, many of the concepts we are trying to supersede in our theorizing are, in fact, widely taken for granted and naturalized, as doxic everyday assumptions.

One of the puzzles to be investigated is: what institutional mechanisms, representational strategies and visual techniques continue to reinforce the naturalization of those city-centric metageographies? And are there not countervailing processes, strategies, experiences and struggles that destabilize them? Consider, for example, modern state cartographies, which are largely reproduced in Google maps and in other digital mapping technologies. Here, the jurisdictional boundaries between different settlements are represented as if they were permanent, natural and pregiven properties of the earth's surface. But, of course, those boundaries are actually constructed through institutions, strategies and struggles; it is through the latter that the operationality of such boundaries is activated, reproduced or reinvented. In this sense, even though these territorial delineations are abstractions, they are obviously "real abstractions" insofar as they massively impact investment, land use and everyday life. At the same time, there are also all kinds of processes that destabilize the image of the world as being composed of neatly bounded, contiguous, non-overlapping territorial containers – for instance, flows of commodities, energy, information, labor and so forth; and a host of economic, political and environmental interdependencies that traverse or supersede such jurisdictional "boxes." These are also key dimensions of contemporary sociospatial relations; they are simply a lot harder to represent using the standard cartographic tools of modern states, with their territorialist visual vocabulary. The challenge is to grasp those different moments, and how they co-evolve across contexts through political strategies, experiments and struggles, as well as through accidents, disasters or unintended consequences.

A big problem for contemporary urban studies is that the field long ago adopted and institutionalized categories of practice – city, urban, suburban, rural and so on – as if they were self-evidently transparent categories of analysis. We are thus often using ideological, "folk" concepts to do conceptual and analytical work for which they are rather blunt, even misleading tools. As Neil Smith recognized long ago, the critique of spatial ideology is thus an essential task for any radical approach to sociospatial theory. Only on this basis can we develop critically reflexive analytic tools that more effectively illuminate the processes that produce sociospatial organization, and their uneven development across contexts.

MA An emerging body of scholarship that draws from Actor-Network Theory (ANT) has also challenged the stable and bounded way in which the urban is traditionally conceived. These scholars, whose work you critically evaluate in Chapter 15, propose to radically decenter the object of urban studies by recasting the city as the relational product of sociomaterial networks that connect myriad spaces and actors, most of which can be thousands of kilometers away from the sites being investigated. Although this "relational turn" in urban studies resonates in some ways with the notion of extended urbanization, it also breaks with some of the methods you build upon in your work, such as geopolitical economy, with its emphasis on the totalizing, world-transforming dynamics of capital. Do you see any potential avenues for the two approaches to mutually reinforce each other in the future, or is the gap between the two becoming increasingly entrenched?

NB It is a big gap, in methodological terms. For me, the issue of totality is essential, but not as an ontological issue. We need to theorize totality because we live in a political-economic system, neoliberalizing capitalism, that is oriented towards totalization – that is, the planetary extension of the commodity form, no matter what the social, political or environmental consequences.[17] Now, obviously, this totality is not a homogenizing one; it is, as Lefebvre recognized, global (or general), hierarchical and fragmented. It is premised upon, and in turn intensifies, differentiation across contexts, and it is always mediated through political institutions, politico-cultural identities, social struggles, and so forth. But, while deciphering specificity, contextuality and the local are important tasks, so too is grasping the totalizing *context* in which such apparent "particularities" are embedded – the "context of context," as Jamie Peck, Nik Theodore and I argue in Chapter 10.

We need a theory that can grapple with both sides of this dialectic. Approaches that veer too far in one or the other direction – structuralism or contextualism – will lose analytical traction in relation to the tricky problems and transformations we are trying to understand. The issues at stake here are not going to be illuminated effectively through a metaphysical debate about whether or not the world is a totality. Rather, the key problem is how to understand the historical specificity of the worldwide economic and environmental system in which we are embedded, how it is evolving, its contradictions and crisis tendencies, and the possibilities for gaining some kind of rational, collective, democratic control over the structural forces and political-economic alliances that are currently appropriating and transforming the conditions for our common planetary life. A theory of totality is only needed under circumstances in which an historical social system exists that totalizes itself; this is a key lesson I learned years ago from Moishe Postone, one of my mentors in social theory when I was in graduate school at the University of Chicago, and whose work on Marx remains a powerful methodological reference point for much of my work.[18]

Aside from the question of totality, another major concern here is that much of the self-proclaimed neo-Latourian scholarship in the social sciences tends to be largely descriptive and almost self-destructively anti-theoretical. Arguments have been made about why those kinds of descriptive analytics are productive, in theoretical terms, but these too often rest upon "straw-person" caricatures of what more structuralist, political-economic arguments actually entail, especially within critical and Marxian theory. There is a long, twisted history of such caricatures, within both leftist and neoconservative strands of political and social theory – consider, for example, the way in which Foucault used to reduce all of Marxism to the position of Althusser. Today it continues, with equally unproductive intellectual consequences, via the ANT discussions. I do not mean to deny the importance of micro-descriptive analysis – for instance, recent work in the microsociology of finance has made some fascinating and productive contributions; and urban ethnography remains a fundamental method for urban studies, not least in the investigation of planetary urbanization. The key challenge, though, is to connect that kind of analysis back up to the macro, the structuring context, or meta-context, within which the texture of everyday life, experience and interaction is embedded. This is an argument that, for example, Berkeley sociologist Michael Burawoy has been making brilliantly in the realm of ethnography for many decades now, and he has devised clear methodological strategies for mediating between experience and social structure, using a kind of geocomparative framework.[19] And, obviously, Pierre Bourdieu's work is basically a reflection on the same issue.

At the risk of overgeneralizing and being perhaps too polemical, I view the recent Latourian turn in the social sciences, and specifically in urban studies, as veering towards a new kind of positivism, albeit one that is generally disguised in more trendy discursive tropes. Here, to use critical-realist terms, the event is thought to exhaust the real, rather than being conditioned by and mediated through underlying mechanisms and structures. I reject this ontology of actualism, based upon the assumption that – as Marx formulated the point in the *Grundrisse* – the concrete is necessarily mediated through manifold determinations, that is to say, through structures and contexts, which are themselves the products of earlier rounds of (structured) practice and (patterned) struggle.[20] This is precisely what an account of the context of context, or the meta-context, is intended to illuminate. Without such an account, I believe, the tools of critical theory are seriously compromised, if not neutralized. This is, obviously, a contentious position to advance in the current academic climate, but it is one I consider essential to the project of critical theory, urban or otherwise.

Of course, the real proof of either position, or any others that might be devised to grapple with the urban question today, is in their potential applications for concrete investigation. We need to move beyond ontological debates or abstract methodological maneuvers, and to demonstrate the analytical and/or political payoffs, or disadvantages, of specific approaches in relation to substantive issues we care about. The debate can only advance if it moves towards more concrete – and political – terrains of analysis.

MA In several chapters of this book, you engage with the question of "alter-urbanization," the challenge of creating a different form of urbanization. Too often, critical urban theory focuses on revealing the uneven, exploitative and environmentally destructive geographies of capitalist urbanization, but stops short of imagining alternative ways of producing, inhabiting and transforming the built and unbuilt environments of the world. But recent efforts by urban scholars to revisit radically alternative political-territorial projects such as the Paris Commune, Rojava in Syria, and Marinaleda in Spain, among many others, reflect the urgency of envisioning what Marxist sociologist Erik Olin Wright refers to as "real utopias."[21] Could you elaborate on the notion of alter-urbanization, and how it relates to your thinking about planetary urbanization?

NB The notion of alter-urbanization is inspired by that of *altermondialisation* – which can be broadly translated as "alternative globalization." Although it has a much longer history, dating back at least to Marx and Engels' 1848 *Communist Manifesto,* the project of an alter-globalization was first explicitly elaborated as such by the broad coalition of social justice, radical democracy and environmentalist movements associated with the World Social Forum in the early 2000s. It continues to serve as a central intellectual focus, strategic orientation and political slogan for diverse New Left and eco-socialist social forces around the world.[22] Amidst a wide range of normative-political agendas, contextually specific concerns and political struggles, such movements have been broadly united in opposition to the neoliberalized, profit-driven, growth-oriented, financialized and highly militarized form of globalization that still currently prevails, and in support of more socially just, democratically managed, peaceful, multipolar, culturally tolerant, solidaristic and ecologically viable ways of organizing the international system.

I have been engaging with an analogous constellation of concerns in the field of critical urban studies for many years, but I only recently began to develop the specific concept of "alter-urbanization" to interpret and explore them. I introduced the concept in some of my teaching during the last year or so, where it immediately proved quite helpful for framing various dimensions of historical and contemporary urban transformation, strategy, ideology and struggle. For instance, in discussing the historical geographies of urban and territorial planning since the 1850s, the concept has helped put into relief the efforts of radical designers, planners and activists, during successive regimes of capitalist development and crisis formation, to pursue a range of "possible urban worlds" whose contours were woven into, but systematically suppressed by, the sociospatial and political-institutional contexts in which they were working.[23] Additionally, I have also begun using the concept of alter-urbanization as a key interpretive rubric for some of our cartographic experiments in the Urban Theory Lab, where students are asked to develop sustained critiques of, and alternatives to, the socially and environmentally disastrous patterns of extended urbanization their work has uncovered in some of the world's most apparently "remote" regions, such as the Arctic, the Amazon, the Gobi desert, the Himalayas, the Pacific Ocean, Siberia and the Sahara desert.

From my point of view, one of the central projects of critical urban theory is to contribute to the imagination and construction of alter-urbanizations. This project is, of course, deeply intertwined with that of deciphering the uneven, variegated geographies of capitalist urbanization, their contradictions and their consequences. But in so doing, it is equally essential to devote sustained attention to the possibilities for radically alternative forms of urbanization – more emancipatory, socially

Figure 17.1: Another city is possible

just, democratic, culturally vibrant, tolerant, ecologically sound – that are latent within, yet systematically suppressed, under current sociospatial arrangements. In Chapter 2 of this book, I argue that critical urban theory is necessarily oriented towards the disjuncture between the actual and the possible – in other words, it has to excavate the suppressed potential for alternative modes of social life, political organization and environmental interdependence that is embedded within extant institutional arrangements. In this specific sense, any critical approach to the urban question is, by definition, oriented towards the project of alter-urbanizations.

This injunction certainly applies to the work we are developing on planetary urbanization: we need to understand not only its oppressive, exclusionary, destructive dynamics, but also the new possibilities it might open up for a different mode of organizing the capacities it has unleashed – for instance, for democratization, interconnection, socialization, appropriation, solidarity, metabolism and differentiation. In this sense, I believe, the *problematique* of alter-urbanizations is absolutely central to any genuinely critical approach to our planetary configuration of urbanization.

During the anti-WTO Seattle protests of 1999, the alter-globalization movements popularized the wonderful slogan, "Another world is possible." A decade later, amidst the Occupy movement, that slogan sometimes reappeared as "Another city is possible" (Figure 17.1). Perhaps urbanization is the key link between those moments of protest and their respective spatial targets – the world and the city. This observation immediately generates a third version of the slogan: *another urbanization is possible*. That, to my mind, is the core project of alter-urbanization: not simply to occupy extant spaces, or even to produce new ones, whether at the scale of the city or that of the world, but to envision new practices and institutions through which the production of space itself may be pursued. Alter-urbanizations, in this sense, involve the occupation, appropriation and continual transformation of the *process* of urbanization, in pursuit of new possibilities for our common yet intensely differentiated planetary life.

Notes

1   See Neil Brenner, *New State Spaces: Urban Governance and the Rescaling of Statehood* (New York: Oxford University Press, 2014; New Brenner, *New Urban Spaces: Urban Theory and the Scale Question* (New York: Oxford University Press, forthcoming) as well as Neil Brenner, Bob Jessop, Martin Jones and Gordon MacLeod, eds., *State/Space: A Reader* (Cambridge, MA: Blackwell, 2003).

2   See Chapter 11 in the present volume; as well as Neil Brenner and Christian Schmid, "Towards a New Epistemology of the Urban," *CITY* 19, no. 2–3 (2015): 151–82.

3   Neil Brenner, "A Thousand Leaves: Notes on the Geographies of Uneven Spatial Development," *Leviathan Undone? The New Political Economy of Scale*, ed. Roger Keil and Rianne Mahon (Vancouver: University of British Columbia Press, 2009), 27–49; Bob Jessop, Neil Brenner and Martin Jones, "Theorizing Socio-spatial Relations," *Environment and Planning D: Society and Space* 26 (2008): 389–401.

4   See, for example, Sallie Marston, John Paul Jones, and Keith Woodward, "Human Geography without Scale," *Transactions of the Institute of British Geographers* 30 (2005): 416–32. For critical counterpoints, see Helga Leitner and Bryon Miller, "Scale and the Limitations of Ontological Debate: A Commentary on Marston, Jones and Woodward," *Transactions of the Institute of British Geographers* 32 (2007): 116–25; and Neil Brenner, "The Limits to Scale? Methodological Reflections on Scalar Structuration," *Progress in Human Geography* 15 (2001): 525–48.

5   Neil Brenner ed., *Implosions/Explosions: Towards a Study of Planetary Urbanization* (Berlin: Jovis, 2014). For further discussion of such visualizations and their analytical implications, see Chapter 12 in the present volume.

6 See, for example, Toban Black, Stephen D'Arcy, Tony Weis and Joshua Kahn Russell, eds., *A Line in the Tar Sands: Struggles for Environmental Justice* (Oakland, CA: PM Press, 2014).

7 See above, all the texts included in Nik Heynen, Maria Kaika and Erik Swyngedouw, eds., *In the Nature of Cities: Urban Political Ecology and the Politics of Urban Metabolism* (New York: Routledge, 2006).

8 Hillary Angelo and David Wachsmuth, "Urbanizing Urban Political Ecology: A Critique of Methodological Cityism," *International Journal of Urban and Regional Research* 39, no. 1 (2015): 16–27.

9 See, for example, Lewis Mumford, "The Natural History of Urbanization," in *Man's Role in Changing the Face of the Earth,* ed. William Thomas Jr. (Chicago: University of Chicago Press, 1956), 382–98; Jane Jacobs, *The Economy of Cities* (New York: Vintage, 1970); and Paul Bairoch, *Cities and Economic Development: From the Dawn of History to the Present,* trans. Christopher Braider (Chicago: Unversity of Chicago Press, 1988).

10 On the historical relation between urbanization and territorial enclosure under capitalism, see Álvaro Sevilla-Buitrago, "Urbs in rure: Historical Enclosure and the Extended Urbanization of the Countryside," in Brenner, *Implosions/Explosions*, 236–59.

11 On the evolution of strategies to appropriate such "free gifts" of nature in relation to systemic cycles of capital accumulation and world ecology, see Jason W. Moore's foundational volume, *Capitalism in the Web of Life: Ecology and the Accumulation of Capital* (New York: Verso, 2015).

12 Neil Brenner, *Extended Urbanization and the Hinterland Question: Towards a Real Subsumption of the Planet?,* unpublished manuscript, Urban Theory Lab, Harvard GSD, December 2015; and Nikos Katsikis, "The Composite Fabric of Urbanization: Agglomeration Landscapes and Operational Landscapes," in *From Hinterland to Hinterglobe: Urbanization as Geographical Organization.* (Doctor of Design Thesis, Harvard University Graduate School of Design, 2016).

13 See Japhy Wilson and Manuel Bayón, "Concrete Jungle: The Planetary Urbanization of the Ecuadorian Amazon," *Human Geography* 8, no. 3 (2015): 1–23; as well as Daniel Buck, "The Subsumption of Space and the Spatiality of Subsumption: Primitive Accumulation and the Transition to Capitalism in Shanghai, China," *Antipode* 39, no. 4 (2007): 757–74. On the application of the Marxian distinction between formal and real subsumption to primary commodity production, see William Boyd, W. Scott Prudham and Rachel Shurman, "Industrial Dynamics and the Problem of Nature," *Society & Natural Resources* 14, no. 7 (2001): 555–70.

14 Henri Lefebvre, "The Worldwide and the Planetary," in *State, Space, World: Selected Essays,* ed. Neil Brenner and Stuart Elden (Minneapolis: University of Minnesota Press, 2009), 196–209.

15 David Wachsmuth, "City as Ideology: Reconciling the Explosion of the City Form with the Tenacity of the City Concept," *Environment and Planning D: Society and Space* 32, no. 1 (2014): 75–90.

16 Christian Schmid, "Networks, Borders, Differences: Towards a Theory of the Urban" and "Traveling Warrior and Complete Urbanization in Switzerland: Landscape as Lived Space," in Brenner, *Implosions/Explosions,* 67–84, 90–102. The issue is also addressed in several other chapters of *Implosions/Explosions.*

17 See, among other works, Moishe Postone, *Time, Labor and Social Domination: A Reinterpretation of Karl Marx's Critical Theory* (New York: Cambridge University Press, 1993); Derek Sayer, *The Violence of Abstraction* (Cambridge, MA: Blackwell, 1987); and Vivek Chibber, *Postcolonial Theory and the Specter of Capital* (New York: Verso, 2013).

18 Postone, *Time, Labor and Social Domination.*

19 See, for example, Michael Burawoy, *The Extended Case Method: Four Countries, Four Decades, Four Great Transformations, and One Theoretical Tradition* (Berkeley: University of California Press, 2009).

20 For a rigorous explication of this idea, see Andrew Sayer, "Abstraction: A Realist Interpretation," *Radical Philosophy* 28 (Summer 1981): 6–15.

21   Erik Olin Wright, *Envisioning Real Utopias* (New York: Verso, 2010).

22   For a useful overview, elaboration and manifesto, see Samir Amin, *The World We Wish to See* (New York: Monthly Review Press, 2008). For critical reflections, see Peter Marcuse, "Are Social Forums the Future of Social Movements," *International Journal of Urban and Regional Research* 29, no. 2 (2005): 417–26. For a more general overview of alter-globalization, at once as a social-theoretical orientation, a social science research perspective and as a political project, see the texts included in Richard Appelbaum and William Robinson, eds., *Critical Globalization Studies* (New York: Routledge, 2005).

23   On the question of "possible urban worlds," see David Harvey, *Justice, Nature and the Geographies of Difference* (Oxford: Blackwell, 1995); and *Spaces of Hope* (Berkeley: University of California Press, 2000).

Sources and Acknowledgments

The images used on the book cover and section divider pages were produced by David Maisel as part of his brilliant 2004 *Oblivion* series (http://davidmaisel.com/portfolio-item/oblivion/). My sincerest thanks are due to the artist for his collegiality and generosity in permitting the use of his work for this project.

During the last fifteen years, I have been fortunate to collaborate with an extraordinary group of critical urbanists in North America and Europe, including my teachers and my students, spanning quite a few generations of lived experience, creative thinking and dedicated critical scholarship. Many of the chapters included in this book are the products of those collaborations. Deepest thanks are due to my coauthors on these texts for their generous permission to include them in this volume. They are, in order of their appearance here: Nik Theodore, Roger Keil, David Wachsmuth, Peter Marcuse, Margit Mayer, Jamie Peck, Christian Schmid and David J. Madden. A warm thank-you is also due to Daniel Ibañez and Martín Arboleda for working with me on the two "dialogues" included in this book. Martín deserves an additional note of gratitude for offering his wise counsel on a range of substantive, organizational and editorial issues, and for crafting such a thoughtful, incisive preface.

Christian Schmid, Margit Mayer, David J. Madden, David Wachsmuth and Álvaro Sevilla Buitrago provided essential advice and critical feedback at key stages in the development of this project. The plan for the book also benefited immensely from discussions with the doctoral researchers affiliated with the Urban Theory Lab at the Graduate School of Design, Harvard University – especially Kian Goh, Dani Ibañez, Nikos Katsikis and Mariano Gomez Luque. Max Welch Guerra energetically supported this book's inclusion in the Bauwelt Fundamente Series. Elisabeth Blum, my editor at Bauwelt Fundamente, offered friendly encouragement and valuable suggestions as the book took shape. Katharina Kulke of Birkhäuser Verlag has been a supportive, reliable and efficient project editor. Amanda Miller provided meticulous assistance with bibliography and endnotes. Thank you, friends and colleagues, for helping me bring this project to fruition.

We gratefully acknowledge the publishers of the original texts for permitting their inclusion in this book. Source information is below; chapters not listed are original to this volume.

Ch. 2: Neil Brenner, "What Is Critical Urban Theory?," *CITY* 13, no. 2–3 (2009): 195–204. © Taylor & Francis; reprinted with permission from Taylor & Francis.

Ch. 3: Neil Brenner and Nik Theodore, "Cities and the Geographies of 'Actually Existing Neoliberalism,'" *Antipode,* 34, no. 3 (2002): 356–86. © Wiley-Blackwell; reprinted with permission from Wiley-Blackwell.

Ch. 4: Neil Brenner and Roger Keil, "From Global Cities to Globalizing Cities," in *The City Reader,* ed. Richard LeGates and Fred Stout, 5th ed. New York: Routledge, 2011, 599–608. © Taylor & Francis; reprinted with permission from Taylor & Francis.

Ch. 5: Neil Brenner and David Wachsmuth, "Territorial Competitiveness: Lineages, Practices, Ideologies," *Planning Ideas That Matter,* ed. Bishwapriya Sanyal, Lawrence Vale and Christina Rosen. Cambridge, MA: MIT Press, 2012, 179–206. © 2012 Massachusetts Institute of Technology; reprinted with permission from the MIT Press.

Ch. 6: Neil Brenner, "'Good Governance': Ideologie eines nachhaltigen Neoliberalismus?" originally published in German in *Reader zum Weltbericht (Für die Zukunft der Städte – URBAN 21),* ed. *Mieter-Echo. Zeitschrift der Berliner MieterGemeinschaft e.V.,* Summer 2000. © Neil Brenner.

Ch. 7: Neil Brenner, "Open City or the Right to the City?," *TOPOS: The International Review of Landscape Architecture and Urban Design* 85 (2013): 42–45. Reprinted with permission.

Ch. 8: Neil Brenner, "Is 'Tactical Urbanism' an Alternative to Neoliberal Urbanism?," website essay commissioned for *POST: notes on modern and contemporary art around the globe* (Museum of Modern Art/MoMA), April 2015. © Neil Brenner.

Ch. 9: Neil Brenner, Peter Marcuse and Margit Mayer, "Cities for People, Not for Profit: An Introduction," *CITY* 13, no. 2–3 (2009): 173–81. © Taylor & Francis; reprinted with permission from Taylor & Francis.

Ch. 10: Neil Brenner, Jamie Peck and Nik Theodore, "After Neoliberalization?," *Globalizations,* 7, no. 3 (2010): 313–30. © Taylor & Francis; reprinted with permission from Taylor & Francis.

Ch. 11: Neil Brenner and Christian Schmid, "Planetary Urbanization," in *Urban Constellations,* ed. Matthew Gandy. Berlin: Jovis, 2012, 10–13. © Neil Brenner and Christian Schmid.

Ch. 12: Neil Brenner, "Introduction: Urban Theory without an Outside," in *Implosions/Explosions: Towards a Study of Planetary Urbanization,* ed. Neil Brenner. Berlin: Jovis, 2014, 14–31. © Neil Brenner.

Ch. 13: Neil Brenner, "The Hinterland, Urbanized?," *Architectural Design/AD,* 2016. © Neil Brenner.

Ch. 15: Neil Brenner, David J. Madden and David Wachsmuth, "Assemblage Urbanism and the Challenges of Critical Urban Theory," *CITY* 15, no. 2 (2011): 225–240. © Taylor & Francis; reprinted with permission from Taylor & Francis.

Author

Neil Brenner Professor of Urban Theory, Graduate School of Design, Harvard University, Cambridge, USA.

Coauthors

Mártin Arboleda Urban Studies Foundation Postdoctoral Fellow, Urban Theory Lab, Graduate School of Design, Harvard University, Cambridge, USA.

Daniel Ibañez Doctor of Design candidate and Research Manager, Urban Theory Lab, Graduate School of Design, Harvard University, Cambridge, USA.

Roger Keil York Research Chair in Global Sub/Urban Studies and Professor, Faculty of Environmental Studies, York University, Toronto, Canada.

David J. Madden Assistant Professor of Sociology and faculty member in the Cities Programme, London School of Economics, United Kingdom.

Peter Marcuse Professor Emeritus of Urban Planning, Graduate School of Architecture, Planning and Preservation, Columbia University, New York, USA.

Margit Mayer Senior Fellow, Center for Metropolitan Studies, Technical University Berlin, formerly Professor of Political Science, Freie University, Berlin, Germany.

Jamie Peck Canada Research Chair in Urban and Regional Political Economy and Professor of Geography, University of British Columbia, Vancouver, Canada.

Christian Schmid Titular Professor of Sociology, Department of Architecture, ETH Zurich, Switzerland.

Nik Theodore Professor, Department of Urban Planning and Policy and Senior Fellow, Great Cities Institute, University of Illinois at Chicago, USA.

David Wachsmuth Assistant Professor, School of Urban Planning, McGill University, Montreal, Canada.

Picture credit

Figure 8.1: Source: © 2016 The Museum of Modern Art, New York. Photograph: Thomas Griesel

Figure 8.2: Source: © 2016 The Museum of Modern Art, New York. Photograph: Thomas Griesel

Figure 8.3: Source: © 2016 Ensamble Studio/MIT-POPlab and URBZ: user-generated cities

Figure 8.4: Source: © 2016 Cohabitation Strategies/CohStra

Figure 8.5: Source: © 2016 Atelier d'Architecture Autogérée

Figure 12.1: Source: Henri Lefebvre, *La révolution urbaine.* Paris: Gallimard, 1970, 26

Figure 12.2: Source: © Constantinos and Emma Doxiadis Foundation

Figure 12.3: Source: Nikos Katsikis, Urban Theory Lab-GSD and terraurbis.com, based on data from the National Imagery Mapping Agency/NIMA 1997 and the National Center for Ecological Analysis and Synthesis/NCEAS

Figure 12.5: Source: © Garth Lenz

Figure 17.1: Source: © Ange Tran, *Not an Alternative*

Bauwelt Fundamente (selected titles)

All titles are available as well as e-book.
More Bauwelt Fundamente on: degruyter.com